THE BEST

CHORD CHANGES

FOR THE

MOST POPULAR SONGS

100 OF THE MOST POPULAR SONGS WITH PROFESSIONALLY ALTERED CHORDS

By FRANK MANTOOTH

ISBN 0-7935-7339-4

Visit Hal Leonard Online at
www.halleonard.com

Contents

Acknowledgments

I would like to extend a personal and public thanks to Tom Johns and Gary Meisner for editing and monitoring this project.

About the Author

Frank Mantooth is currently active as a pianist, composer, arranger, clinician and educator residing in Garden City, Kansas. Frank's four albums, **Suite Tooth, Persevere, Dangerous Precedent, and Sophisticated Lady** have garnered a total of nine Grammy nominations in both writing and playing categories.

As an author, Frank has recently published "The Best Chord Changes for the World's Greatest Standards", Vols. I-5 for the Hal Leonard Corporation. This is in addition to over 130 works for combo and jazz ensemble which have been published with five major publishing houses since 1978.

Frank has taught at numerous summer jazz camps and in residence at various universities and high schools. Recent writing commissions have come from the Kansas City Symphony, the Madison Symphony Orchestra, Doc Severinsen, Pete Christlieb, Louie Bellson, and the Airmen of Note.

Recently released on the Seabreeze label is Frank's latest project, **Sophisticated Lady** which features Pete Christlieb, Kevin Mahogany, Randy Brecker, Pat LaBarbera, Bobby Shew, Nick Brignola and other jazz artists. Notice has been received of **Sophisticated Lady's** receipt of Grammy nominations in three categories.

Foreword

In preparation for harmonically altering the chord changes to 100 beloved standards, the arranger will have to answer two questions:

The first question addresses the issue of subjectivity: What makes one set of altered changes preferable to the original changes or to another set of alterations?

Answer: There is no one definitive set of altered changes to any given tune. Alterations are unequivocally subjective and personal. In fact, jazz musicians may improvise different harmonies each successive chorus of a song.

The second question addresses the issue of tradition: To what extent, if any, should the altered changes acknowledge the original harmonic motion?

Unfortunately, the answer is not simple. "After You've Gone" appeared in an earlier volume of altered standards. Let's combine the first four measures of melody with the following altered harmonies.

These altered changes sound good, they move logically, and they don't interfere with the melody. However, as a consequence of our harmonies, there is now little resemblance to the original song, "After You've Gone".

Therefore certain parameters will be adhered to in the interest of harmonic restraint.

1. The melodies are the originals and are never altered to accommodate an altered harmony.

2. The melodies will cadence in their original keys. From this point on, no subsequent harmonies (original or altered) have been offered. The appropriate "turnaround" returning to the initial harmony of the song for subsequent choruses is discussed in the Introduction.

3. Common usage will prevail. The "common usage" factor refers to an evolutionary process whereby changes over the course of time become the accepted or standardized changes to a particular song. Frequently, these harmonies are not the originals by any means. Anyone who has learned a song solely by ear may be surprised by the dissimilarities between their learned changes and the originals.

Common turnarounds from the Tonic (I) to the

I vi
C Ami7

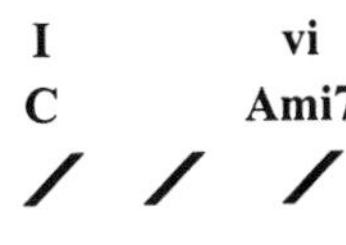

I ii
C Dmi7

From Tonic (I) to Submediant (ii):

I IV
C FMa7

I VII7
C B7

Harmonic Devices

Every arranger has his or her own "bag of tric
in their arrangements. A harmonic predilectio
dominant (llth chord) constructed on the sam

We could split these measures as follows if th

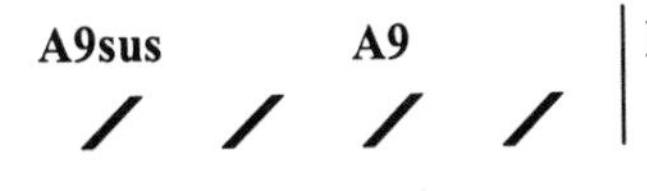

This "device" has a twofold purpose:

1. Frequently the suspended dom
measure. This allows for a smo

2. More inner voice movement is

Introduction

(an explanation of terms, harmonic devices, and symbols used)

Chord Symbol Notation

The chord symbols that accompany printed sheet music are frequently incorrect. One shortcoming is a tendency for publishers to analyze only the right-hand structures. The harmonic contribution(s) of the tone(s) in the bass clef is generally ignored.

This chord could obviously be analyzed as a Dmi6.

However, over the following bass notes, the Dmi6 gets renamed by being incorporated into a larger structure. For example:

On piano sheet music and lead sheets (melody and chord symbols only), dominants are often expressed simply as 7th chords, even though the melody may pass through the 9th or 13th. For example, if analyzed with"G" as the tonic, the following dominant structure would simply be called a G7 although the melody passes through the 9th and 13th of the chord:

One final shortcoming of most chord symbol notation is that altered tones that occur in the melody are not always represented by the chord symbol.

This example at the right shows how a melody over a D dominant might simply be called a D7 despite the presence of both the ♯11 and ♯5.

It is the objective of this text to provide the most accurate chord symbols for all vertical harmonies.

Diagonal Slashes

A diagonal slash is used in this text when t
indicate that the single note "G" is played i

Diagonal slashes with nothing above the d
previous harmony remains unchanged. In t
harmony for the two entire measures while

Ami
/

Cadences

After the final cadence to the tonic, no sul
contingent upon the initial harmony and th

Turnarounds

Turnarounds have two functions:

- They are harmonic devices u
- They provide a logical harmo

For example, in a 32-bar AABA form we v
is usually accomplished in the last two me
turnaround is contingent upon the destina

Common turnarounds from Tonic (I) to To

Diatonic Harmonies
For ex. in the Key of C

Two other harmonic devices that are occasionally used in this volume are the pedal dominant and the tritone substitute (tritone sub.).

Let's arbitrarily pick the key of E♭ Major and take a look at a common cyclical progression over the pedal dominant, B♭.

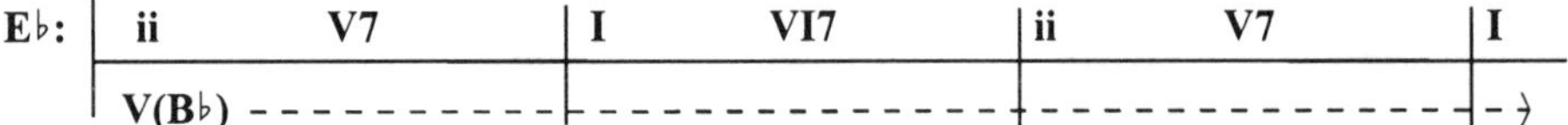
E♭:
ii
V7
I
VI7
ii
V7
I
V(B♭)

The pedal dominant is a great tension inducer, adding a little spice to a common cyclical progression. The pedal dominant device is often employed at the bridge (B section) of an AABA tune.

The next four measures effectively demonstrate the use of tritone substitutions. Observe the basic harmonic motion of these four measures.

Gmi7
C7
Fmi7
B♭7
E♭:
iii
VI7
ii
V7

Now, let's split each bar by adding dominant or altered dominant harmonies a tritone removed from each of the basic harmonies:

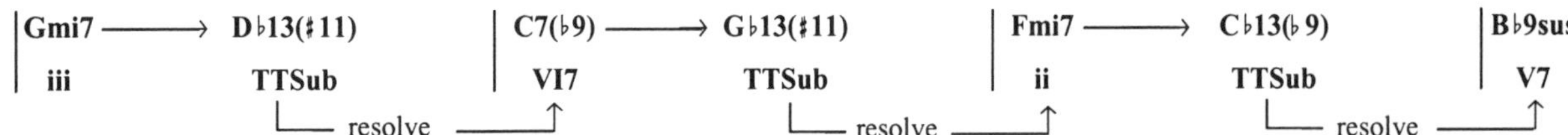
Gmi7
D♭13(♯11)
C7(♭9)
G♭13(♯11)
Fmi7
C♭13(♭9)
B♭9sus
iii
TTSub
VI7
TTSub
ii
TTSub
V7
resolve
resolve
resolve

The success and resultant popularity of tritone substitutions are due solely to their capability to generate extra harmonic motion between cyclical changes. The following suggestions are best heeded if tritone substitutions are to be effective:

- Dominants work best as the substituted harmony.
- If applicable, the melody will influence the harmony and possible alterations of the substituted chord.
- The Tritone Sub will always resolve to a harmony 1/2 step lower.

Logical Root Movement

Even in the highly subjective area of harmonic alteration, there are certain irrefutable facts. Written music (from Palestrina to Pearl Jam) adheres to certain constants. One of these, governing how roots move between adjacent harmonies, has been catalogued according to frequency of occurrence. For lack of a better label, we'll call this Logical Root Movement.

The most frequent root movement between adjacent harmonies is cyclical (by fourths or fifths). Next in frequency is chromatic root movement, followed by diatonic (stepwise) movement, and finally the tritone leap with a downward resolution of a half step. This last movement is primarily a device of the jazz idiom.

Logical Root Movement

(Listed in terms of frequency of occurrence)

1. Cyclical
2. Chromatic
3. Diatonic
4. Tritone leap with a half-step resolution

Logical Root Movement is an essential ingredient of logical harmonic alteration. Logical Root Movement is usually the apparent differential between novice and professional versions of altered changes.

"Hot Notes"

Parenthetical melody notes may infrequently appear. These notes clash with the altered harmony (i.e. are not consonant chord tones). These alterations are intended more for solo improvisation.

The Right Arrow ➔

If the altered harmony is continued or sustained where the original harmonies were in motion, the right arrow may appear. This informs the reader that this alteration is intended until the next altered harmony.

Altered Changes

The altered changes will appear in red above the originals. Either the original changes or the altered changes may be played from measure 1 to the final cadence. Original and altered harmonies are provided from top to bottom, even in instances where the harmonies are identical. This should facilitate sight reading for those finding themselves in that situation. Also, please know that the altered changes are offered solely as alternatives (options) to the originals.

AIN'T SHE SWEET

Words by JACK YELLEN
Music by MILTON AGER

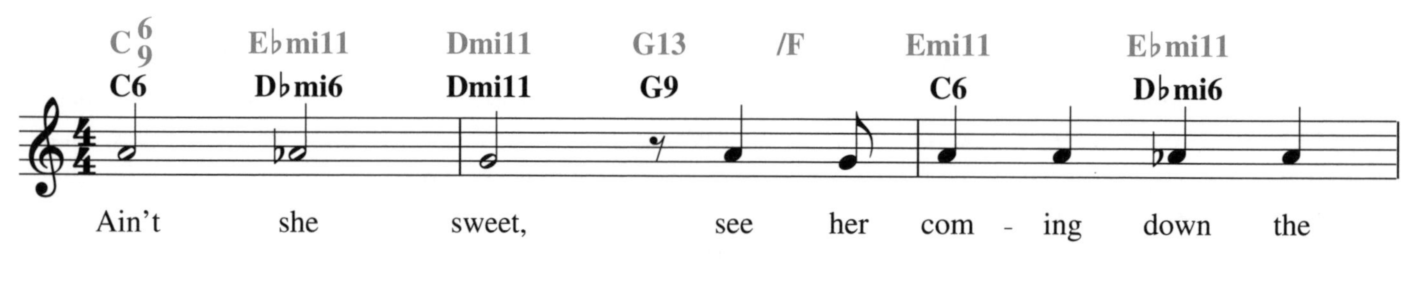

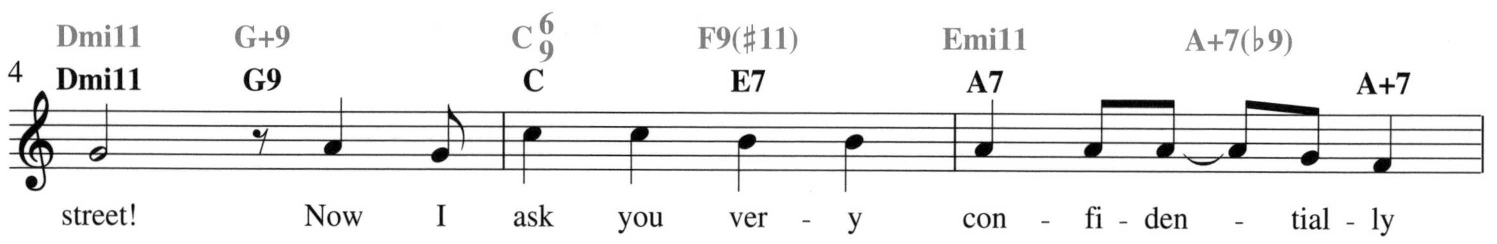

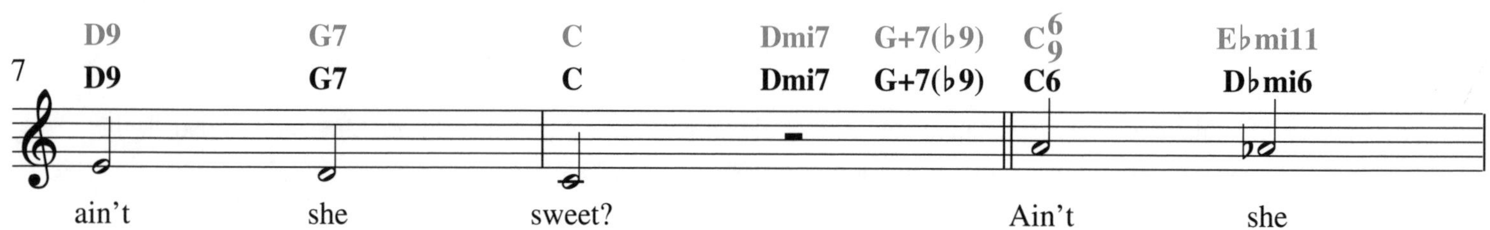

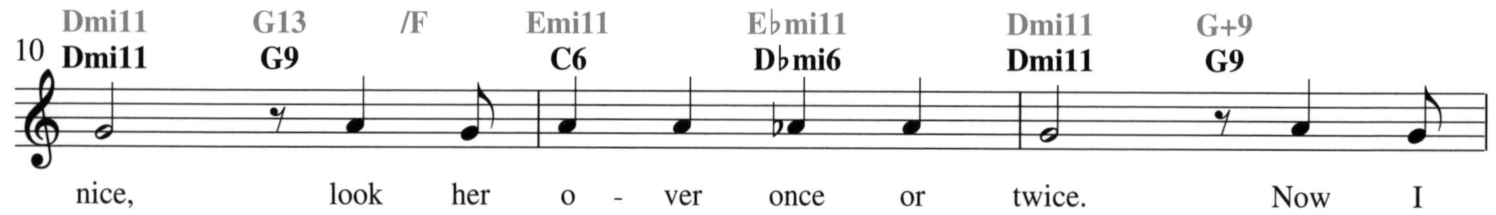

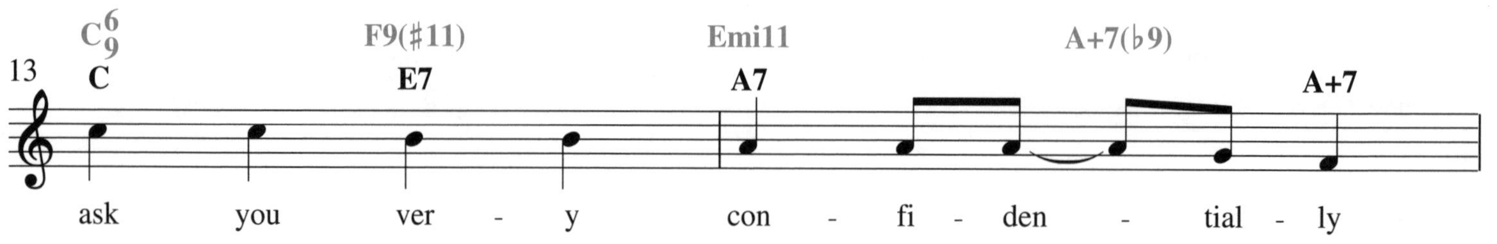

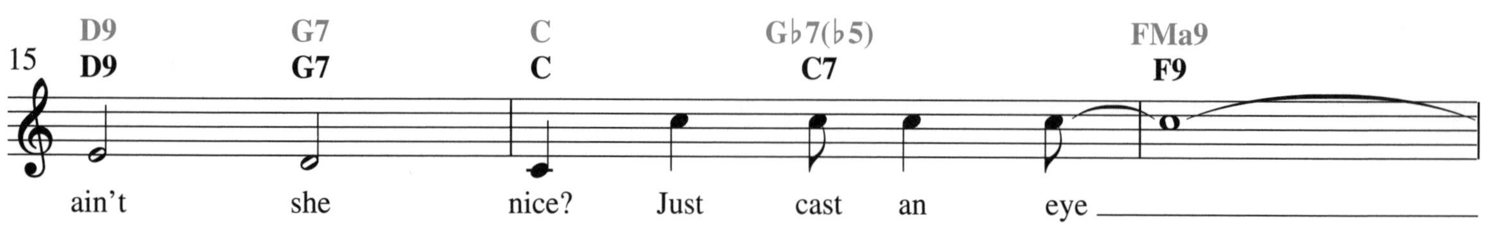

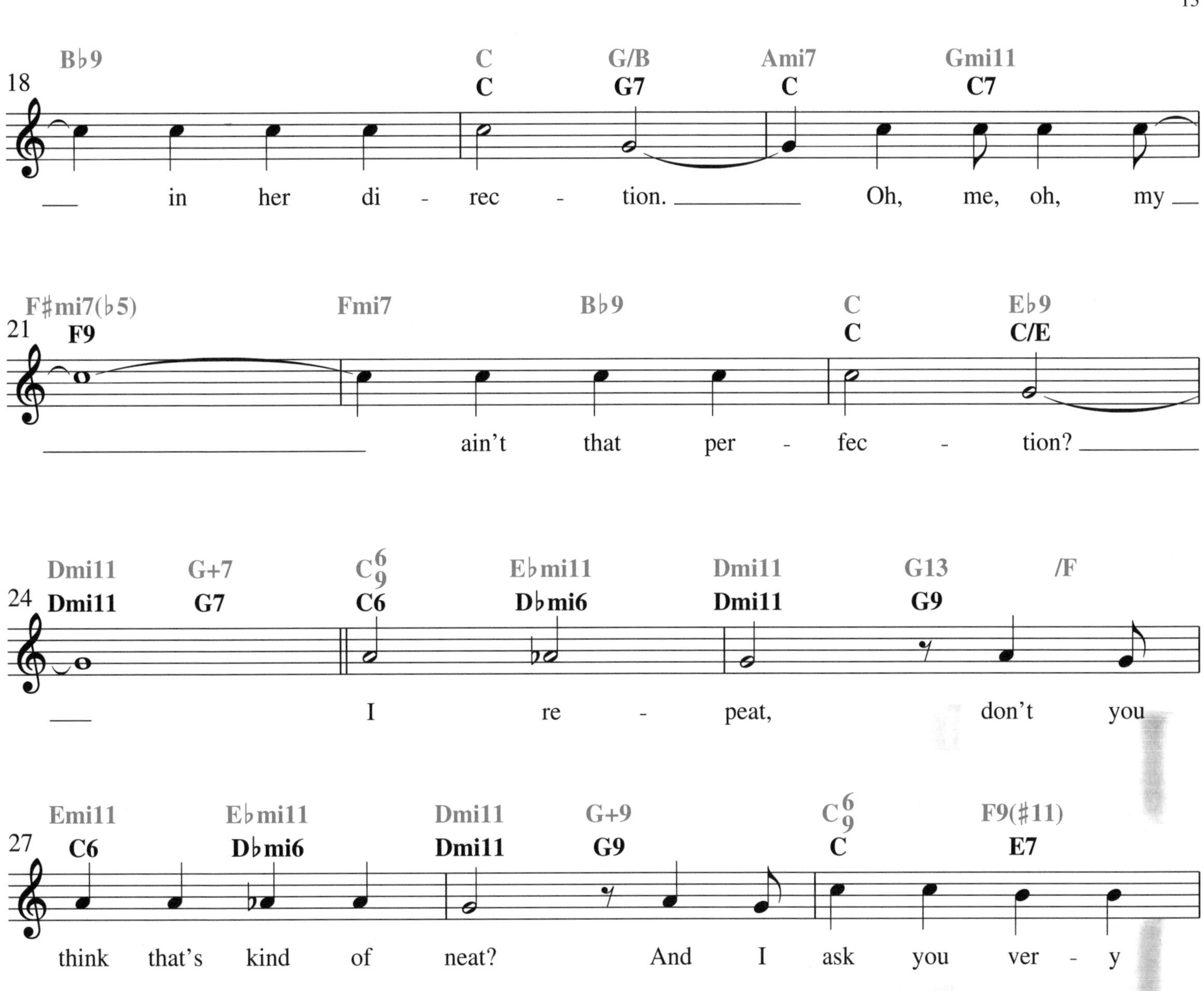
18
B♭9 C G/B Ami7 Gmi11
C G7 C C7
in her di - rec - tion. Oh, me, oh, my
21
F♯mi7(♭5) Fmi7 B♭9 C E♭9
F9 C C/E
ain't that per - fec - tion?
24
Dmi11 G+7 C6/9 E♭mi11 Dmi11 G13 /F
Dmi11 G7 C6 D♭mi6 Dmi11 G9
I re - peat, don't you
27
Emi11 E♭mi11 Dmi11 G+9 C6/9 F9(♯11)
C6 D♭mi6 Dmi11 G9 C E7
think that's kind of neat? And I ask you ver - y
30
Emi11 A+7(♭9) D9 G7 C
A7 A+7 D9 G7 C
con - fi - den - tial - ly ain't she sweet?

AVALON

Words by AL JOLSON and B.G. DeSYLVA
Music by VINCENT ROSE

BLACK COFFEE

Words and Music by PAUL FRANCIS WEBSTER
and SONNY BURKE

13
F7(♯9) Gb7(♯9) F7(♯9) Gb7(♯9)
talk - in' to the shad - ows, one o' - clock to four, and
talk - in' to the shad - ows, one o' - clock to four, and
15
F7(♯9) Gb7(♯9) F7(♯9) Cmi11 B9(♯11)
F7(♯9) Gb7(♯9) F7(♯9) B9
Lord, how slow the mo - ments go when all I do is pour black
Lord, how slow the mo - ments go when all I do is pour black
17
Bb9 Eb9sus F7(♯9) Bb9
Bb9 Bb°7 Bb9 F7(♯9) Gb7(♯7)
3
3
cof - fee. Since the blues caught my eye.
cof - fee. Love's a sor - ry af - fair.
20
Ami7(b5) D+7(♯9) Gmi7 D7(♯9)
F7(♯9) D7(♯9) Gmi7 C13sus
I'm hang - in' out on Mon - day
I know where all the blues are,
22
G13(b9) C7sus F7(♯9) Gb7(♯9) F13sus B9(♯11)
Gmi7 C7sus F7(♯9) Gb7(♯9) F B7(b5)
my Sun - day dreams to dry. Now a
'cause, ba - by, I've been there. Now a
25
Bbmi9 /Ab Gmi7(b5) Gb13(♯11) Fmi7/Eb D+7(♯9)
Bbmi9 Fmi7
man is born to go a - lov - in', A
man is born to love a wom - an, To
27
Gmi7(b5) C+7(b9) (♯9) FMa7 Gmi11 Ami7
Bbmi7 C+7(b9) (♯9) Ami7 Dmi7 Ami7
wom - an's born to weep and fret To
work and slave to pay her debts. And

29
A♭mi11
D♭+7(♯9)
B♭mi11
A13(♭9)
A♭mi11
G7(♯11)
G♭Ma7
stay at home and tend her ov - en, and
just be - cause he's on - ly hu - man, To
31
A♭mi11
D♭7sus
D♭7
Gmi11
C7sus
C7
A♭mi11
D♭9
Gmi11
C7
drown her past re - grets in cof - fee and cig - a - rettes!
drown his past re - grets in cof - fee and cig - a - rettes!
I'm
33
F7(♯9)
G♭7(♯9)
F7(♯9)
G♭7(♯9)
moon - in' all the morn - in' and mourn - in' all the night, and
35
F7(♯9)
G♭7(♯9)
F7(♯9)
Cmi11
B9(♯11)
B9
in be - tween it's nic - o - tine and not much heart to fight black
37
B♭9
E♭9sus
F7(♯9)
B♭9
B♭°7
G♭7(♯9)
cof - fee. Feel - in' low as the ground.
can be.
40
F6/A
D7(♭9 ♭5)
Gmi7
D7(♯9)
FMa7
D7(♭9)
C13sus
It's driv - in' me cra - zy, this wait - in' for my ba - by,
42
G13(♭9)
C7sus
Gmi7
It's driv - in' me cra - zy, this wait - in' for my ba - by,
to may - be come a - round.

BEYOND THE BLUE HORIZON

from the Paramount Picture MONTE CARLO

Words by LEO ROBIN
Music by RICHARD A. WHITING
and W. FRANKE HARLING

G/A♭ A♭Ma9 G♭13(♯11) G♭7
18
A♭°7 A♭ D♭mi(♯7) E♭7
new ho - ri - zon.

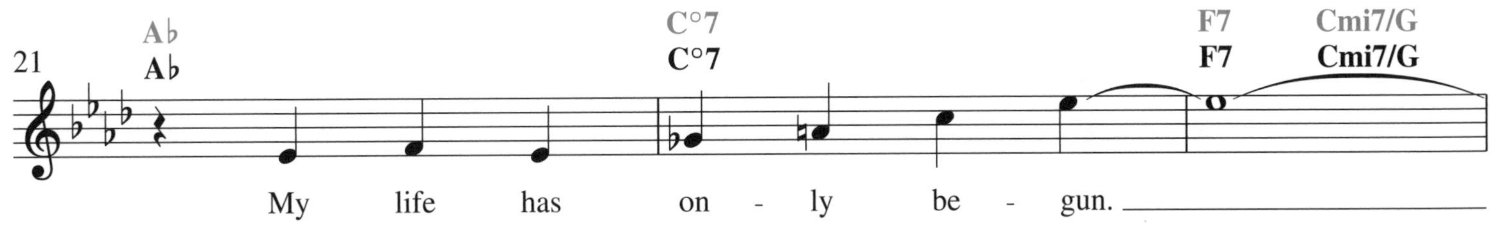
A♭ C°7 F7 Cmi7/G
21
A♭ C°7 F7 Cmi7/G
My life has on - ly be - gun.

A♭mi6 F7/A B♭mi11 G♭7 E♭9sus
24
A♭mi6 F7/A B♭mi11 B♭mi7(♭5) B♭mi7
Be - yond the blue ho -

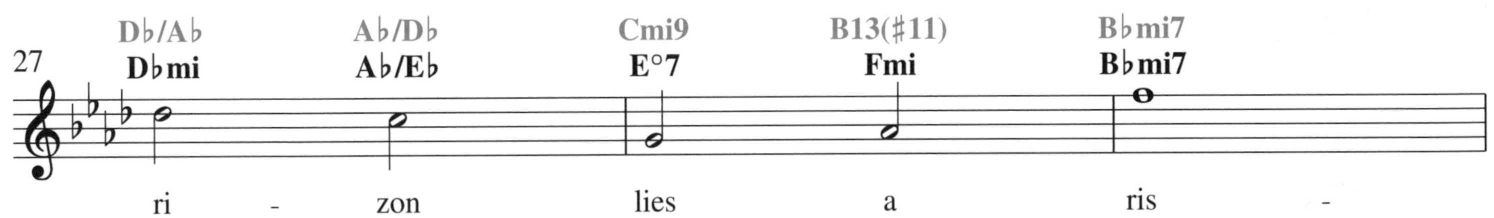
D♭/A♭ A♭/D♭ Cmi9 B13(♯11) B♭mi7
27
D♭mi A♭/E♭ E°7 Fmi B♭mi7
ri - zon lies a ris -

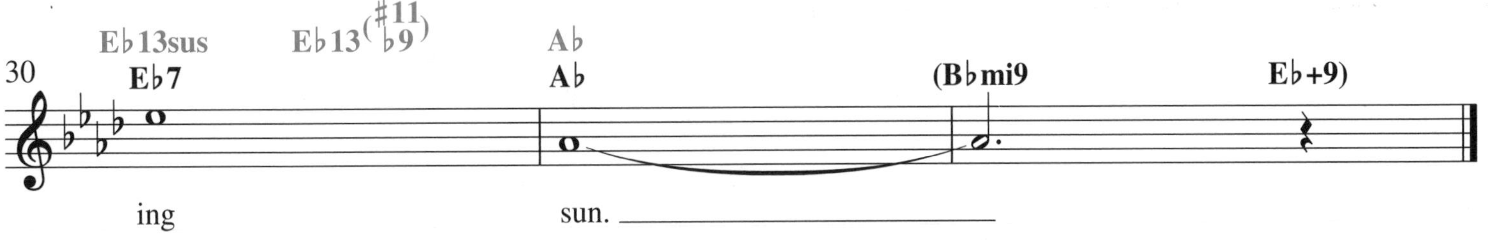
E♭13sus E♭13(♯11 ♭9) A♭
30
E♭7 A♭ (B♭mi9 E♭+9)
ing sun.

BILL BAILEY, WON'T YOU PLEASE COME HOME

Words and Music by
HUGHIE CANON

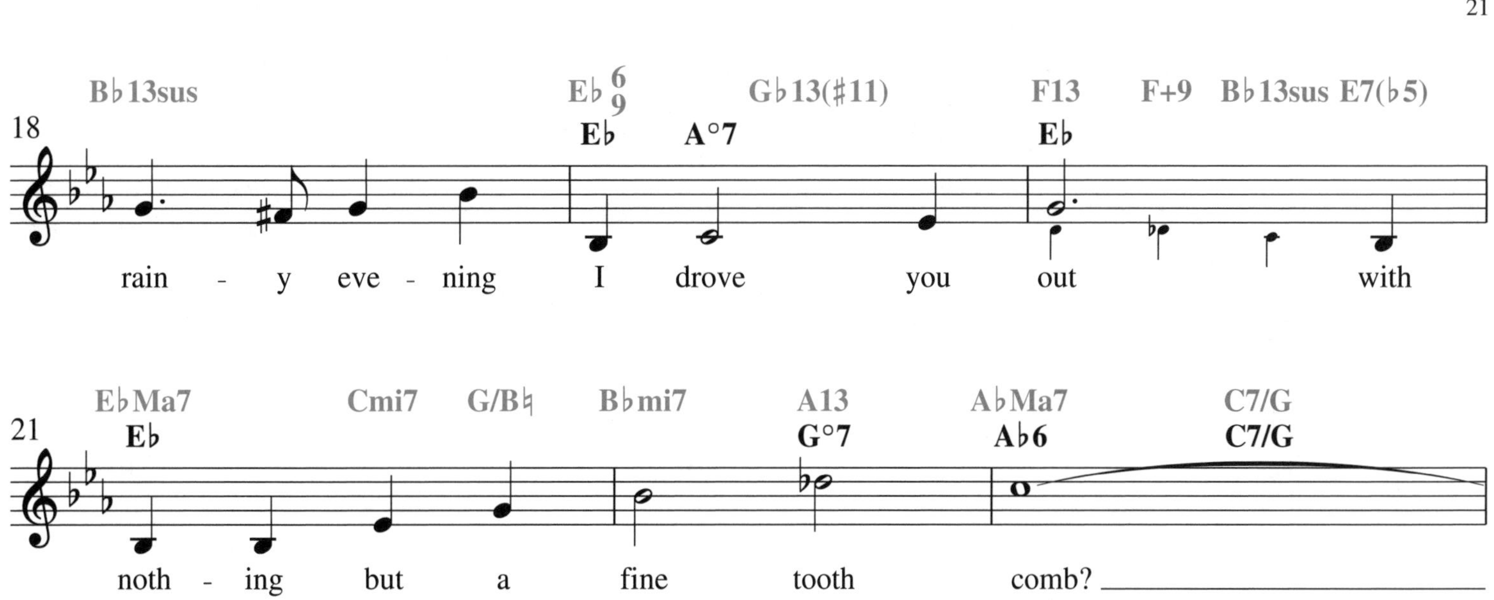
B♭13sus E♭6/9 G♭13(♯11) F13 F+9 B♭13sus E7(♭5)
E♭ A°7 E♭
rain - y eve - ning I drove you out with
E♭Ma7 Cmi7 G/B♮ B♭mi7 A13 A♭Ma7 C7/G
E♭ G°7 A♭6 C7/G
noth - ing but a fine tooth comb?

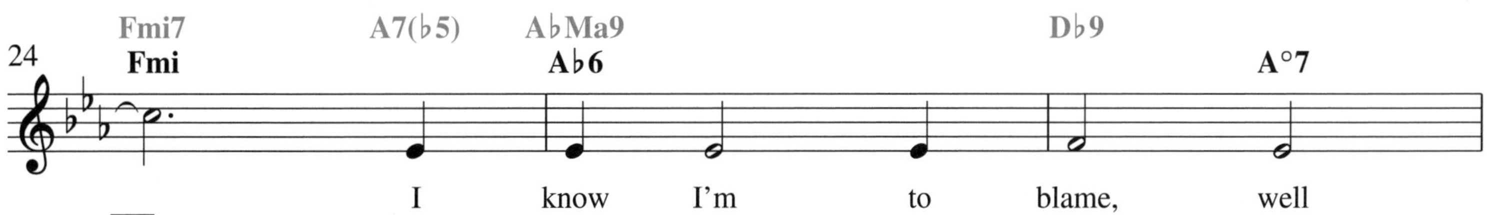
Fmi7 A7(♭5) A♭Ma9 D♭9
Fmi A♭6 A°7
I know I'm to blame, well

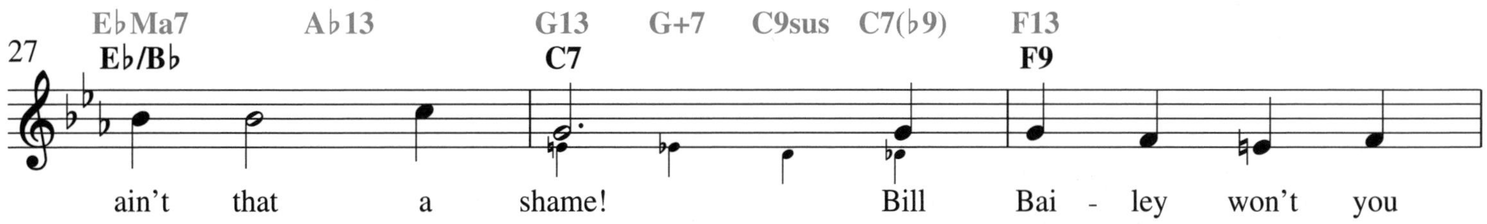
E♭Ma7 A♭13 G13 G+7 C9sus C7(♭9) F13
E♭/B♭ C7 F9
ain't that a shame! Bill Bai - ley won't you

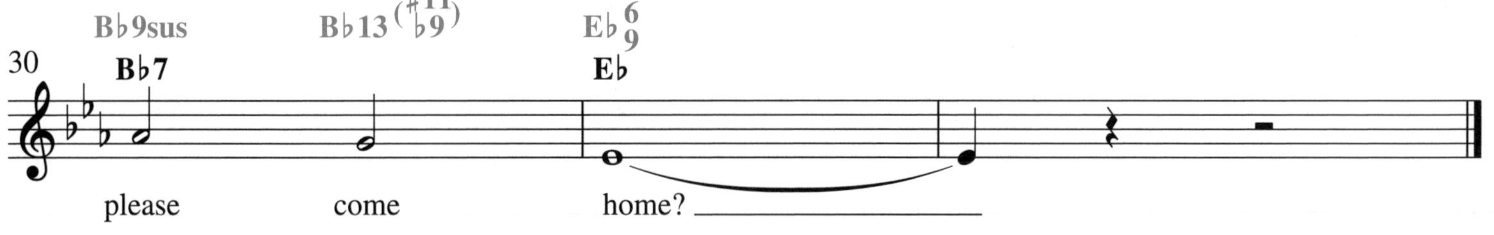
B♭9sus B♭13(♯11 ♭9) E♭6/9
B♭7 E♭
please come home?

THE BIRTH OF THE BLUES

from GEORGE WHITE'S SCANDALS OF 1924

Words by B.G. DeSYLVA and LEW BROWN
Music by RAY HENDERSON

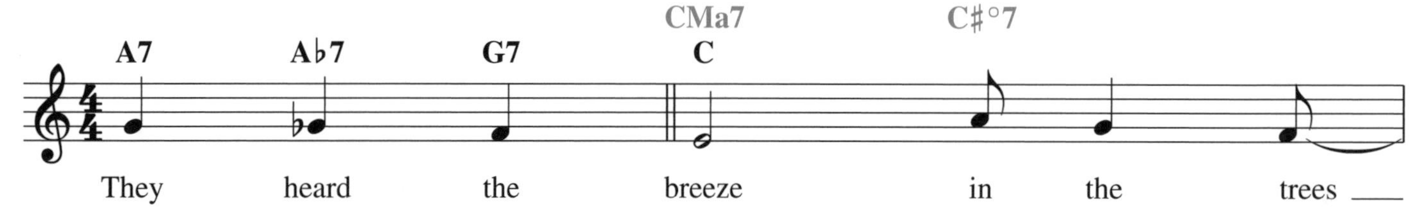

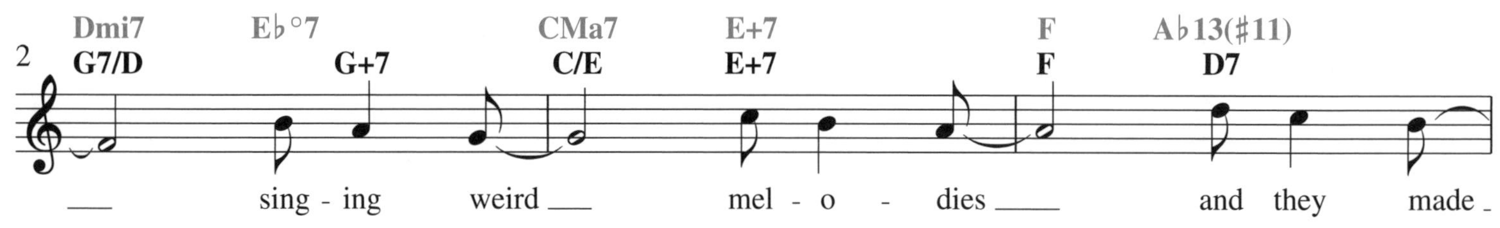

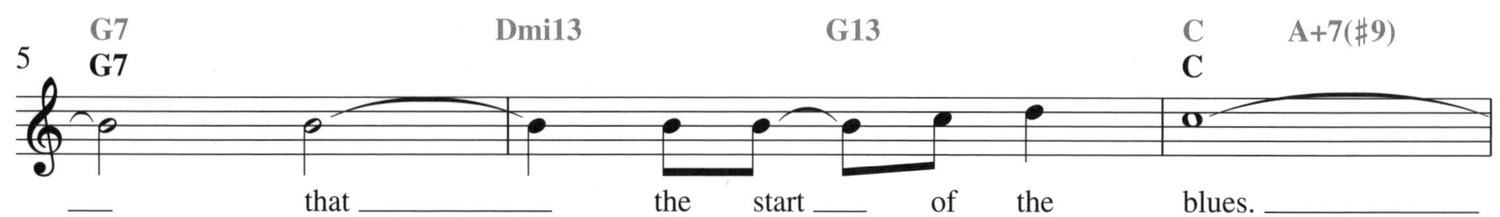

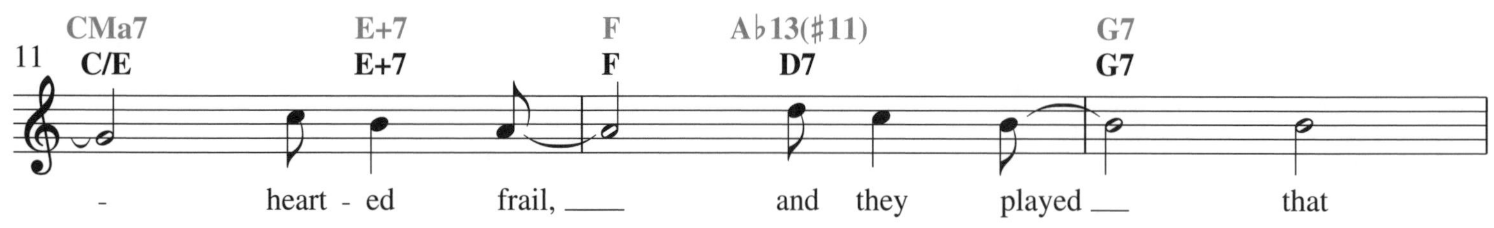

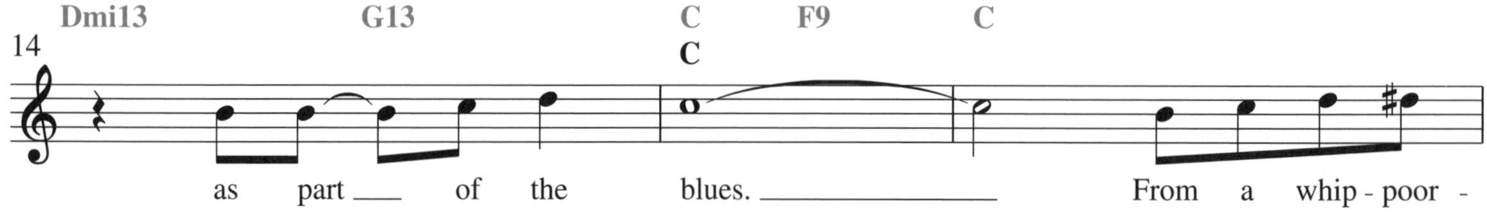

17
Bmi11 F13(♯11) E9 F13(♯11)
E7 Bmi7(♭5) E7 Bmi7(♭5)
will out on a hill they took a new
19
Bmi7 F13(♯11) E9
E7 Bmi7(♭5) E7 (N.C.)
note pushed it through a
21
A13 Emi13 A13sus E♭9(♯11) D9sus A♭13(♭9)
A7 D7sus D7
horn 'til it was worn in - to a blue note!
24
G9sus (N.C.) CMa7 C♯°7 Dmi7 E♭°7
G9 Ami7 A♭7 G7 C G7 G+9
And then they nursed it, re - hearsed it, and gave
27
CMa7 E+7 F A♭13(♯11) G7
C/E E+7 F D7 G7
out the news that the south - land
30
Dmi13 G7 C
C
gave birth to the blues!

BY THE TIME I GET TO PHOENIX

Words and Music by
JIMMY WEBB

C7(♭9 ♭5)
Cmi
To Coda
1
Fmi7
Fmi7
(♯7)
Fmi7
Fmi6
'cause I've left that girl so man - y times be -
off the
tho'
D♭9
D♭
B♭7sus
B♭7
2
Fmi7
Fmi7
fore. By the wall,
D♭9
D♭
B♭7sus
B♭7
D.S. al Coda
that's all. By the
CODA
Fmi
Fmi7
(♯7)
B♭9sus
B♭7
B♭9
time and time I've tried to tell her
E♭Ma7
E♭Ma7
A7(♭5)
A♭Ma7
A♭Ma7
Dmi7(♭5)
Fmi
so. She just did - n't know,
G7sus
G7
G+7
CMa7
C
B♭Ma7/C
B♭6
I would real - ly go.
CMa7
C
B♭Ma7/C
B♭6
CMa9
C

BYE BYE BABY

from GENTLEMEN PREFER BLONDES

Words by LEO ROBIN
Music by JULE STYNE

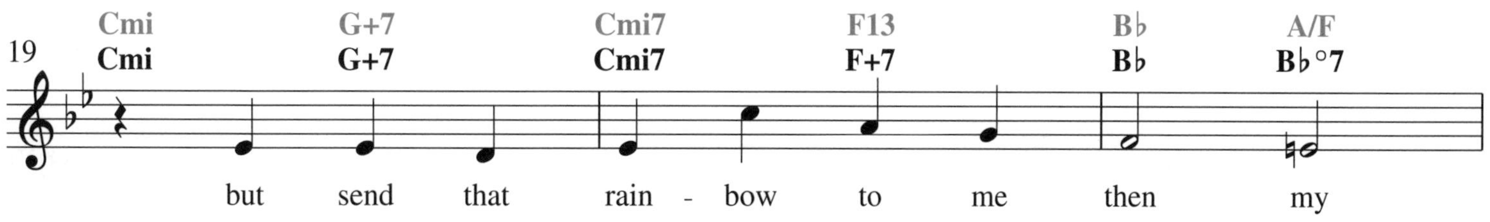
19
Cmi G+7 Cmi7 F13 B♭ A/F
Cmi G+7 Cmi7 F+7 B♭ B♭°7
but send that rain - bow to me then my

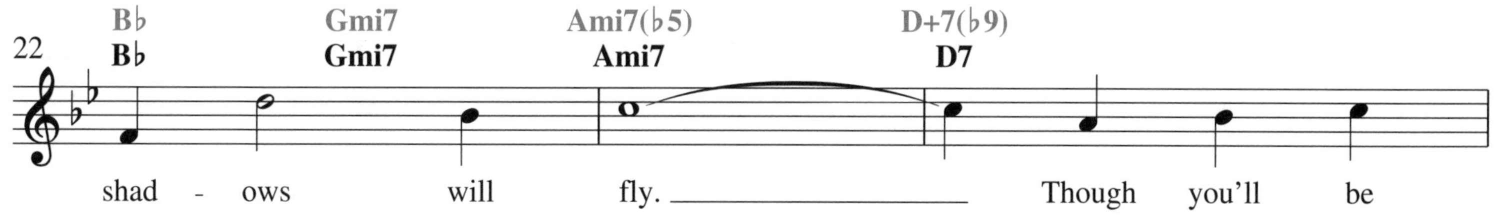
22
B♭ Gmi7 Ami7(♭5) D+7(♭9)
B♭ Gmi7 Ami7 D7
shad - ows will fly. Though you'll be

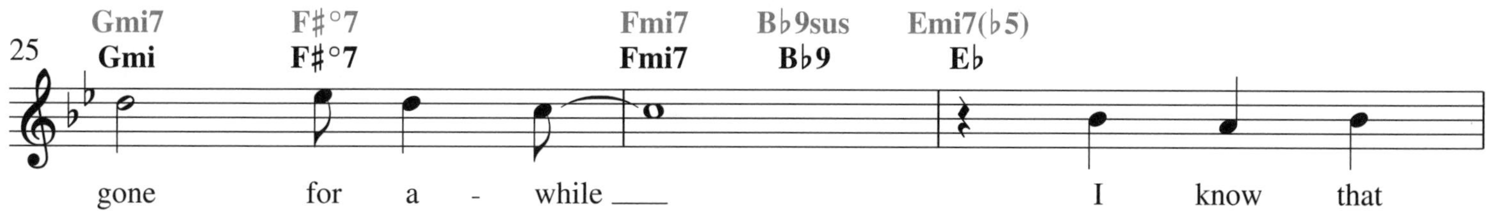
25
Gmi7 F♯°7 Fmi7 B♭9sus Emi7(♭5)
Gmi F♯°7 Fmi7 B♭9 E♭
gone for a - while I know that

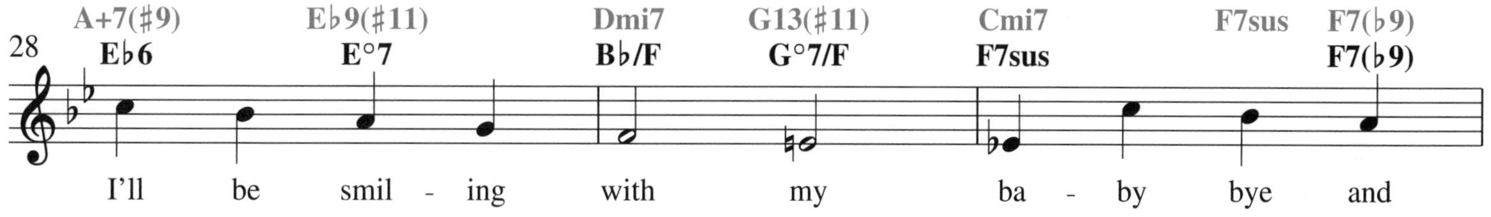
28
A+7(♯9) E♭9(♯11) Dmi7 G13(♯11) Cmi7 F7sus F7(♭9)
E♭6 E°7 B♭/F G°7/F F7sus F7(♭9)
I'll be smil - ing with my ba - by bye and

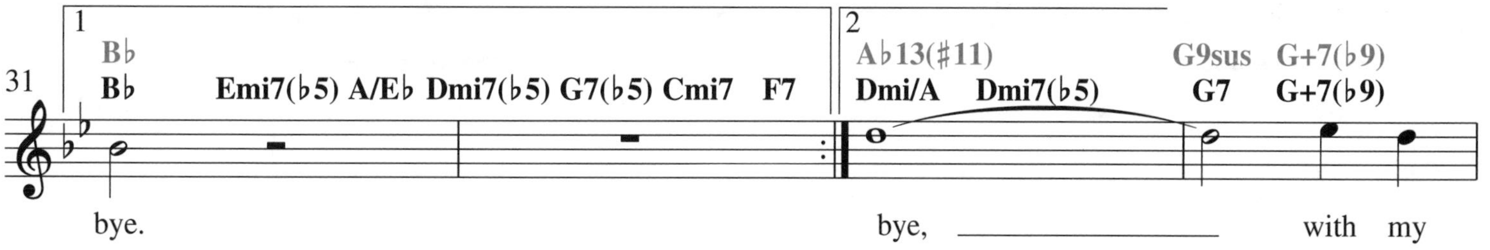
31
1
B♭
B♭ Emi7(♭5) A/E♭ Dmi7(♭5) G7(♭5) Cmi7 F7
2
A♭13(♯11) G9sus G+7(♭9)
Dmi/A Dmi7(♭5) G7 G+7(♭9)
bye. bye, with my

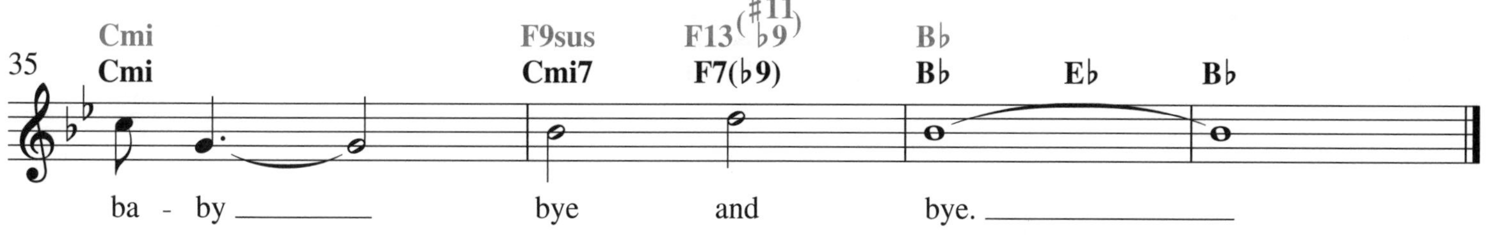
35
Cmi F9sus F13(♯11 ♭9) B♭
Cmi Cmi7 F7(♭9) B♭ E♭ B♭
ba - by bye and bye.

CALL ME

Words and Music by
TONY HATCH

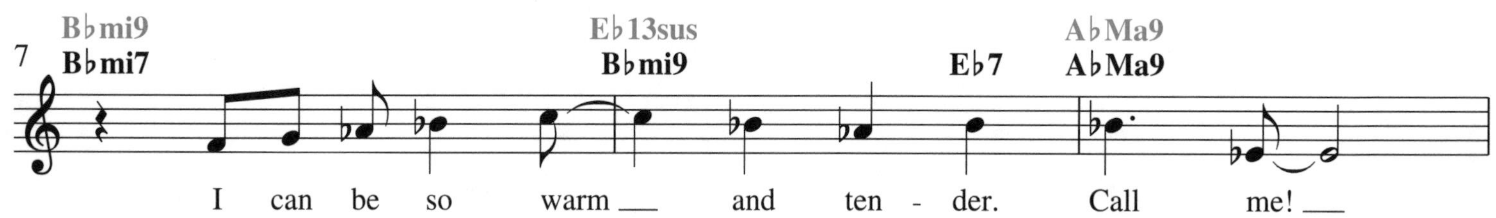

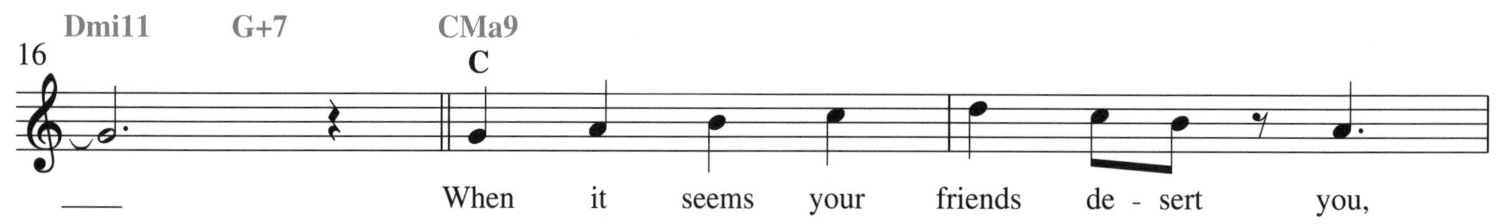

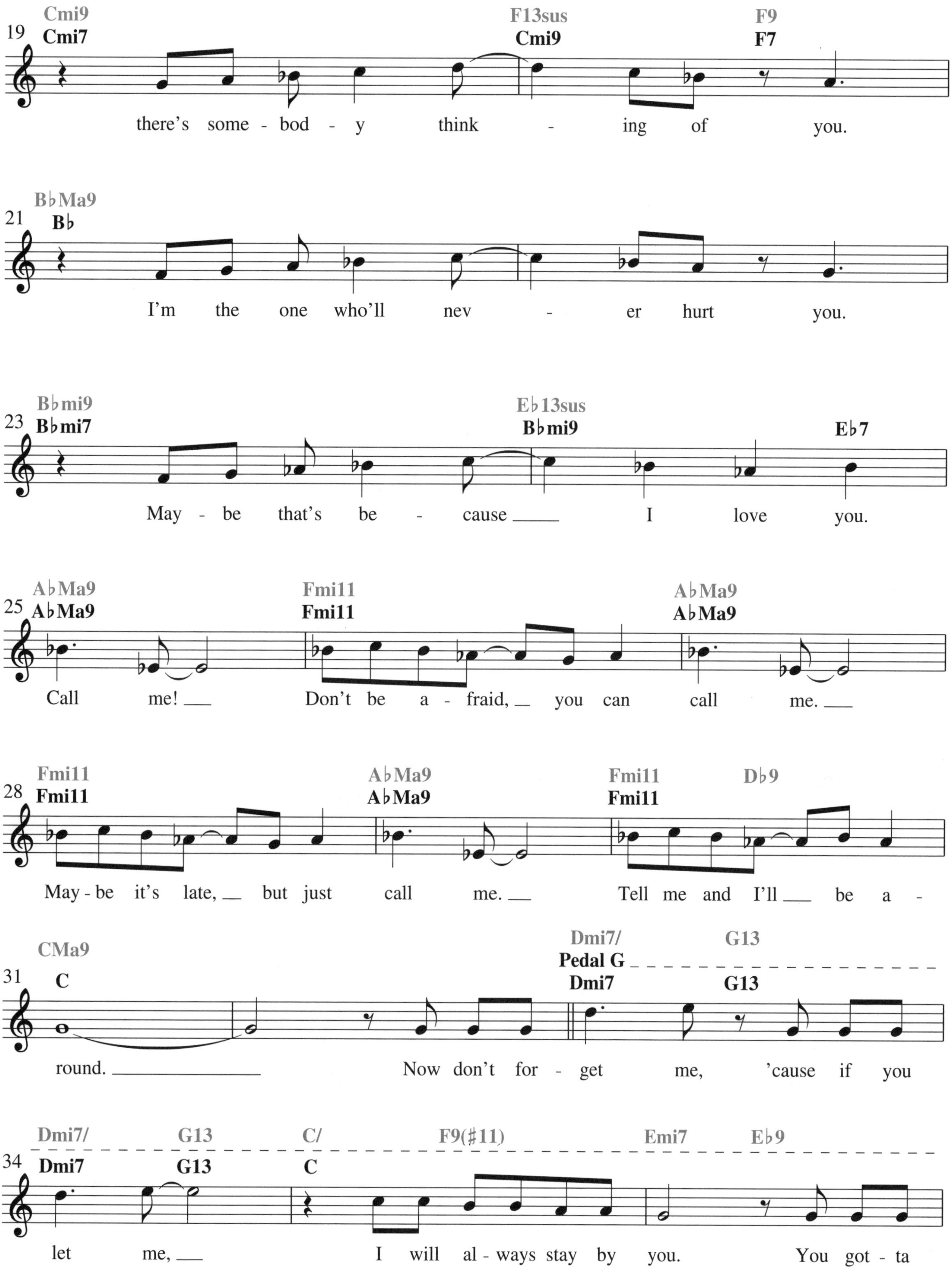

Cmi9 F13sus F9
19 Cmi7 Cmi9 F7
there's some - bod - y think - ing of you.

B♭Ma9
21 B♭
I'm the one who'll nev - er hurt you.

B♭mi9 E♭13sus
23 B♭mi7 B♭mi9 E♭7
May - be that's be - cause ___ I love you.

A♭Ma9 Fmi11 A♭Ma9
25 A♭Ma9 Fmi11 A♭Ma9
Call me! ___ Don't be a - fraid, ___ you can call me. ___

Fmi11 A♭Ma9 Fmi11 D♭9
28 Fmi11 A♭Ma9 Fmi11
May - be it's late, ___ but just call me. ___ Tell me and I'll ___ be a -

CMa9 Dmi7/ Pedal G G13
31 C Dmi7 G13
round. ___ Now don't for - get me, 'cause if you

Dmi7/ G13 Dmi7/ G13 C
37 Dmi7 G13 Dmi7 G13 C
trust me, that's how it must be. There's so much that I can
D13sus D+7 G7sus G7(♭9) CMa9
40 Dmi7 G7 C
do. If you call I'll
Cmi9 F13sus F9
43 Cmi7 Cmi9 F7
be right with you. You and I should be to - geth - er.
B♭Ma9 B♭mi9
46 B♭ B♭mi7
Take this love I long to give you, I'll be at your side
E♭13sus A♭Ma9 Fmi11
49 B♭mi9 E♭7 A♭Ma9 Fmi11
for - ev - er. Call me! Don't be a - fraid, you can
A♭Ma9 Fmi11 A♭Ma9
52 A♭Ma9 Fmi11 A♭Ma9
call me. May - be it's late, but just call me.
Fmi11 D♭9 CMa9
55 Fmi11 C
Tell me and I'll be a - round.

IT WAS A VERY GOOD YEAR

Words and Music by
ERVIN DRAKE

CHICAGO
(That Toddlin' Town)

Words and Music by
FRED FISHER

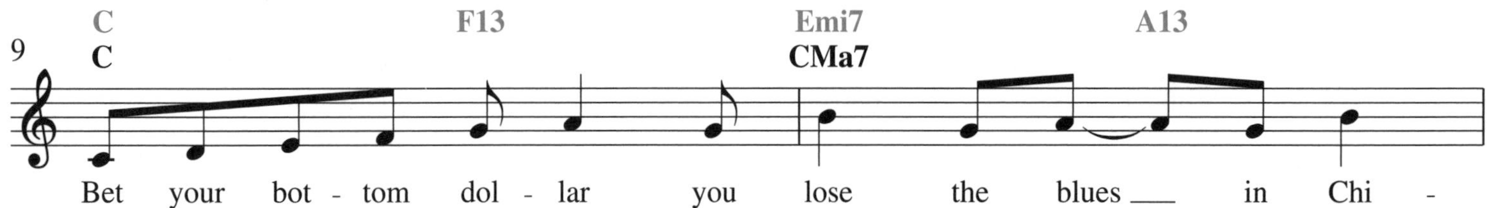

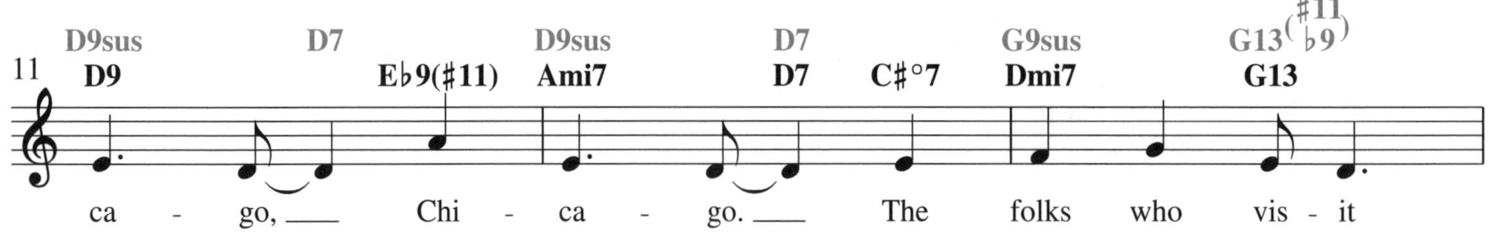

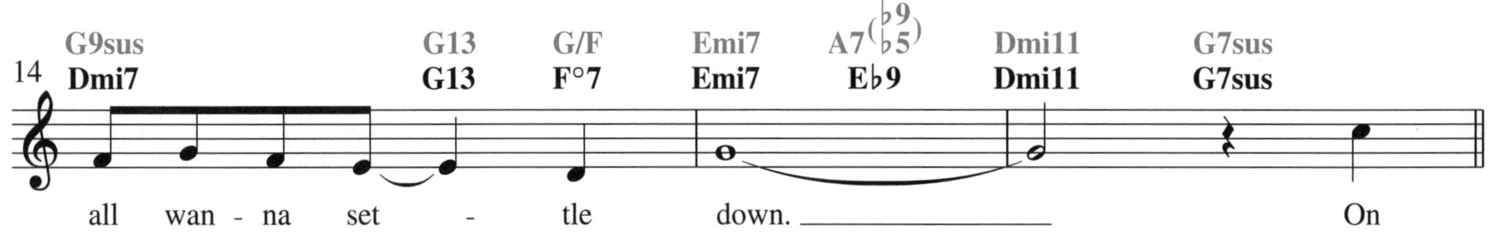

CMa7
17 CMa7
F13
Dmi7
Emi7
Emi7
A13
A7
State Street, that great street, I
Dmi7
19 Dmi7
G13
G7
Dmi7
Dmi7
G13
G7
A+7
just wan - na say, (just wan - na say,) they
Dmi9
21 Dmi9
G7
G7
E7sus
Bmi11
B♭9(♯11)
E7
Ami7
Ami
do things they don't do on Broad - way.
A7(♭9)
24 A7
Dmi9
FMa7
Say, you'll have the time, the time
Fmi6
26 B♭9(♯11)
B♭9
C/G
B+7(♯9)
G+7
of your life. Bring all your friends, your kids
Gmi/B♭
28 C/G
A7(♭9)
E♭13(♯11)
E♭°7
Dmi13
G7/D
A♭13(♭9)
G9
A♭7
and your wife to Chi - ca - go, Chi -
G7
30 G7
G9sus
G7(♭9)
C
C
ca - go, my home - town.

THE CHRISTMAS SONG

(Chestnuts Roasting on an Open Fire)

Words and Music by MEL TORME
and ROBERT WELLS

17
E♭13sus
B♭mi7 E♭9 B♭mi7 E♭9
San - ta's on his way; he's load - ed
19
A♭Ma9/E♭
B♭mi7 E♭9 A♭Ma9
lots of toys and good - ies on his sleigh. And ev - 'ry
21
D♭13sus G♭Ma9/D♭
A♭mi7 D♭9 G♭Ma9
moth - er's child is gon - na spy to see if
23
Cmi11 B9(♯11) B♭7sus E+7(♯9)
Cmi11 F7 B♭7sus B♭7
rein - deer real - ly know how to fly. And
25
Ami7(♭5) A♭13(♯11) Gmi7 Fmi9 E7(♯9)
E♭6 B♭7 E♭6 B♭13sus B♭13
so I'm of - fer - ing this sim - ple phrase to
27
E♭13sus B♭mi7 A+7(♯9) A♭Ma9 D♭9sus Cmi7 D♭7
E♭6 E♭9 A♭ A♭7 G+7 Cmi /B♭ A♭mi6
kids from one to nine - ty - two. Al - tho' it's been said man - y
30
Cmi7 /B♭ Ami11 A♭13 Gmi7 Cmi7 Fmi7 B♭7(♭9) E♭6/9
E♭/B♭ Ami11 A♭7 E♭/B♭ Fmi7 B♭7(♭9) E♭6
times, man - y ways, "Mer - ry Christ - mas to you."

COCKTAILS FOR TWO

from the Paramount Picture MURDER AT THE VANITIES

Words and Music by ARTHUR JOHNSTON
and SAM COSLOW

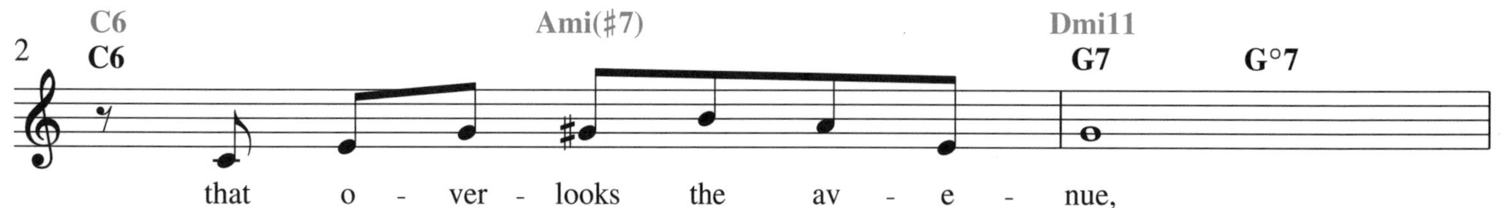

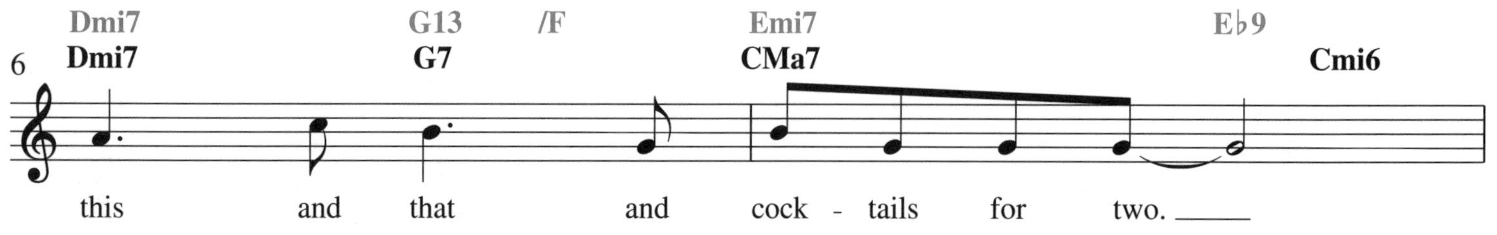

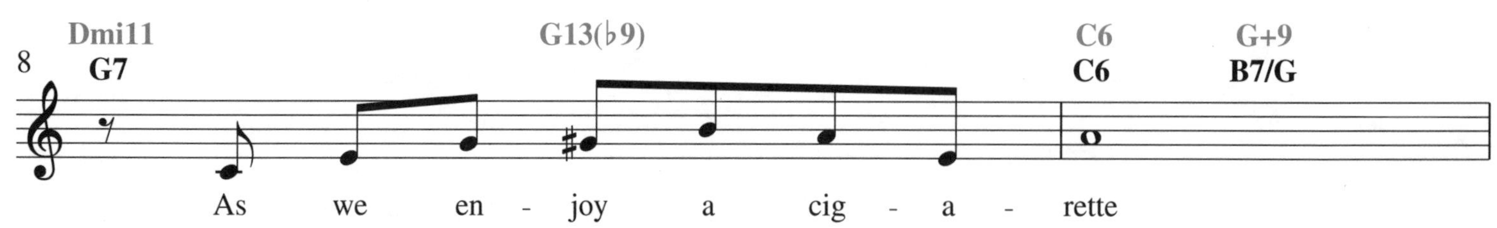

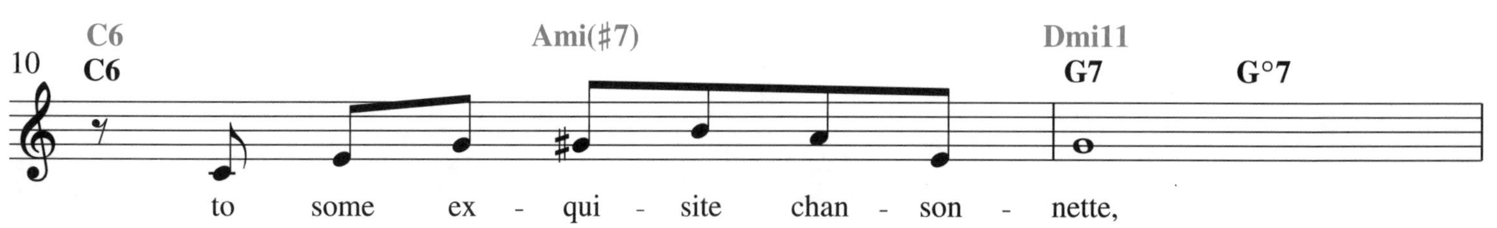

12
G13sus Dmi7 G13 Dmi7 G13
G7 Dmi7 G7 Dmi7 G7
two hands are sure to sly - ly meet be - neath a ser - vi - ette with
15
C9sus A♭°7 Gmi7 C+7 FMa7
C9 B+7 C7 3 FMa7 F6
cock - tails for two. My head may go reel - ing,
18
B♭9(♯11) CMa9 F13 C/E E♭°7
Fmi6 CMa9 C E♭°7
but my heart will be o - be - di - ent, with in - tox - i - cat - ing
21
Dmi7 G13 Dmi7 G13 /F Emi11 E♭9
Dmi7 G7 G9 G7 C6 C♯°7
kiss - es for the prin - ci - pal in - gre - di - ent.
24
Dmi11 G13(♭9) C6 G+9 C6 Ami(♯7)
G7/D C6 B7/G C6
Most an - y af - ter - noon at five we'll be so glad we're both a -
27
Dmi11 G13sus Dmi7 G13
G7 G°7 G7 Dmi7 G7
live. Then may - be for - tune will com - plete her plan that
30
Dmi7 G13 CMa9
Dmi7 G7 C
all be - gan with cock - tails for two.

COME SUNDAY

from BLACK, BROWN & BEIGE

By DUKE ELLINGTON

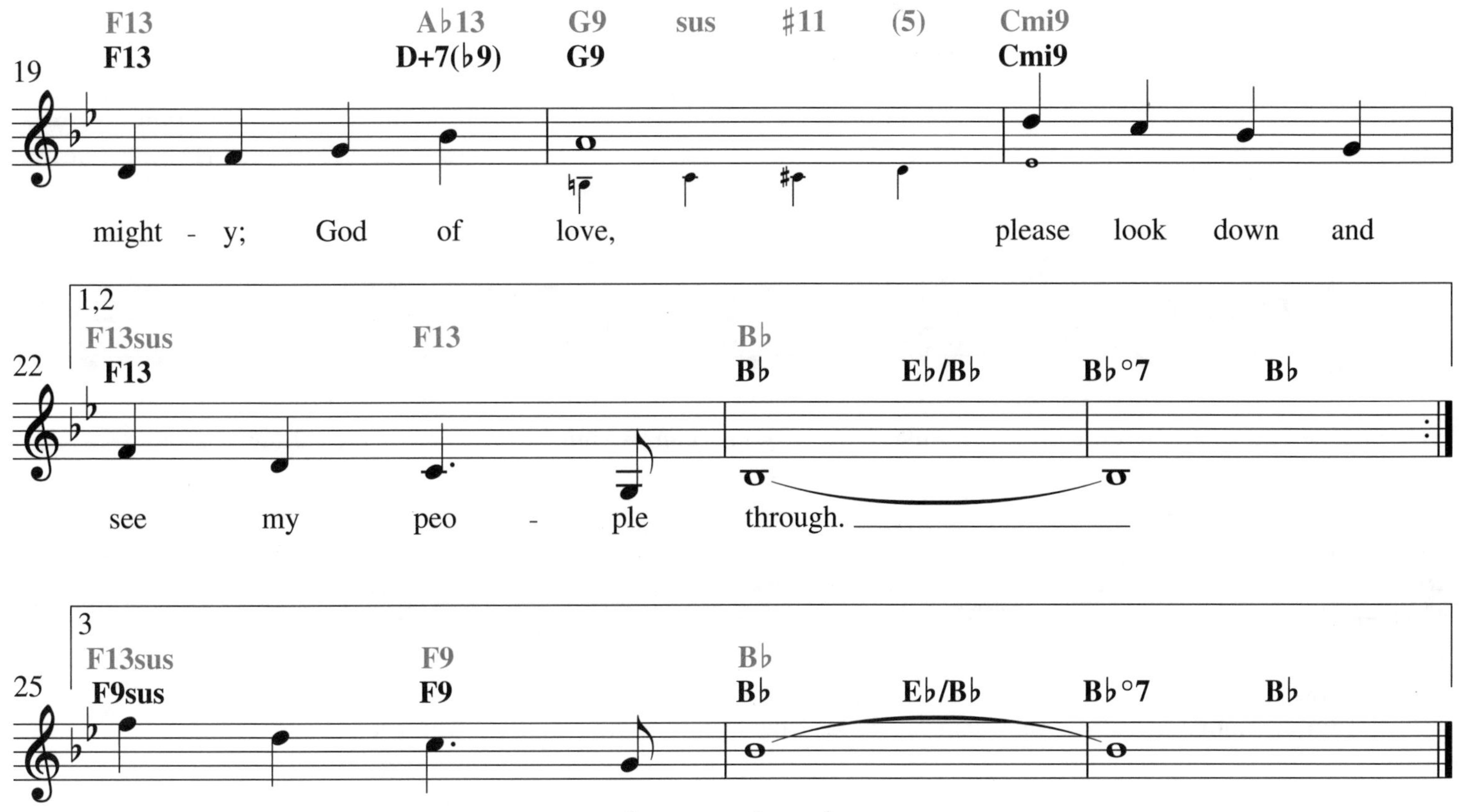

F13
F13
A♭13
D+7(♭9)
G9
G9
sus
♯11
(5)
Cmi9
Cmi9
19
might - y; God of love, please look down and
1,2
F13sus
F13
F13
B♭
B♭
E♭/B♭
B♭°7
B♭
22
see my peo - ple through.
3
F13sus
F9sus
F9
F9
B♭
B♭
E♭/B♭
B♭°7
B♭
25
see my peo - ple through.

COMES LOVE

Words and Music by LEW BROWN,
SAM H. STEPT and CHARLIE TOBIAS

17
G7 G+7 Cmi
G7 G+7 Cmi G7/D Cmi/E♭ G7/D
Don't try hid - in' 'cause there is - n't an - y use.
That's all, broth - er if you've ev - er been in love.
20
F13 E♭13(♯11)
Cmi F7 D7
You'll start slid - in'
That's all, broth - er!
23
D13sus B♭13 Ami11 A♭7(♭5) Gmi9
D7 Gmi
when your heart turns on the juice. Comes a head - ache you can
You know what I'm speak - ing of! Comes a night - mare you can
26
D7
D7
lose it in a day. Comes a tooth - ache see your den - tist right a - way. Comes
al - ways stay a - wake. Comes de - pres - sion you may get an - oth - er break. Comes
29
Ami11 D7alt.
D7 C/E F°7 D7/F♯ E♭7 D7
1
Gmi
Gmi
love, noth - ing can be done!
love, noth - ing can be
32
2
Gmi
Gmi
Comes a done!

DON'T BLAME ME

Words by DOROTHY FIELDS
Music by JIMMY McHUGH

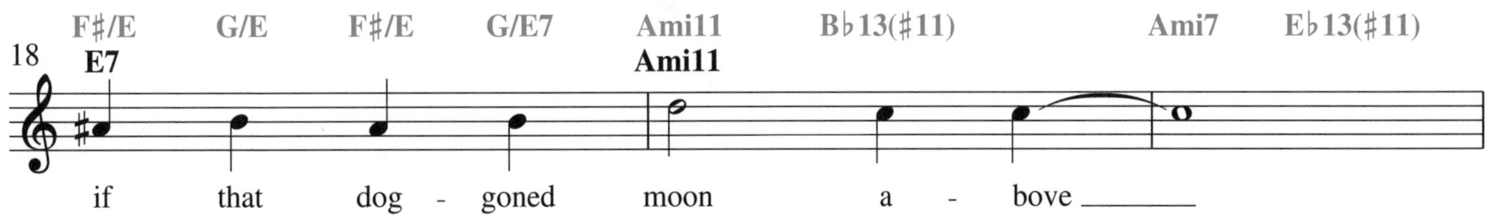
F♯/E G/E F♯/E G/E7 Ami11 B♭13(♯11) Ami7 E♭13(♯11)
18
E7 Ami11
if that dog - goned moon a - bove

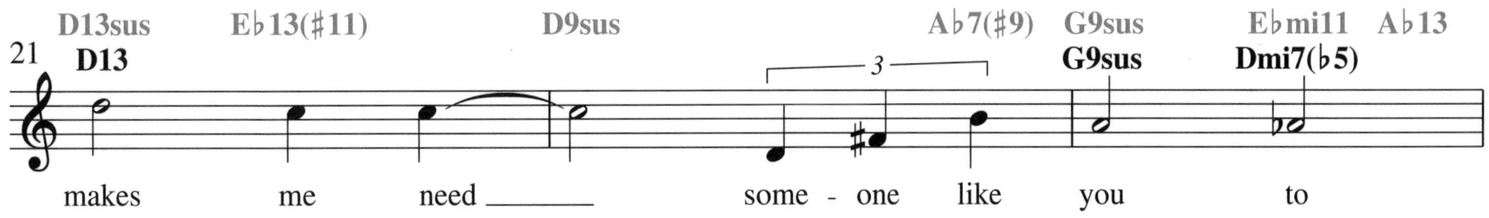
D13sus E♭13(♯11) D9sus A♭7(♯9) G9sus E♭mi11 A♭13
21
D13 G9sus Dmi7(♭5)
3
makes me need some - one like you to

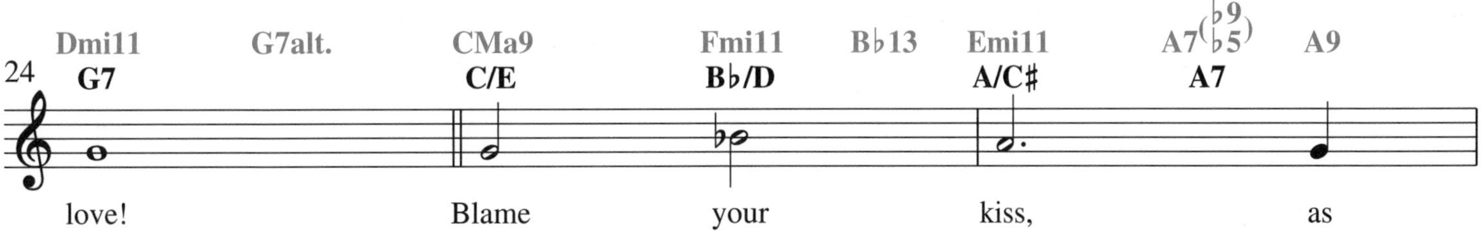
Dmi11 G7alt. CMa9 Fmi11 B♭13 Emi11 A7(♭9 ♭5) A9
24
G7 C/E B♭/D A/C♯ A7
love! Blame your kiss, as

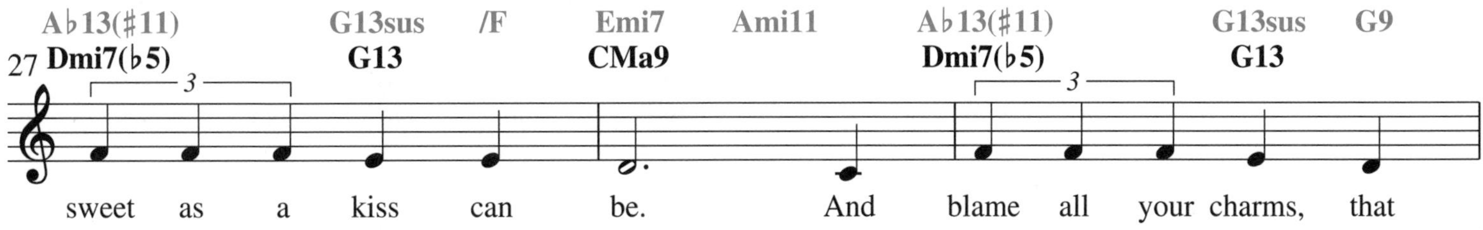
A♭13(♯11) G13sus /F Emi7 Ami11 A♭13(♯11) G13sus G9
27
Dmi7(♭5) G13 CMa9 Dmi7(♭5) G13
3
3
sweet as a kiss can be. And blame all your charms, that

B♭13(♯11) A+7 A7(♭9) G9sus G+9 C6/9
30
Emi7(♭5) A+7 Dmi7 G+9 C
3
melt in my arms but don't blame me.

DON'T SIT UNDER THE APPLE TREE

(With Anyone Else but Me)

Words and Music by LEW BROWN,
SAM H. STEPT and CHARLIE TOBIAS

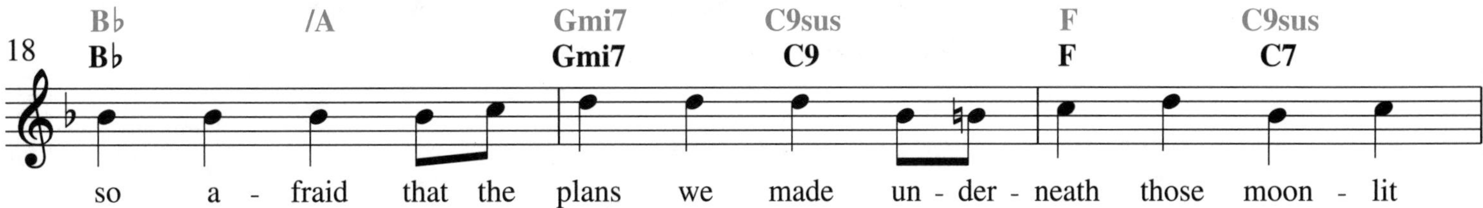
B♭ /A Gmi7 C9sus F C9sus
18
B♭ Gmi7 C9 F C7
so a - fraid that the plans we made un - der - neath those moon - lit

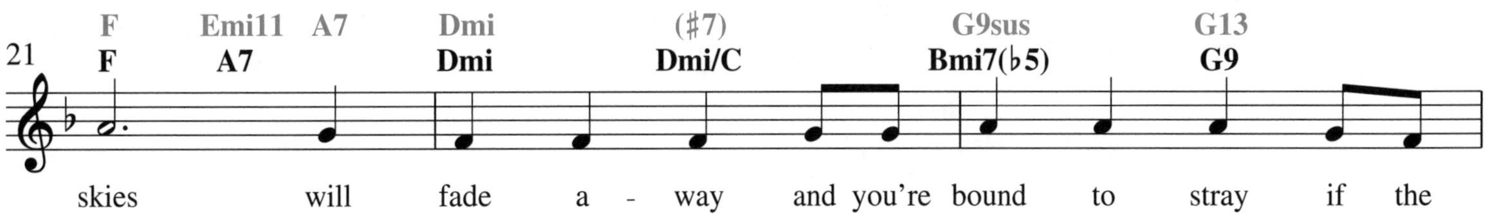
F Emi11 A7 Dmi (♯7) G9sus G13
21
F A7 Dmi Dmi/C Bmi7(♭5) G9
skies will fade a - way and you're bound to stray if the

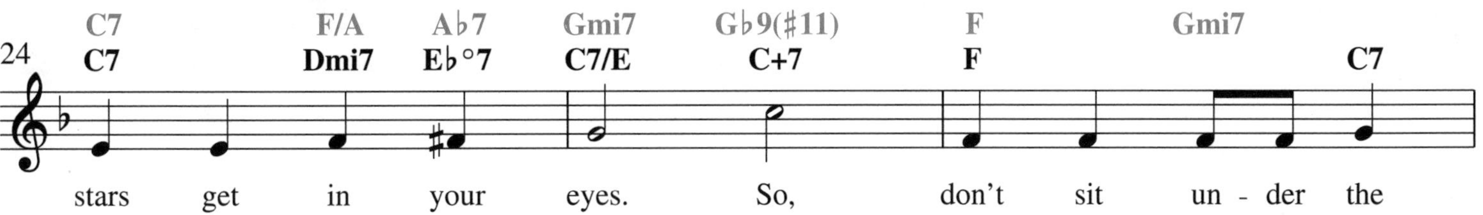
C7 F/A A♭7 Gmi7 G♭9(♯11) F Gmi7
24
C7 Dmi7 E♭°7 C7/E C+7 F C7
stars get in your eyes. So, don't sit un - der the

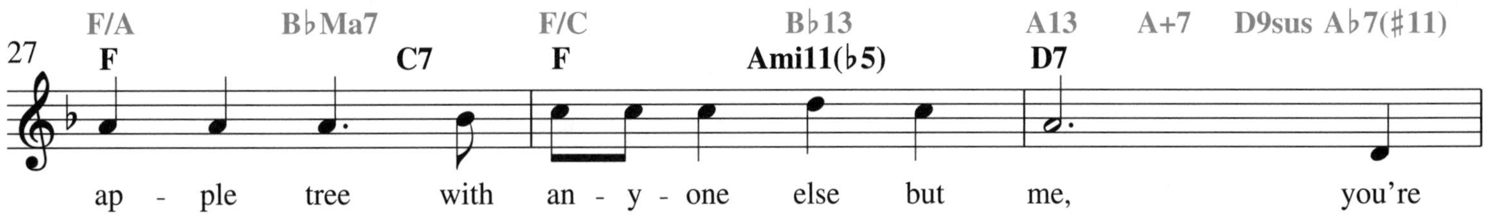
F/A B♭Ma7 F/C B♭13 A13 A+7 D9sus A♭7(♯11)
27
F C7 F Ami11(♭5) D7
ap - ple tree with an - y - one else but me, you're

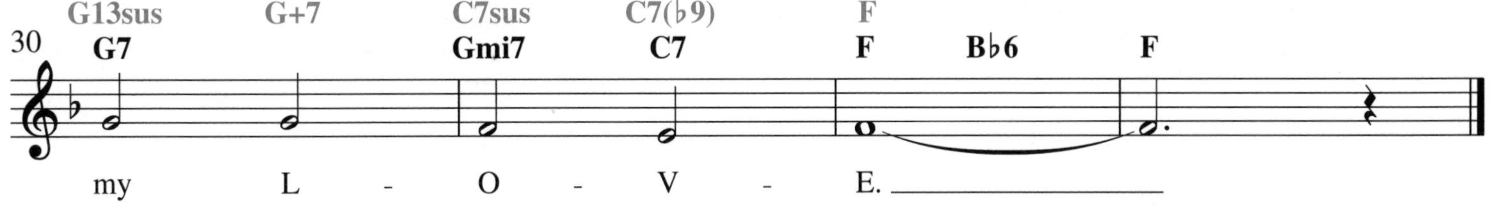
G13sus G+7 C7sus C7(♭9) F
30
G7 Gmi7 C7 F B♭6 F
my L - O - V - E.

DON'T TAKE YOUR LOVE FROM ME

Words and Music by
HENRY NEMO

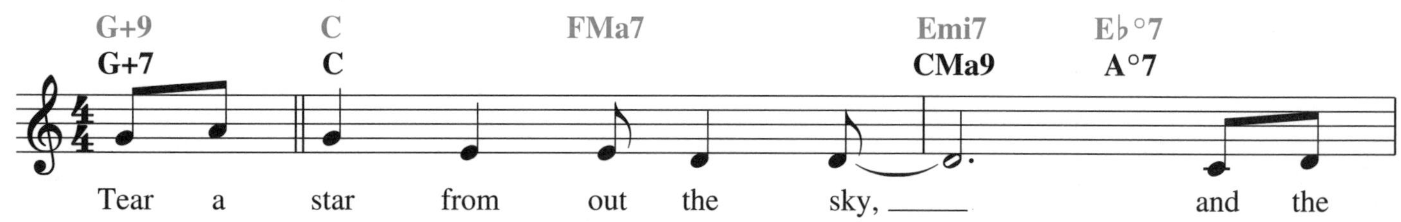
G+9 C FMa7 Emi7 E♭°7
G+7 C CMa9 A°7
Tear a star from out the sky, and the

3
Dmi6 G9 Dmi7 A♭13(♯11)
G9 Dmi7
sky feels blue. Tear a pet - al from a rose

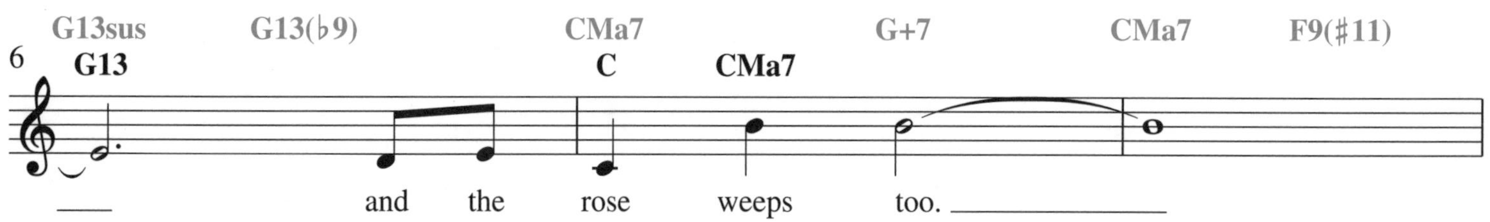
6
G13sus G13(♭9) CMa7 G+7 CMa7 F9(♯11)
G13 C CMa7
and the rose weeps too.

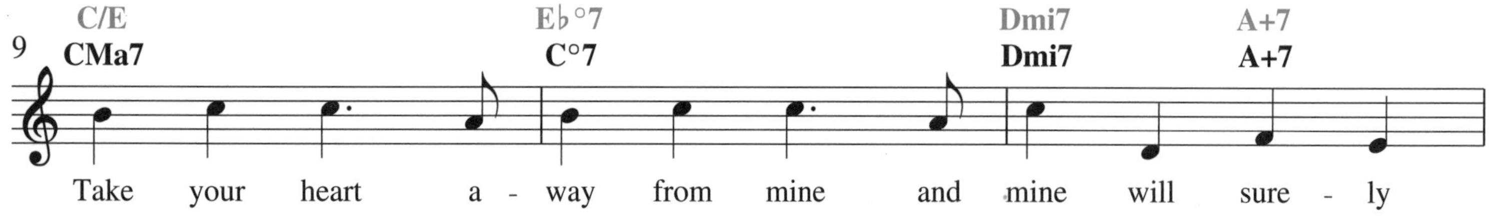
9
C/E E♭°7 Dmi7 A+7
CMa7 C°7 Dmi7 A+7
Take your heart a - way from mine and mine will sure - ly

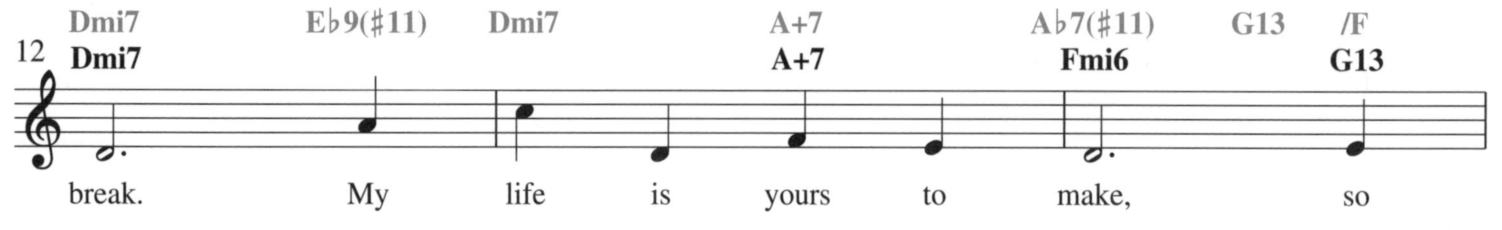
12
Dmi7 E♭9(♯11) Dmi7 A+7 A♭7(♯11) G13 /F
Dmi7 A+7 Fmi6 G13
break. My life is yours to make, so

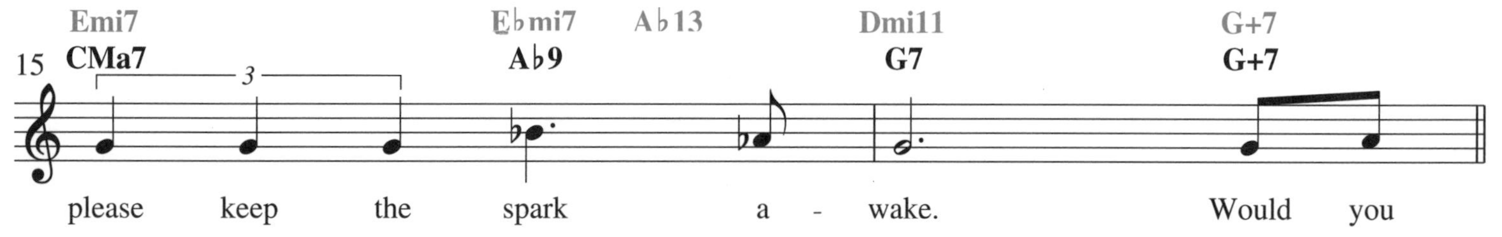
15
Emi7 E♭mi7 A♭13 Dmi11 G+7
CMa7 A♭9 G7 G+7
3
please keep the spark a - wake. Would you

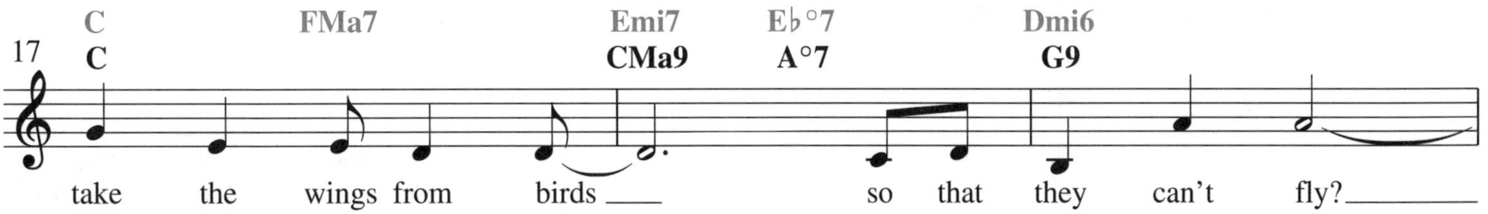
17
C
FMa7
Emi7
E♭°7
Dmi6
C
CMa9
A°7
G9
take the wings from birds ___ so that they can't fly? ___

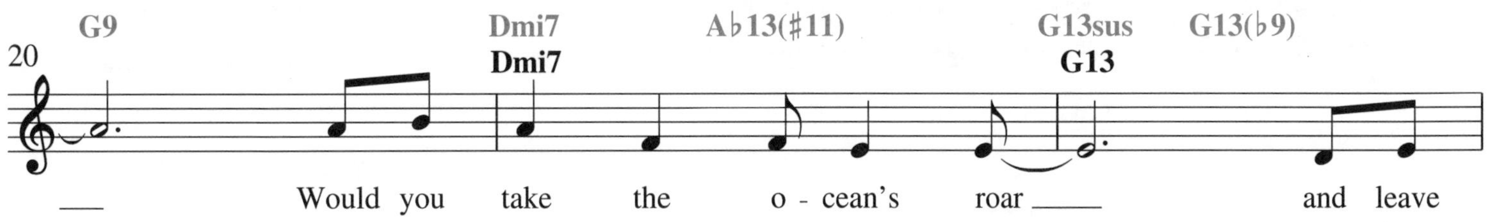
20
G9
Dmi7
A♭13(♯11)
G13sus
G13(♭9)
Dmi7
G13
___ Would you take the o - cean's roar ___ and leave

23
C
A♭13
Gmi11
G♭13(♯11)
FMa7
C6
C7
C+7
FMa7
just a sigh? ___ All this your heart won't

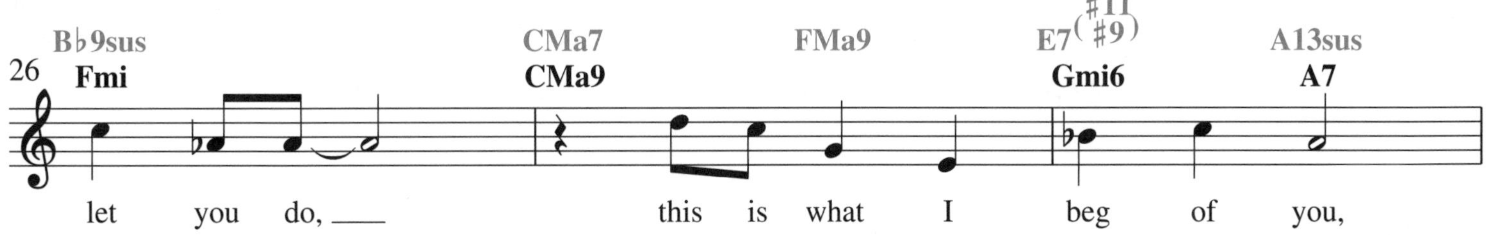
26
B♭9sus
CMa7
FMa9
E7(♯11 ♯9)
A13sus
Fmi
CMa9
Gmi6
A7
let you do, ___ this is what I beg of you,

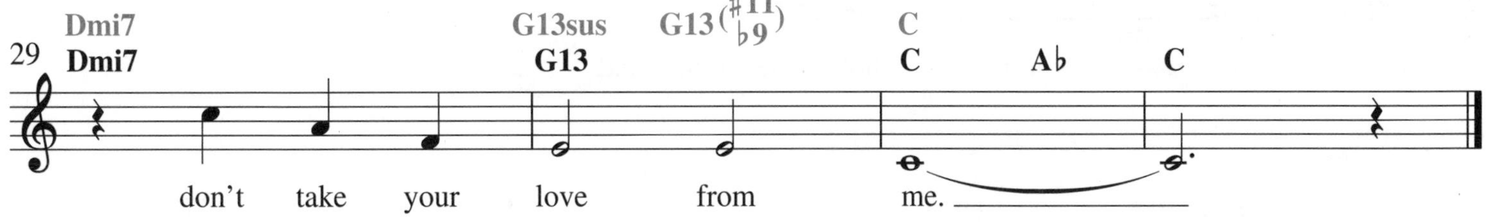
29
Dmi7
G13sus
G13(♯11 ♭9)
C
Dmi7
G13
C
A♭
C
don't take your love from me. ___

DREAM A LITTLE DREAM OF ME

Words by GUS KAHN
Music by WILBUR SCHWANDT
and FABIAN ANDREE

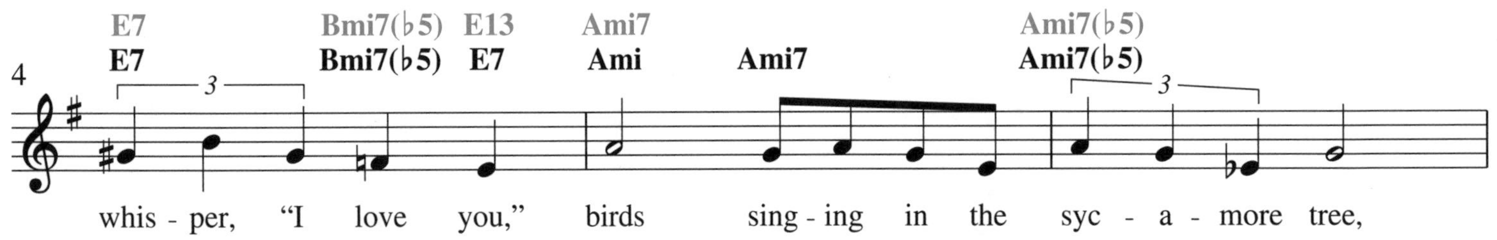

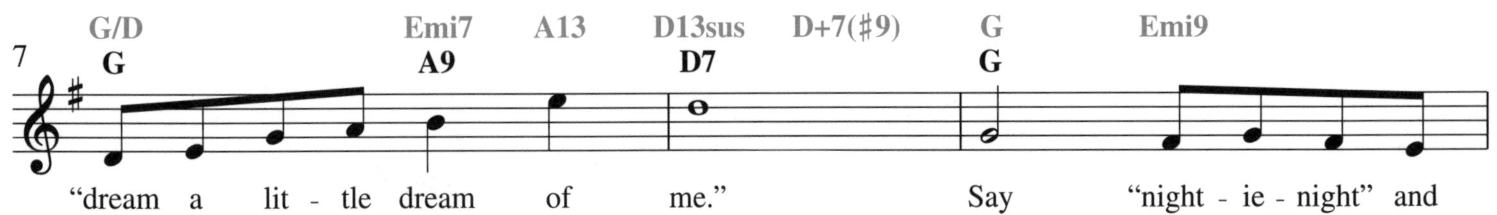

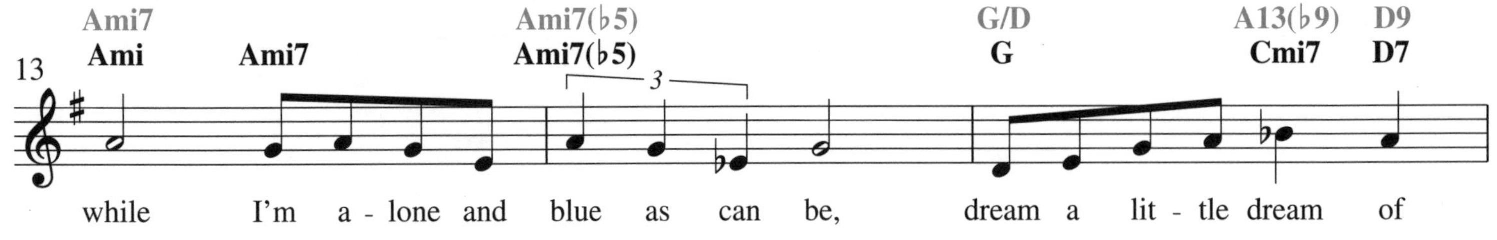

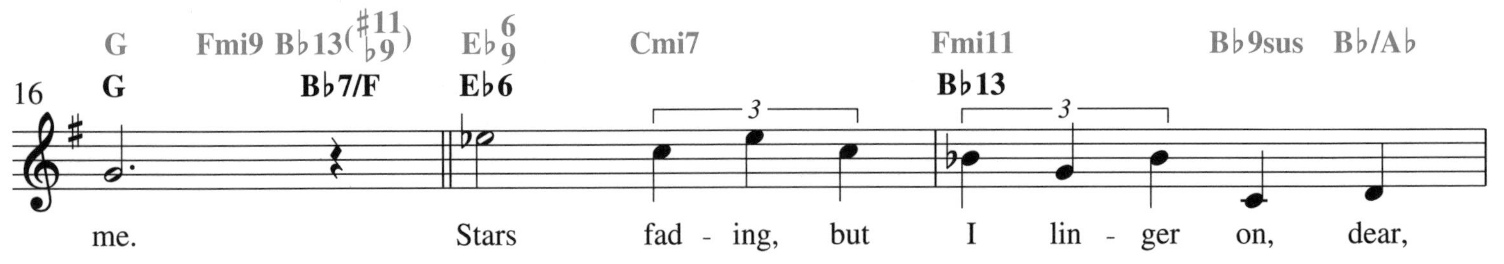

19
E♭/G G♭13(♯11) Fmi11 B♭13(♯11/♭9) E♭6/9 Cmi7
E♭6 B♭7 B♭°7 B♭7 E♭6
still crav - ing your kiss. I'm long - ing to
22
Fmi11 B♭9sus B♭7 E♭ Cmi7 B♭13 Ami11 D+7(♯9)
B♭13 E♭6 D7
lin - ger till dawn, dear, just say - ing this:
25
G Emi9 E♭7 D7 G C9(♯11)
G E♭7 D7 G
Sweet dreams till sun - beams find you, sweet dreams that leave all
28
E7 Bmi7(♭5) E13 Ami7
E7 Bmi7(♭5) E7 Ami Ami7
wor - ries be - hind you, but in your dreams what -
30
Ami7(♭5) G/D A13(♭9) D9 G
Ami7(♭5) G Cmi7 D7 G
ev - er they be, dream a lit - tle dream of me.

ELMER'S TUNE

Words and Music by ELMER ALBRECHT,
SAMMY GALLOP and DICK JURGENS

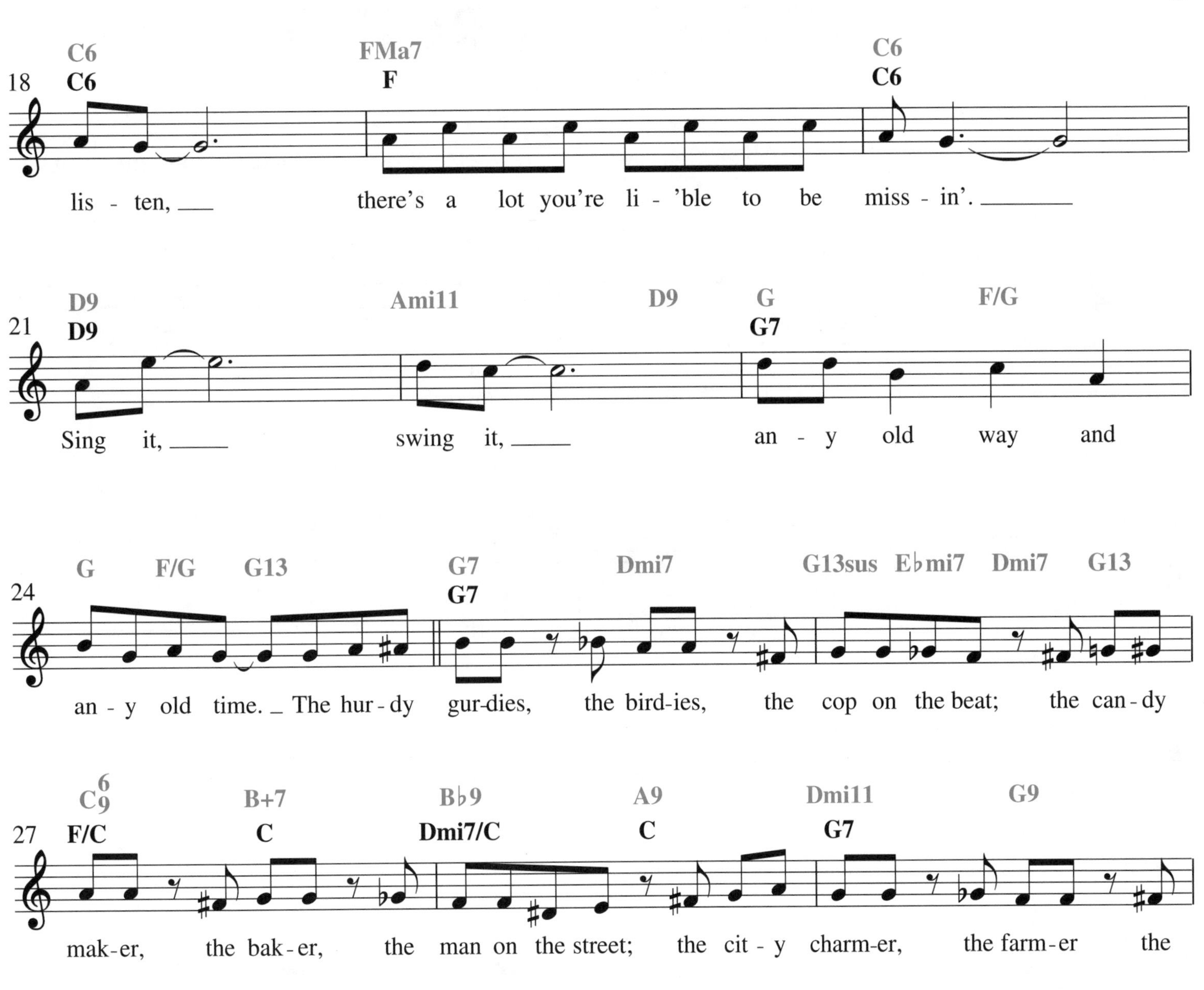
18
C6 FMa7 C6
C6 F C6
lis - ten, there's a lot you're li - 'ble to be miss - in'.
21
D9 Ami11 D9 G F/G
D9 G7
Sing it, swing it, an - y old way and
24
G F/G G13 G7 Dmi7 G13sus E♭mi7 Dmi7 G13
G7
an - y old time. The hur - dy gur-dies, the bird-ies, the cop on the beat; the can - dy
27
C6/9 B+7 B♭9 A9 Dmi11 G9
F/C C Dmi7/C C G7
mak-er, the bak - er, the man on the street; the cit - y charm-er, the farm-er the
30
Dmi11 G9 D9 G13sus G13(♯11 ♭9) C
D9 G13 C
man in the moon all sing El - mer's Tune.

GET ME TO THE CHURCH ON TIME

from MY FAIR LADY

Words by ALAN JAY LERNER
Music by FREDERICK LOEWE

Emi11 A13 D7 Ami/E F7 D9/F♯
23 A7sus A7 D7 Ami/E F7 D9/F♯
whis - tling, *whewt* me out the door! For
G(add2)
27 G
I'm get - ting mar - ried in the morn - ing.
D7sus G(add2) G /F
30
Ding! dong! the bells are gon - na chime.
Bmi7(♭5)/E E7(♭9) Ami7 E/D D/C
34 G/F E7 C6 CMa7 C+ C6 C♯°7
Kick up a rum - pus, but
B+7 E7(♭9 ♭5) E7(♭9) Ami11 Cmi9 F13
37 G Gmi G Bmi C
don't lose the com - pass. And get me to the church,
Bmi7 E+7(♯9) B♭13(♯11) Ami11 G/B CMa9 A9/C♯
41 G/D Emi7 A9 G/D Bmi G7 A7
get me to the church, for Pete's sake, get me to the
D7sus D7(♭9) G
45 Ami7 D7 G
church on time!

GETTING TO KNOW YOU

from THE KING AND I

Lyrics by OSCAR HAMMERSTEIN II
Music by RICHARD RODGERS

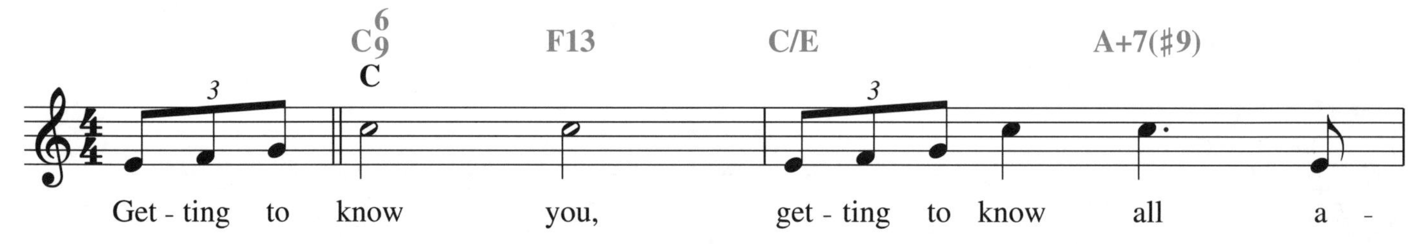

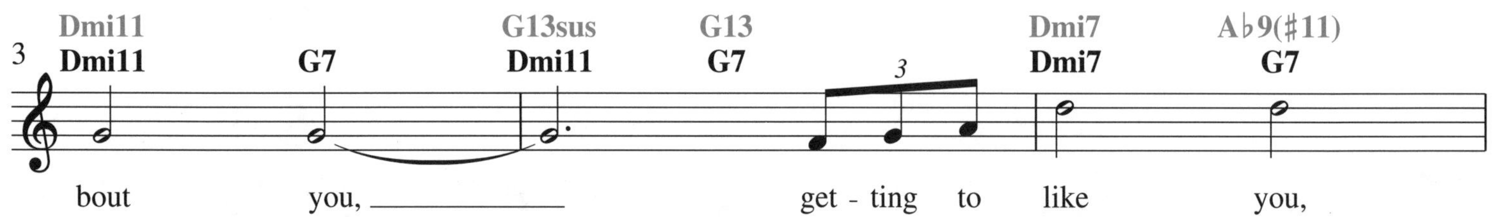

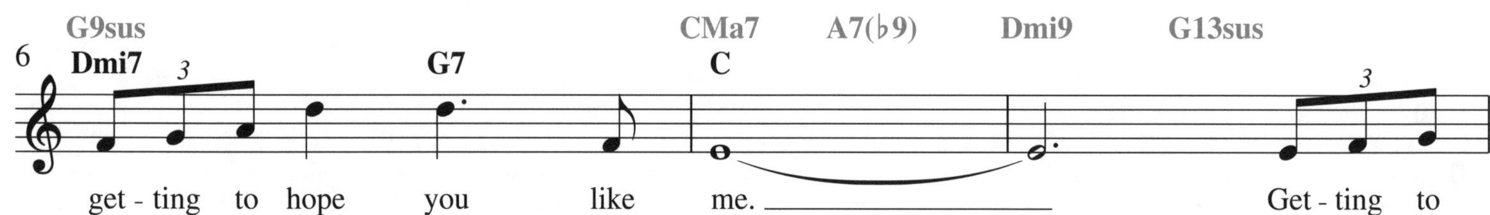

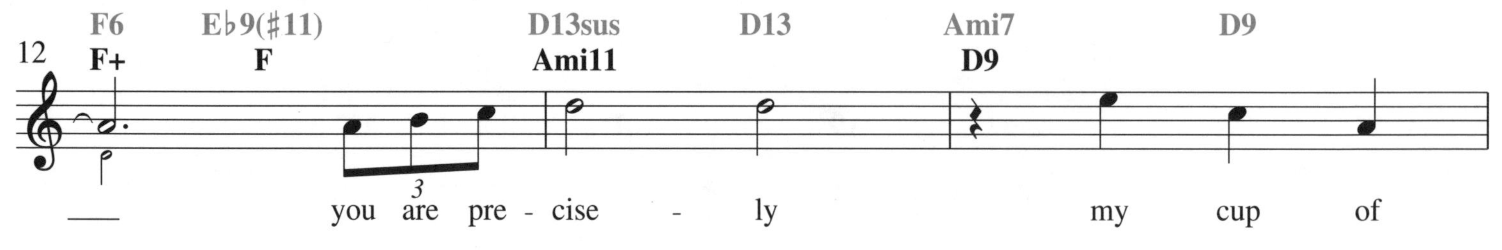

C/E A+7(♯9) Dmi11 G13sus G13
18 Dmi11 G7 Dmi11 G7
get - ting to feel free and eas - y when I am
Dmi7 A♭9(♯11) G9sus CMa7 A♭°7
21 Dmi7 G7 Dmi7 G7 C7
with you, get - ting to know what to say.
Gmi6 C7 FMa7 /E Dmi13 G9sus
24 FMa7 F6 Dmi7 G7
Have-n't you no - ticed? Sud - den - ly I'm bright and
CMa7 G♭7(♯11) FMa7 G9sus CMa7 A7(♭9)
27 CMa7 C7 FMa7 C
breez - y, be - cause of all the
Dmi9 G13sus F13 Emi11 Ami7 E♭13(♯11)
30 Dmi7 G7 C6 Ami7 D7
beau - ti - ful and new things I'm learn - ing a - bout you
D13sus D13 G7sus(add3) G7(♭9) C
33 Dmi7 G7 C F C
day by day.

GIGI

from GIGI

Words by ALAN JAY LERNER
Music by FREDERICK LOEWE

C
C
Gi - gi, am I a fool with - out a mind or have I

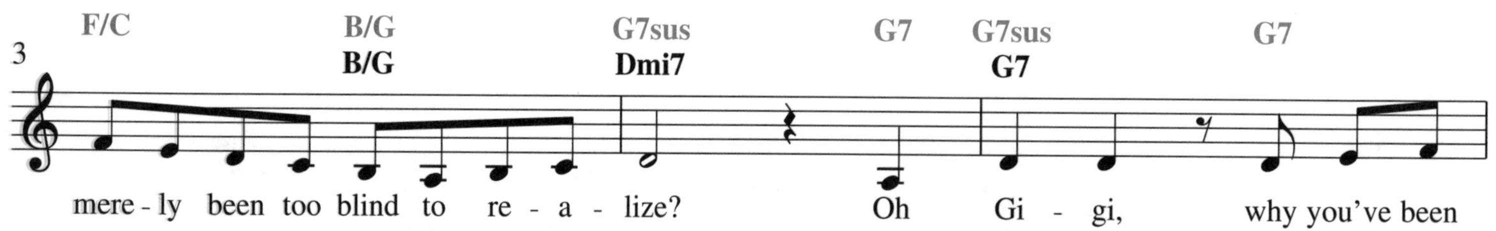
3
F/C B/G G7sus G7 G7sus G7
B/G Dmi7 G7
mere - ly been too blind to re - a - lize? Oh Gi - gi, why you've been

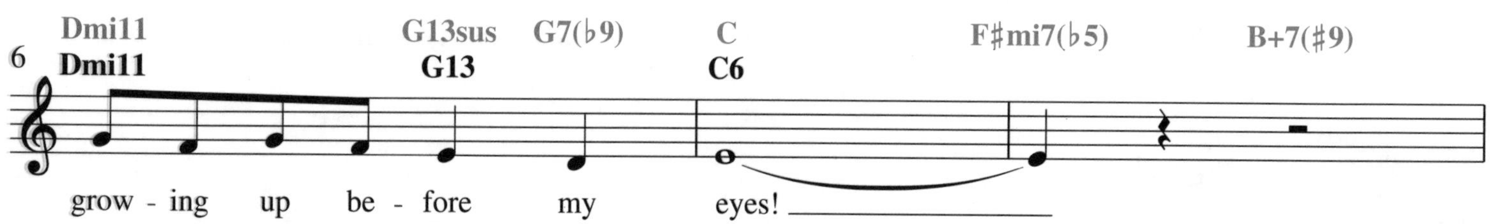
6
Dmi11 G13sus G7(♭9) C F♯mi7(♭5) B+7(♯9)
Dmi11 G13 C6
grow - ing up be - fore my eyes!

9
E E♭7/E
E E°7
Gi - gi, you're not at all that fun - ny, awk - ward lit - tle

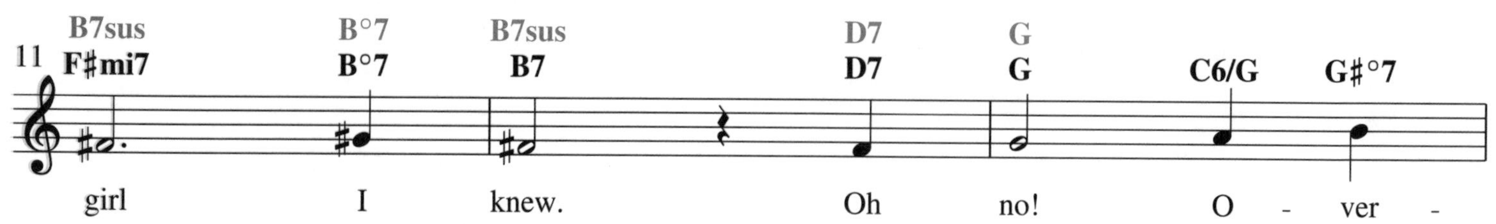
11
B7sus B°7 B7sus D7 G
F♯mi7 B°7 B7 D7 G C6/G G♯°7
girl I knew. Oh no! O - ver -

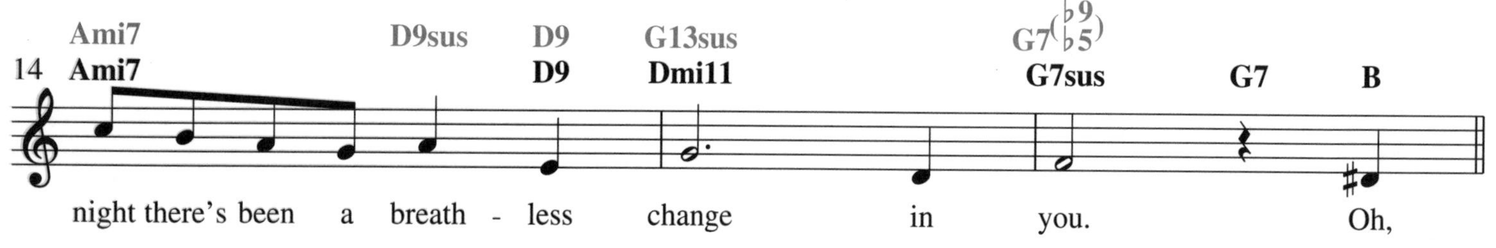
14
Ami7 D9sus D9 G13sus G7(♭9 ♭5)
Ami7 D9 Dmi11 G7sus G7 B
night there's been a breath - less change in you. Oh,

17
C
C
Gi - gi, while you were trem - bling on the brink, was I out
19
F/C B/G G7sus A7(♭9) Dmi (♯7)
B/G F6 A7 Dmi Dmi7
yon - der some-where blink - ing at a star? Oh, Gi - gi, have I been
22
Emi11(♭5) A+7 A7 Dmi (♯7)
Emi11(♭5) A+7 A7 Dmi
stand - ing up too close or back too far?
24
Dmi7 (6) FMa7 B♭9 CMa9
Dmi7 F Fmi6 C/E Emi7
When did your spar - kle turn to fi - re and your
27
F6 B♭9 CMa9 Fmi/A♭ CMa7/G A7(♭9)
F6 Fmi6 CMa9/G Fmi/A♭ C/G G°7
warmth be - come de - si - re? Oh, what mi - ra - cle has
30
Dmi11 G7sus G7(♭9) C
Dmi11 G7 C (Dmi7 G7)
made you the way you are?

THE GIRL THAT I MARRY

from the Stage Production ANNIE GET YOUR GUN

Words and Music by
IRVING BERLIN

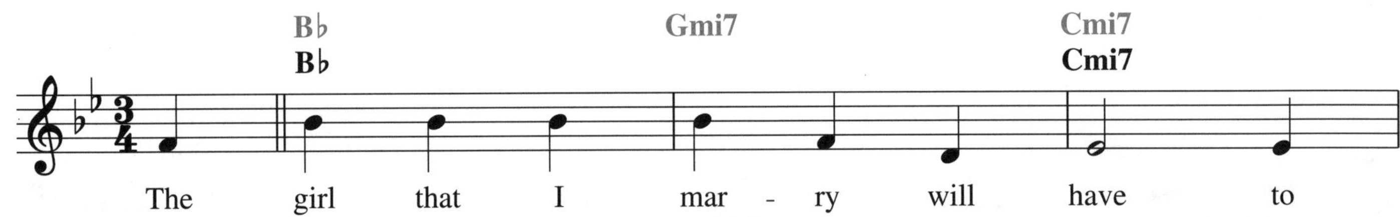
B♭ Gmi7 Cmi7
B♭ Cmi7
The girl that I mar - ry will have to

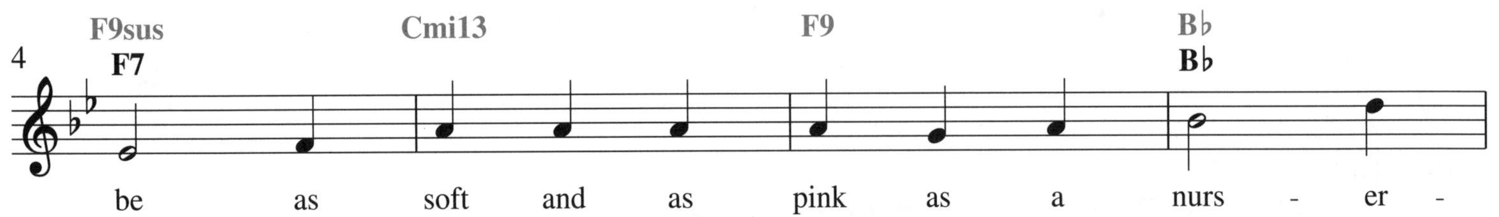
4
F9sus Cmi13 F9 B♭
F7 B♭
be as soft and as pink as a nurs - er -

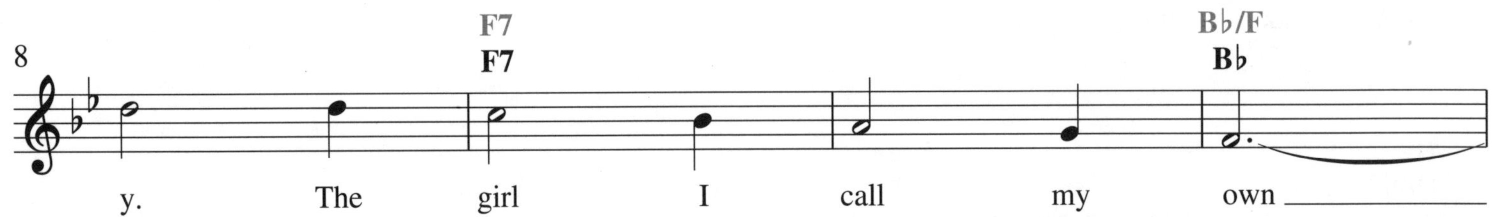
8
F7 B♭/F
F7 B♭
y. The girl I call my own

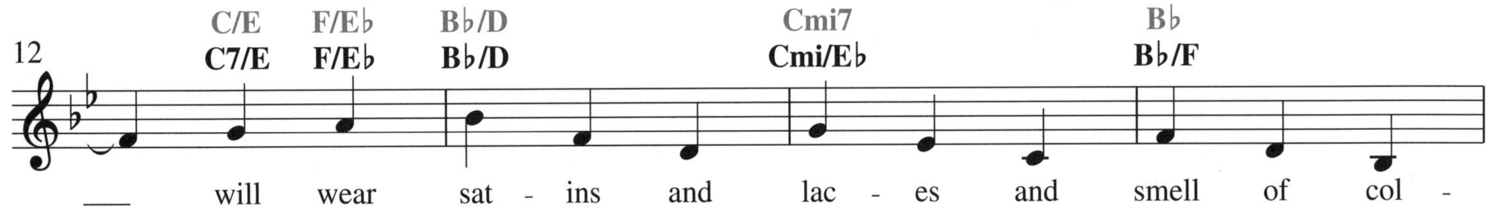
12
C/E F/E♭ B♭/D Cmi7 B♭
C7/E F/E♭ B♭/D Cmi/E♭ B♭/F
will wear sat - ins and lac - es and smell of col -

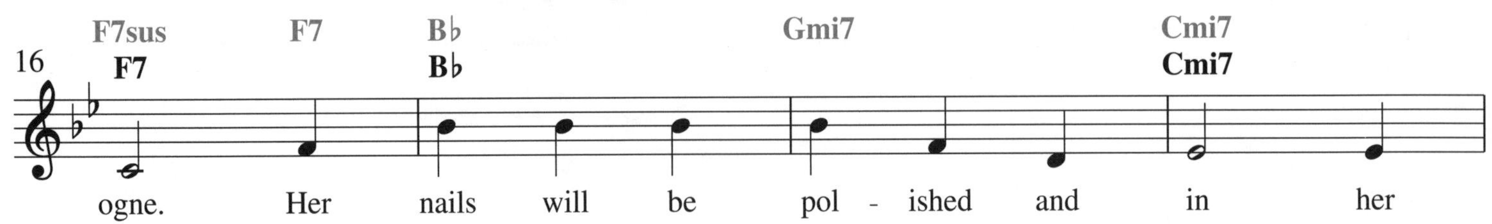
16
F7sus F7 B♭ Gmi7 Cmi7
F7 B♭ Cmi7
ogne. Her nails will be pol - ished and in her

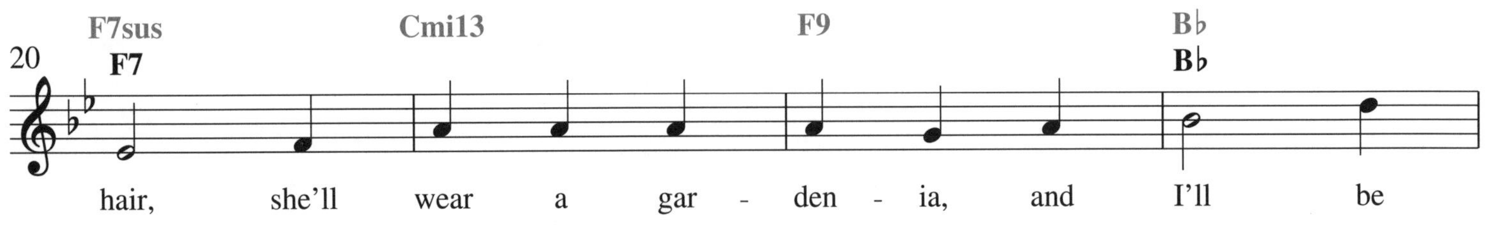
20
F7sus Cmi13 F9 B♭
F7 B♭
hair, she'll wear a gar - den - ia, and I'll be

24
Gmi7 D/F♯ Fmi13 B♭+9 E♭6
B♭9 E♭6
there 'stead of flit - tin' I'll be sit - tin'

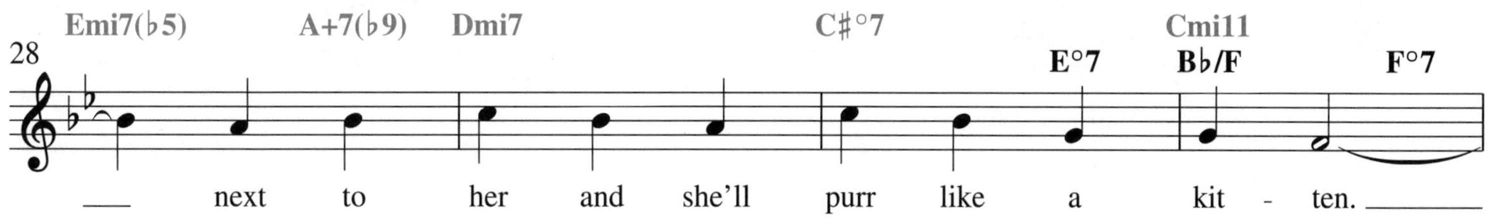
28
Emi7(♭5) A+7(♭9) Dmi7 C♯°7 Cmi11
E°7 B♭/F F°7
next to her and she'll purr like a kit - ten.

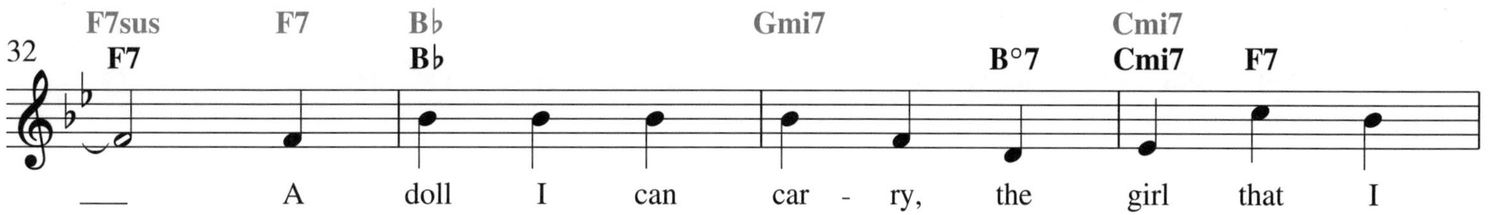
32
F7sus F7 B♭ Gmi7 Cmi7
F7 B♭ B°7 Cmi7 F7
A doll I can car - ry, the girl that I

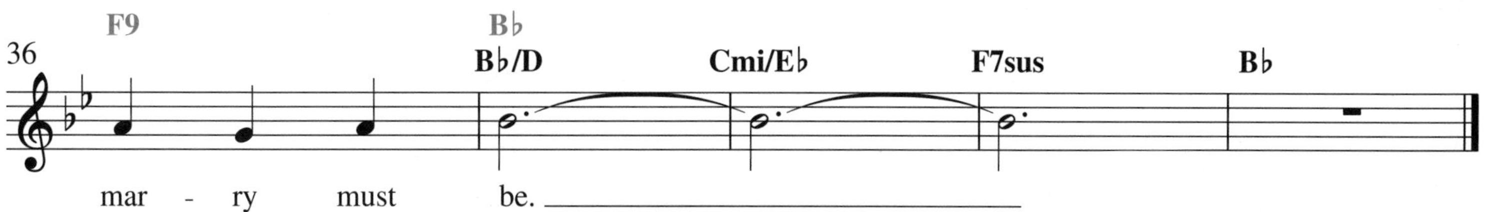
36
F9 B♭
B♭/D Cmi/E♭ F7sus B♭
mar - ry must be.

GOOD MORNING HEARTACHE

Words and Music by DAN FISHER,
IRENE HIGGINBOTHAM and ERVIN DRAKE

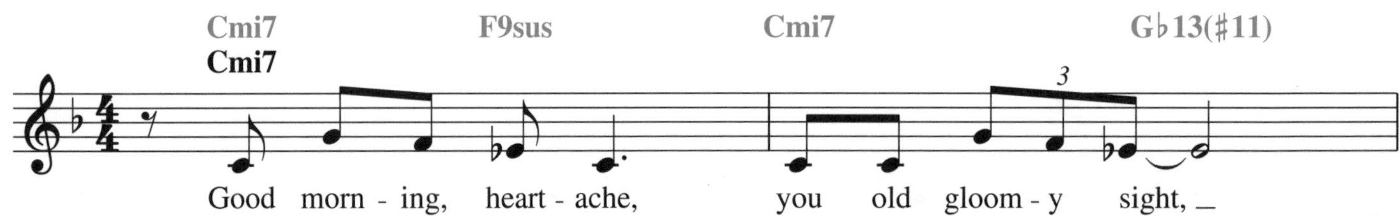

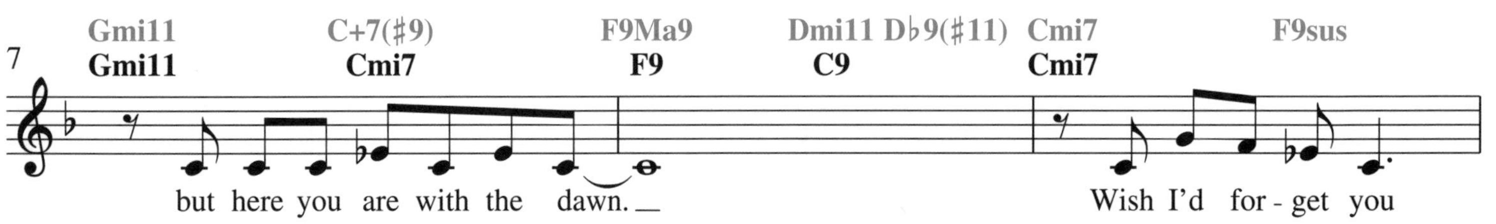

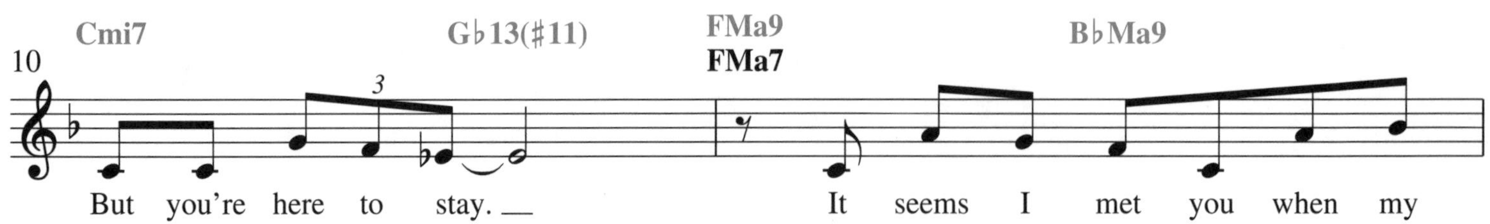

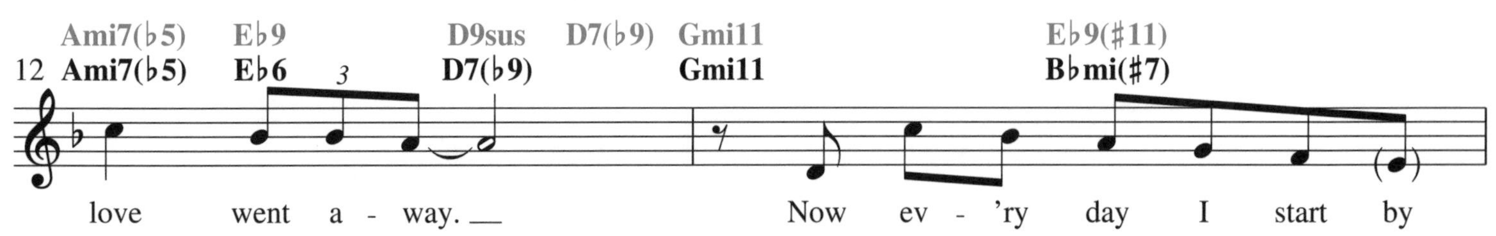

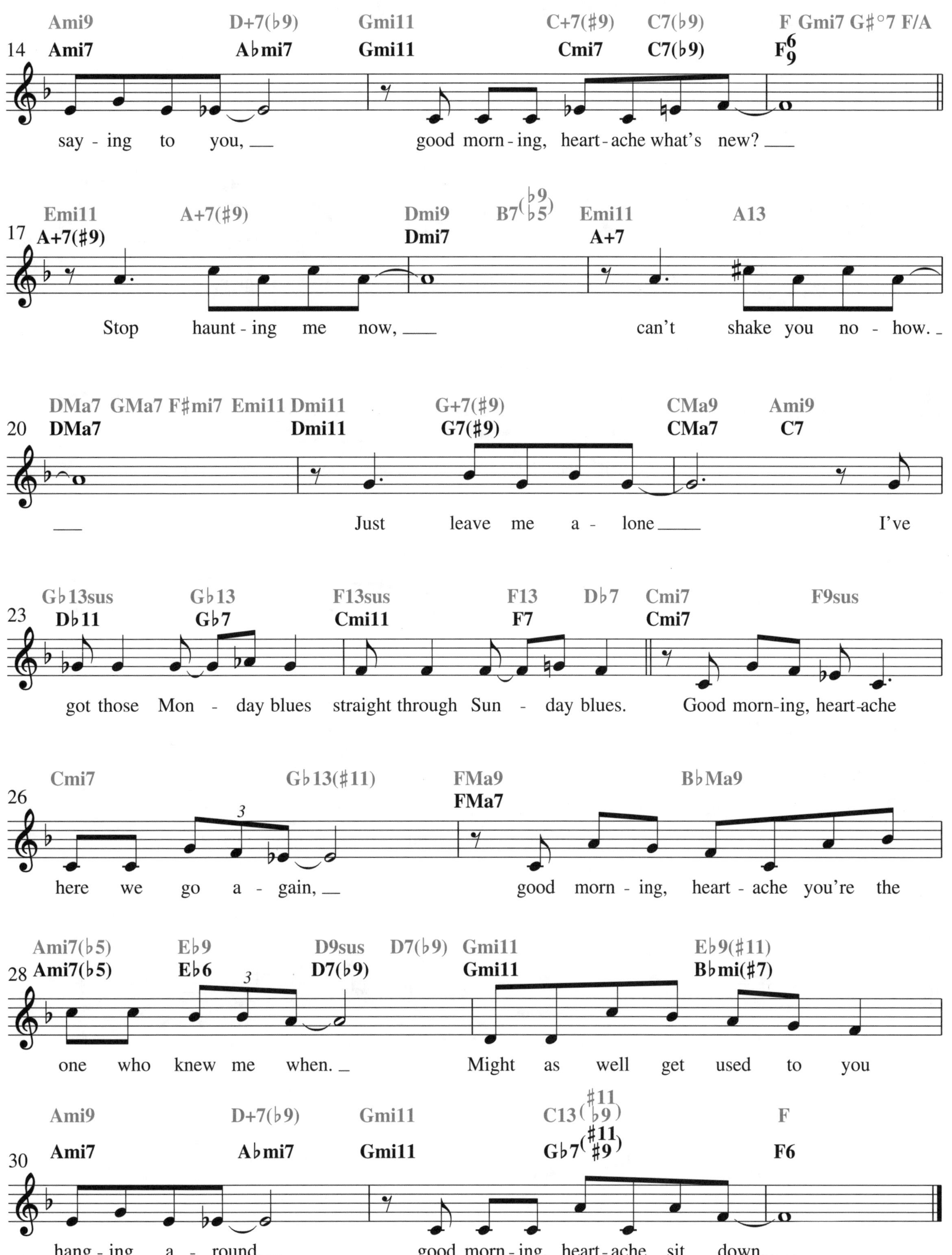
14
Ami9 D+7(♭9) Gmi11 C+7(♯9) C7(♭9) F Gmi7 G♯°7 F/A
Ami7 A♭mi7 Gmi11 Cmi7 C7(♭9) F6/9
say - ing to you, __ good morn - ing, heart - ache what's new? __
17
Emi11 A+7(♯9) Dmi9 B7(♭9/♭5) Emi11 A13
A+7(♯9) Dmi7 A+7
Stop haunt - ing me now, __ can't shake you no - how. _
20
DMa7 GMa7 F♯mi7 Emi11 Dmi11 G+7(♯9) CMa9 Ami9
DMa7 Dmi11 G7(♯9) CMa7 C7
__ Just leave me a - lone __ I've
23
G♭13sus G♭13 F13sus F13 D♭7 Cmi7 F9sus
D♭11 G♭7 Cmi11 F7 Cmi7
got those Mon - day blues straight through Sun - day blues. Good morn-ing, heart-ache
26
Cmi7 G♭13(♯11) FMa9 B♭Ma9
FMa7
here we go a - gain, _ good morn - ing, heart - ache you're the
28
Ami7(♭5) E♭9 D9sus D7(♭9) Gmi11 E♭9(♯11)
Ami7(♭5) E♭6 D7(♭9) Gmi11 B♭mi(♯7)
one who knew me when. _ Might as well get used to you
30
Ami9 D+7(♭9) Gmi11 C13(♯11/♭9) F
Ami7 A♭mi7 Gmi11 G♭7(♯11/♯9) F6
hang - ing a - round, _ good morn - ing, heart - ache sit down. __

GRAVY WALTZ

Lyrics by STEVE ALLEN
Music by RAY BROWN

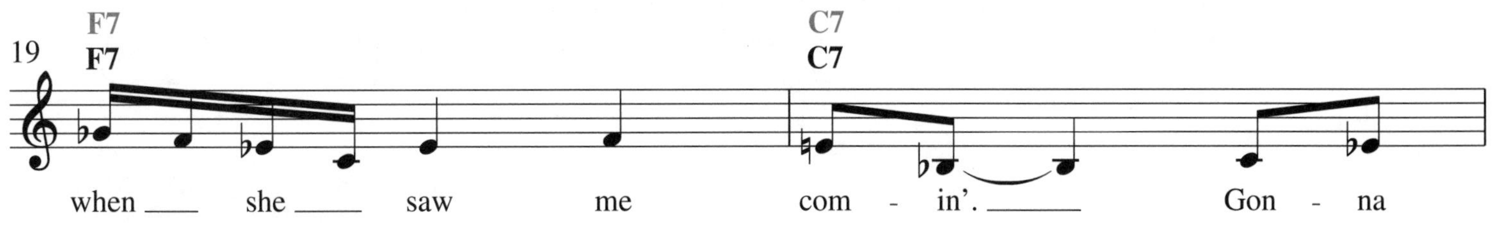
F7 C7
19
F7 C7
when ___ she ___ saw me com - in'. ___ Gon - na

F7 C E♭13 D7 D7sus D7
21
F7 C Ami D C/E D/F♯
get __ a ___ taste be - fore it goes to waste, this hon - ey

G7 G7sus G7 C F /C
24
G F/A G7/B C F
bee's hum - min'. Mis - ter Weep - in' Wil - low, I'm thru with

Bmi11 E7(♭9 ♭5) Ami7 /G F♯mi7(♭5) B7(♯9)
27
C/G E7/G♯ Ami F♯mi7(♭5) Fmi6
all of my faults, 'cause Mir - an - da's
my ba - by's

Emi7(♭5) A+7 D9 G7 C
30
Emi7(♭5) A7 D9 G7 C
3
rea - dy to do the ev - er new gra - vy waltz.

I CAN'T BELIEVE THAT YOU'RE IN LOVE WITH ME

Words and Music by JIMMY McHUGH
and CLARENCE GASKILL

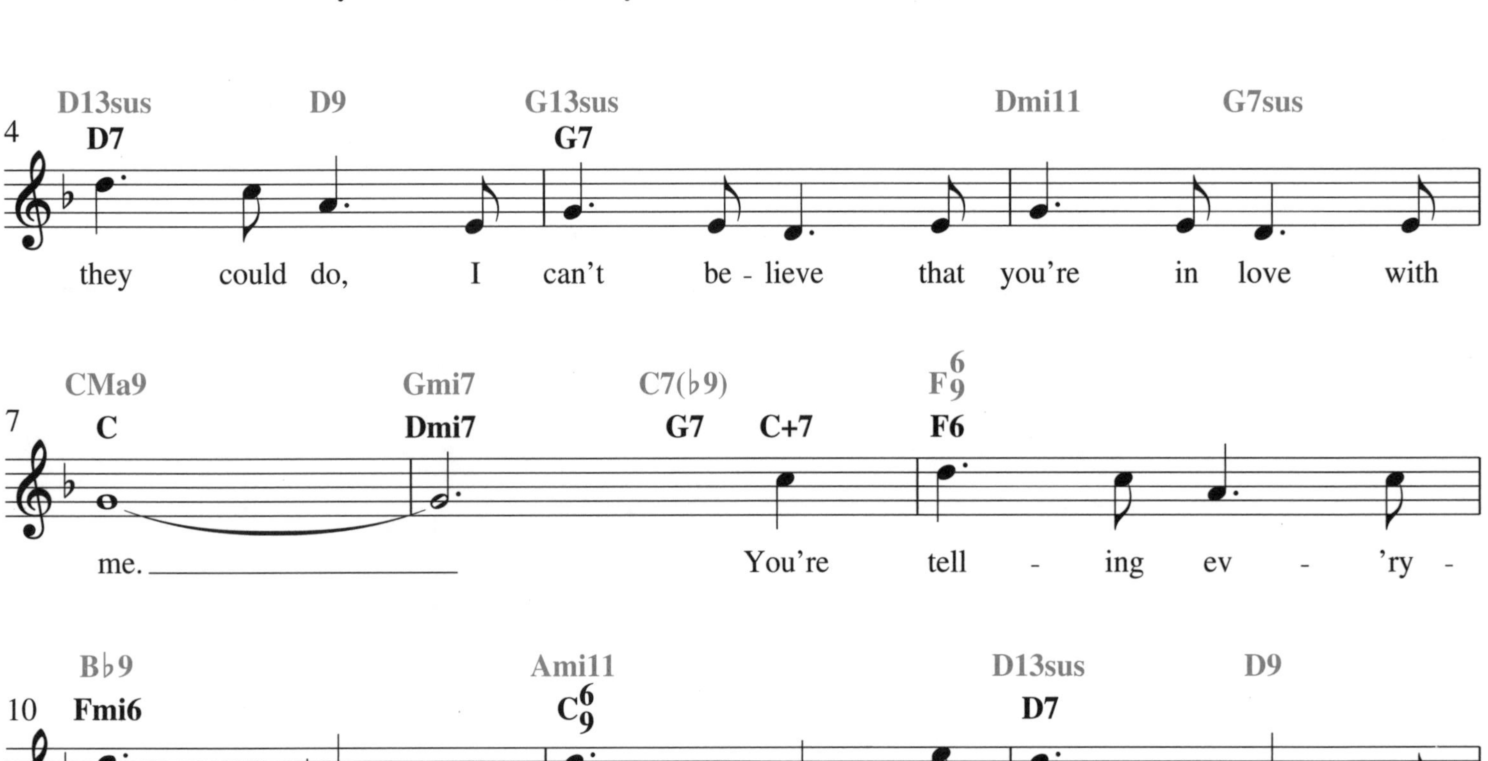

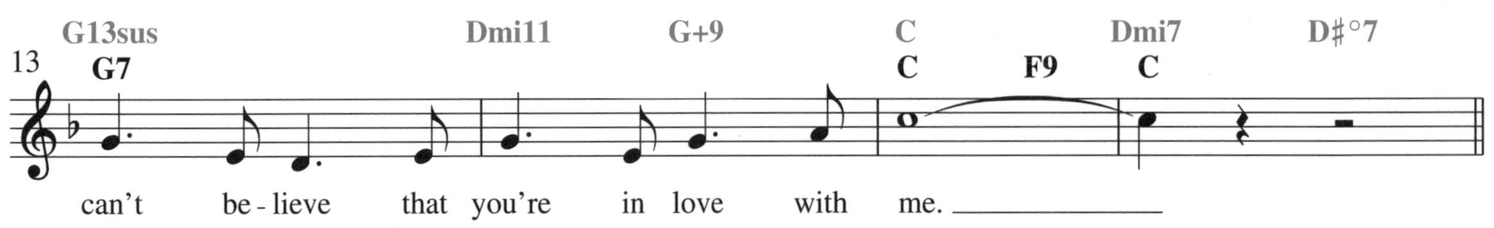

21
D13sus D9 Ami11 D9 G9sus
D7 D9 Dmi7 D7 G9
I just can't i - mag - ine that you love

24
G13 G♭13(♯11) F6/9 B♭9
C+7 F6 Fmi6
me. And af - ter all is said and done, to

27
Ami11 D13sus D9 G13sus
C6/9 D7 G7
think that I'm the luck - y one, I can't be - lieve that

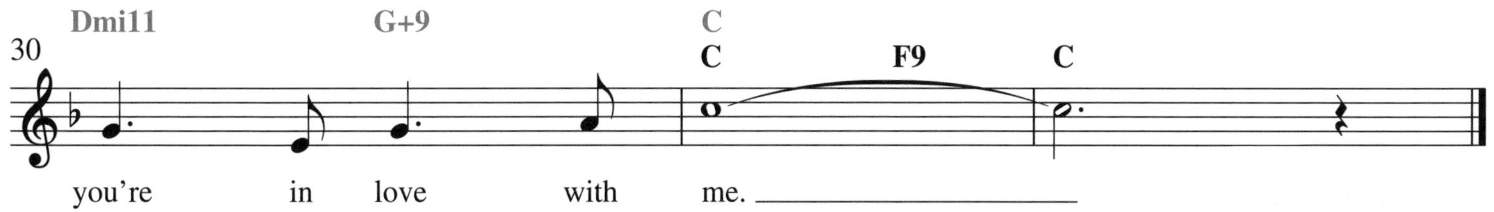
30
Dmi11 G+9 C
C F9 C
you're in love with me.

I COULD HAVE DANCED ALL NIGHT

from MY FAIR LADY

Words by ALAN JAY LERNER
Music by FREDERICK LOEWE

N.C. DMa7
D
I'll nev - er know ___ what made it
A7sus A7(♭9 ♭5) DMa7
Emi7 A7 D DMa7 D6
so ___ ex - cit - ing, ___
C9sus FMa7 D♭9(♯11) C7(♭9)
N.C. F Gmi C7(♭9)
why all at once ___ my heart took
F9 F9sus ⟶ B♭
F9 E♭/B♭ B♭/A Cmi7/G B♭
flight. ___ I on - ly know ___
B♭Ma9 E♭6 B♭/D
B♭Ma7 E♭6
___ when he be - gan to dance ___ with
Cmi7 F13sus F9 F9sus
E♭Ma7 F13sus F9 F7sus
me. I could have danced, danced, danced, ___
F7 B♭
F7 B♭
___ all night. ___

I DON'T STAND A GHOST OF A CHANCE

Words by BING CROSBY and NED WASHINGTON
Music by VICTOR YOUNG

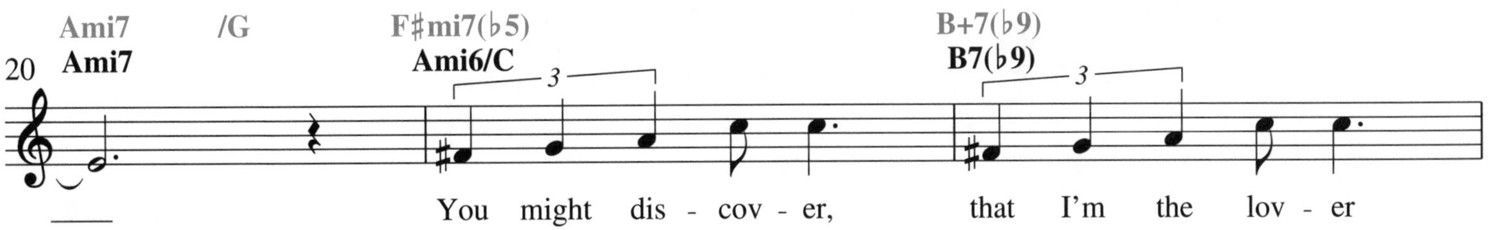
Ami7
/G
F♯mi7(♭5)
B+7(♭9)
20
Ami7
Ami6/C
B7(♭9)
3
3
You might dis - cov - er, that I'm the lov - er

Emi9
A13
Dmi7
G+7
CMa9
23
E9
G+9
C
meant for you, and I'd be true. But what's the good of

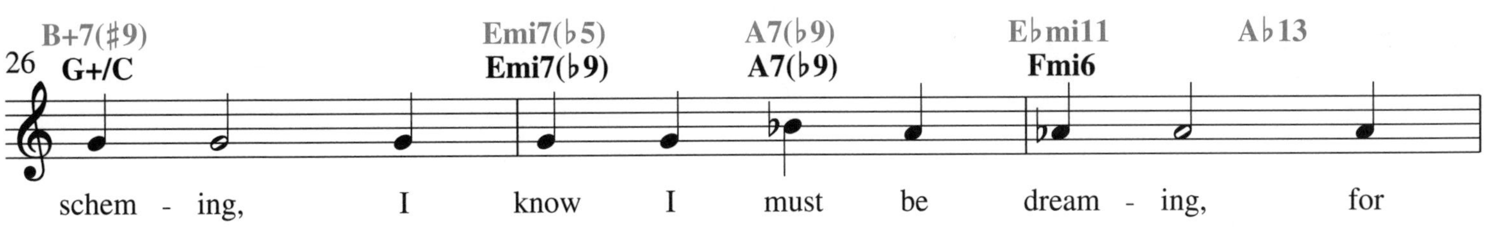
B+7(♯9)
Emi7(♭5)
A7(♭9)
E♭mi11
A♭13
26
G+/C
Emi7(♭9)
A7(♭9)
Fmi6
schem - ing, I know I must be dream - ing, for

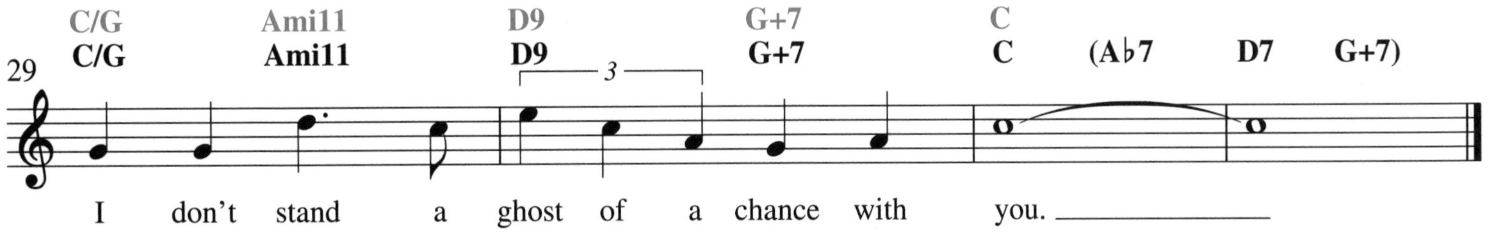
C/G
Ami11
D9
G+7
C
29
C/G
Ami11
D9
G+7
C
(A♭7
D7
G+7)
3
I don't stand a ghost of a chance with you.

I DON'T WANT TO WALK WITHOUT YOU

from the Paramount Picture SWEATER GIRL

Words by FRANK LOESSER
Music by JULE STYNE

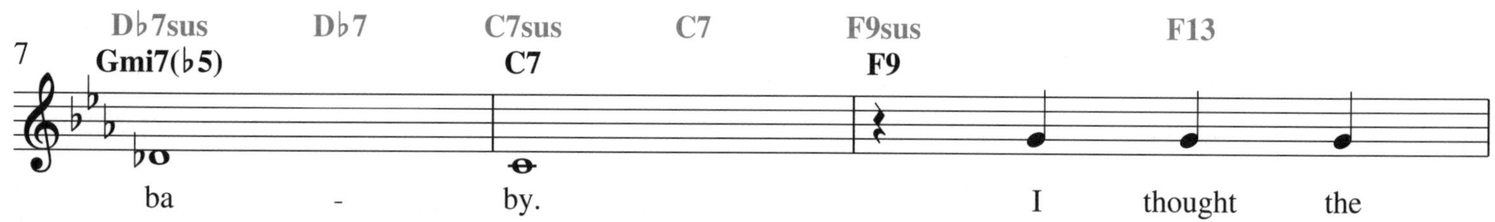

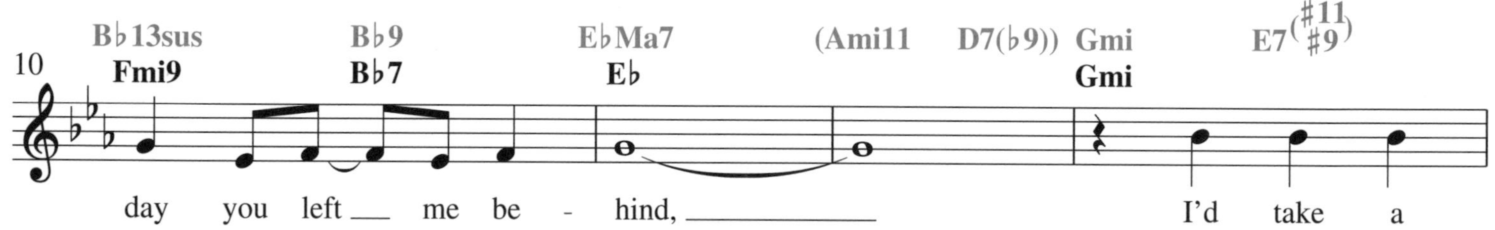

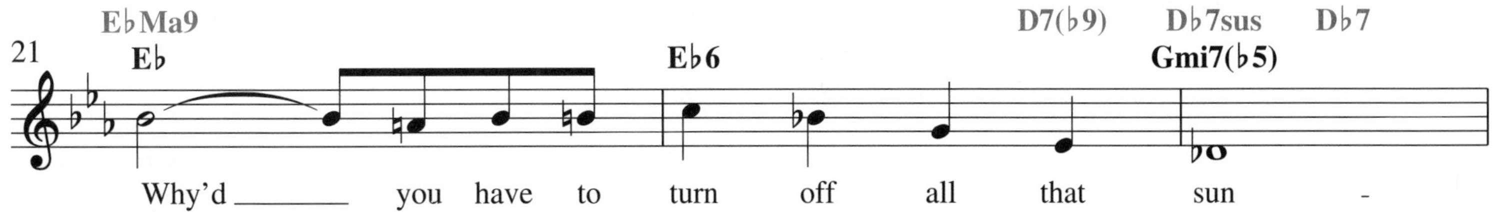
21
E♭Ma9
E♭
E♭6
D7(♭9)
D♭7sus
D♭7
Gmi7(♭5)
Why'd ___ you have to turn off all that sun -

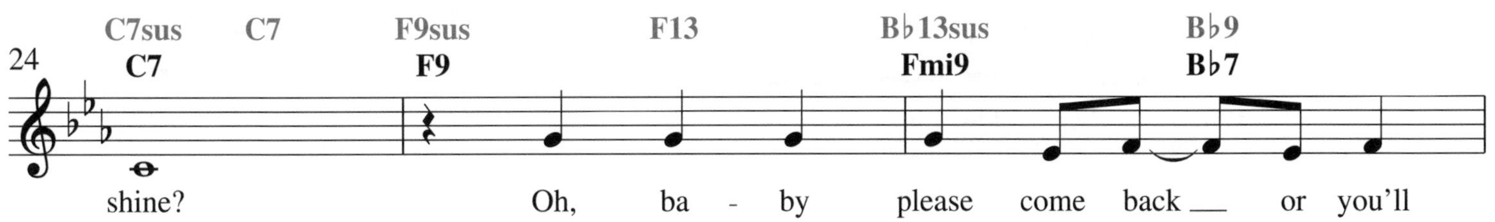
24
C7sus
C7
C7
F9sus
F9
F13
B♭13sus
Fmi9
B♭9
B♭7
shine? Oh, ba - by please come back ___ or you'll

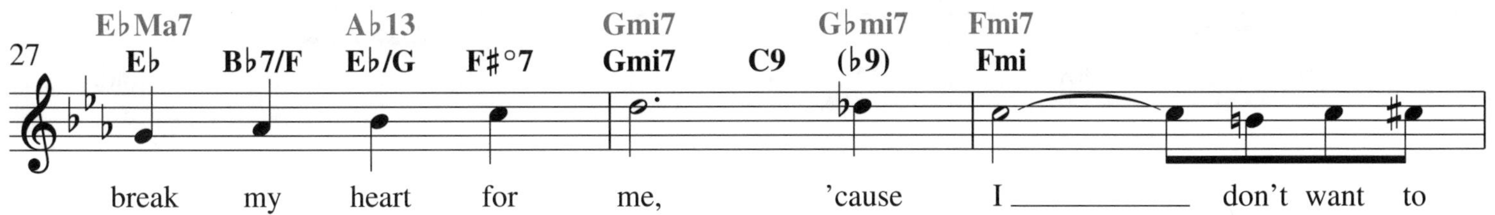
27
E♭Ma7
E♭
B♭7/F
A♭13
E♭/G
F♯°7
Gmi7
Gmi7
C9
G♭mi7
(♭9)
Fmi7
Fmi
break my heart for me, 'cause I ___ don't want to

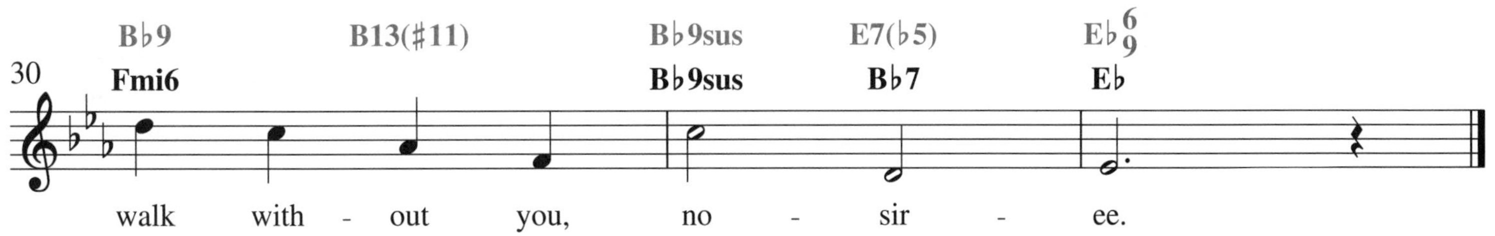
30
B♭9
Fmi6
B13(♯11)
B♭9sus
B♭9sus
E7(♭5)
B♭7
E♭6/9
E♭
walk with - out you, no - sir - ee.

I GOTTA RIGHT TO SING THE BLUES

Words by TED KOEHLER
Music by HAROLD ARLEN

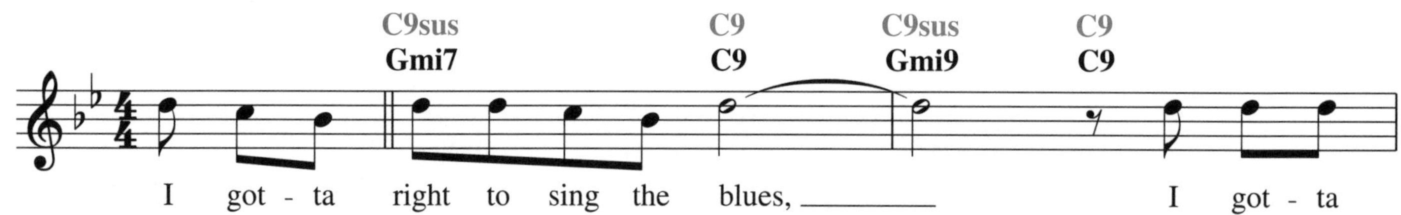
C9sus C9 C9sus C9
Gmi7 C9 Gmi9 C9
I got - ta right to sing the blues, I got - ta

3
F13sus F+7 B♭9sus B♭9
F7 F+7 Fmi7 B♭9
right to feel low down, I got - ta right to hang a - round,

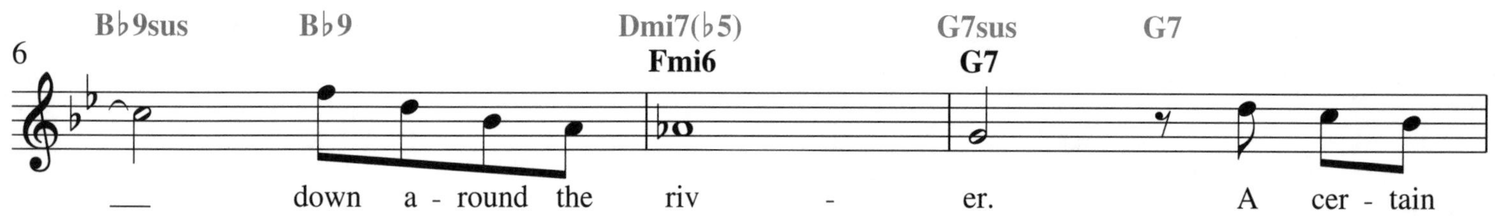
6
B♭9sus B♭9 Dmi7(♭5) G7sus G7
Fmi6 G7
down a - round the riv - er. A cer - tain

9
C9sus C9 C9sus C9 orig.
Gmi7 C9 Gmi9 C9 F6 E7 E♭Ma7 E7
man in this old town keeps drag - gin' my poor heart a - round.

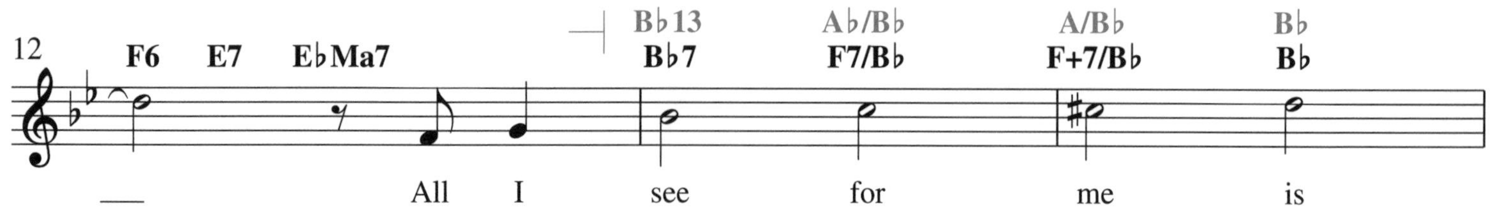
12
B♭13 A♭/B♭ A/B♭ B♭
F6 E7 E♭Ma7 B♭7 F7/B♭ F+7/B♭ B♭
All I see for me is

15
Cmi7/B♭ A/B♭ B♭ N.C. C9sus C9
Cmi7/B♭ B♭°7 F7/B♭ B♭ Gmi7 C9
mis - er - y. I got - ta right to sing the blues,

18
C9sus C9 F13sus F+7
Gmi9 C9 F7 F+7
I got - ta right to moan and sigh, I got - ta

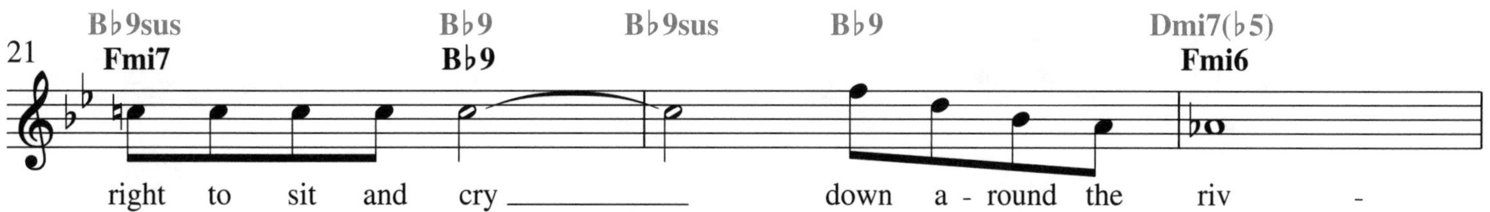
21
B♭9sus B♭9 B♭9sus B♭9 Dmi7(♭5)
Fmi7 B♭9 Fmi6
right to sit and cry down a - round the riv -

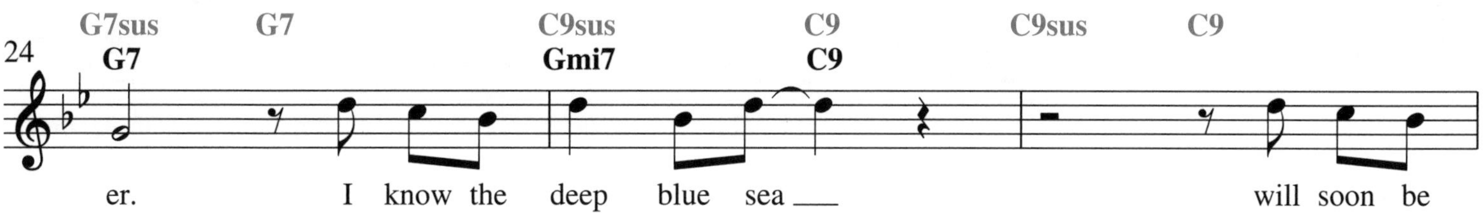
24
G7sus G7 C9sus C9 C9sus C9
G7 Gmi7 C9
er. I know the deep blue sea will soon be

27
A♭13(♯11) C9sus C9
E♭mi(♯7) C7 Gmi7 C9
call - ing me. It must be love say what you choose, I

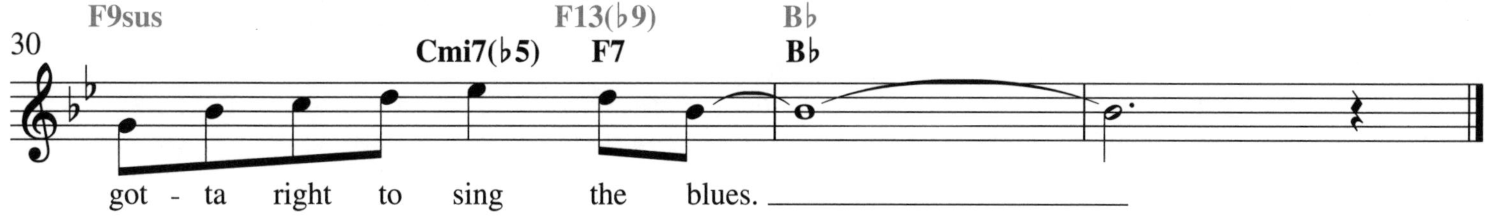
30
F9sus F13(♭9) B♭
Cmi7(♭5) F7 B♭
got - ta right to sing the blues.

I LET A SONG GO OUT OF MY HEART

Words and Music by DUKE ELLINGTON, HENRY NEMO,
JOHN REDMOND and IRVING MILLS

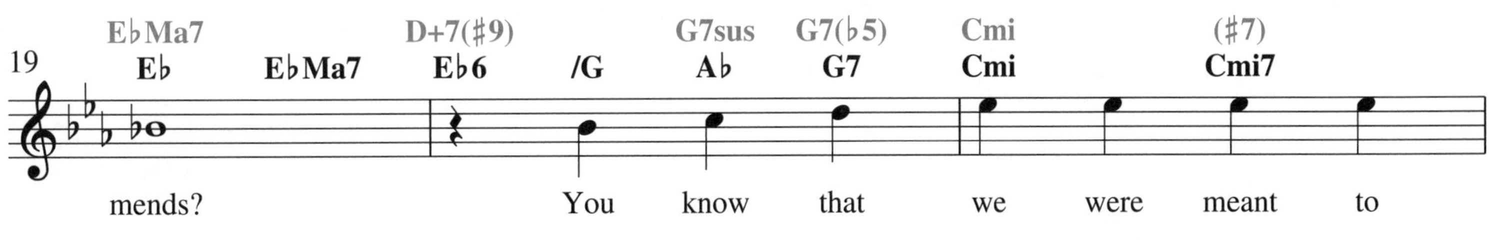
19
E♭Ma7 D+7(♯9) G7sus G7(♭5) Cmi (♯7)
E♭ E♭Ma7 E♭6 /G A♭ G7 Cmi Cmi7
mends? You know that we were meant to

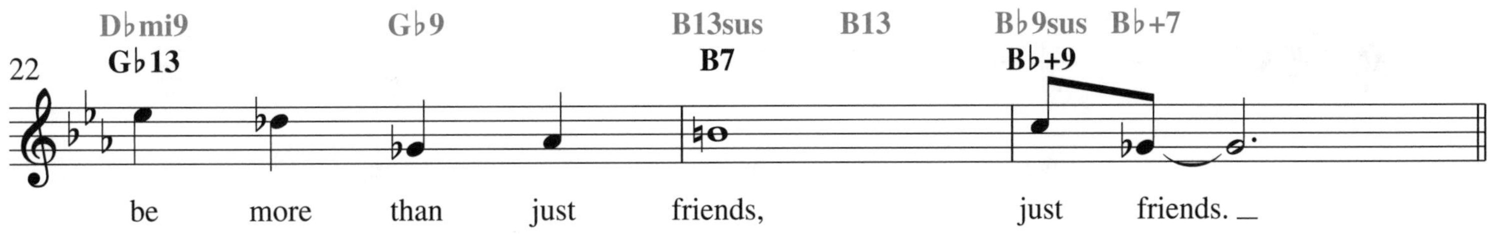
22
D♭mi9 G♭9 B13sus B13 B♭9sus B♭+7
G♭13 B7 B♭+9
be more than just friends, just friends.

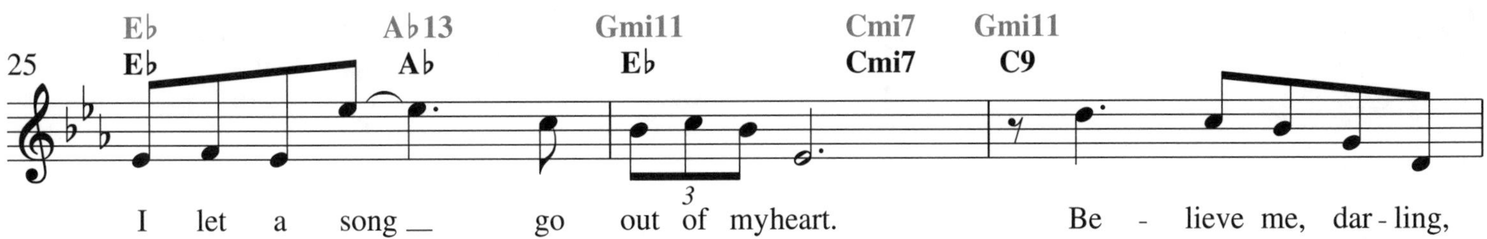
25
E♭ A♭13 Gmi11 Cmi7 Gmi11
E♭ A♭ E♭ Cmi7 C9
I let a song go out of myheart. Be - lieve me, dar - ling,

28
C9sus C7alt. Fmi7 Gmi7 A♭6 A°7 E♭Ma7/B♭
A♭6 Cmi/G Fmi7 F♯°7 E♭/G
when I say I won't know sweet mu -

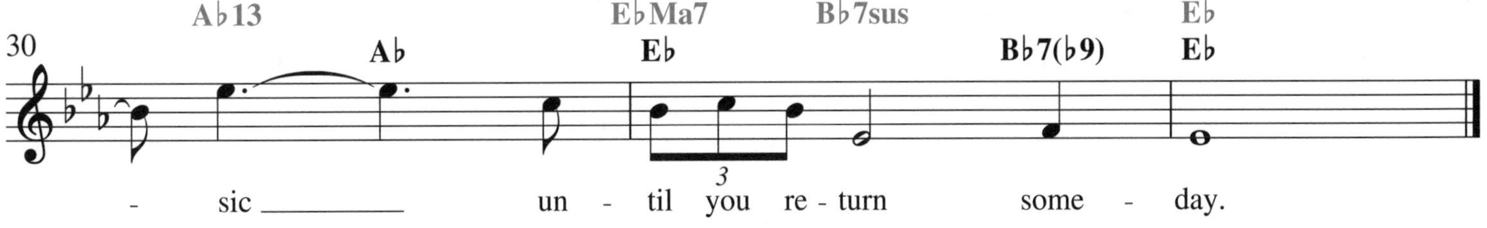
30
A♭13 E♭Ma7 B♭7sus E♭
A♭ E♭ B♭7(♭9) E♭
- sic un - til you re - turn some - day.

I LOVE PARIS

from CAN-CAN

Words and Music by
COLE PORTER

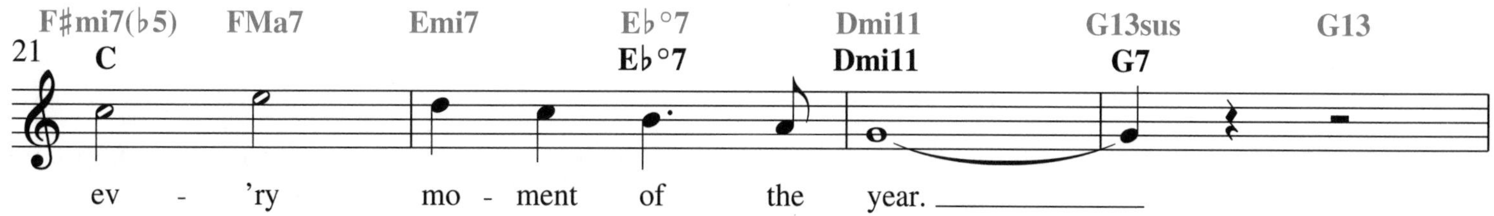
F♯mi7(♭5)
FMa7
Emi7
E♭°7
Dmi11
G13sus
G13
21
C
E♭°7
Dmi11
G7
ev - 'ry mo - ment of the year.

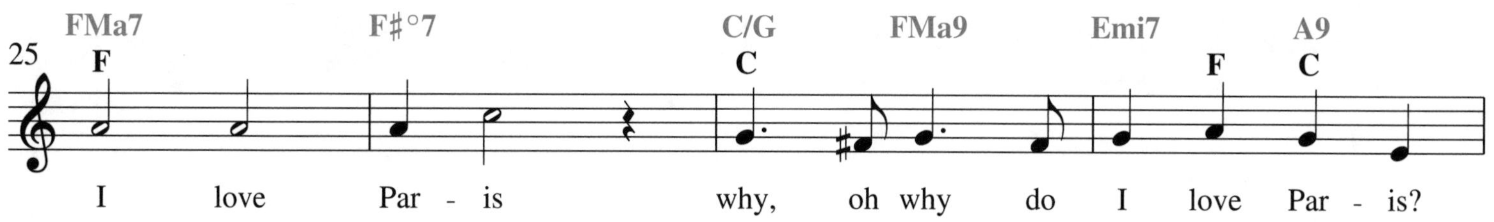
FMa7
F♯°7
C/G
FMa9
Emi7
A9
25
F
C
F
C
I love Par - is why, oh why do I love Par - is?

Dmi7
G13sus
G7(♭9)
C
29
G7
G13
C
Be - cause my love is near.

I MEAN YOU

By THELONIOUS MONK
and COLEMAN HAWKINS

24
G♭7(♯11)
G♭+7
F13
F
D♭9
D♭

28
D7
D
G11
F
C9sus
C13(♭9)

31
F
F
Fine
Interlude
E♭
E♭

34
D♭
D♭
E♭
E♭
D♭
D♭
E♭
E♭
E♭13(♯11)
E♭7
D.S. al Fine

I'LL NEVER FALL IN LOVE AGAIN

Lyric by HAL DAVID
Music by BURT BACHARACH

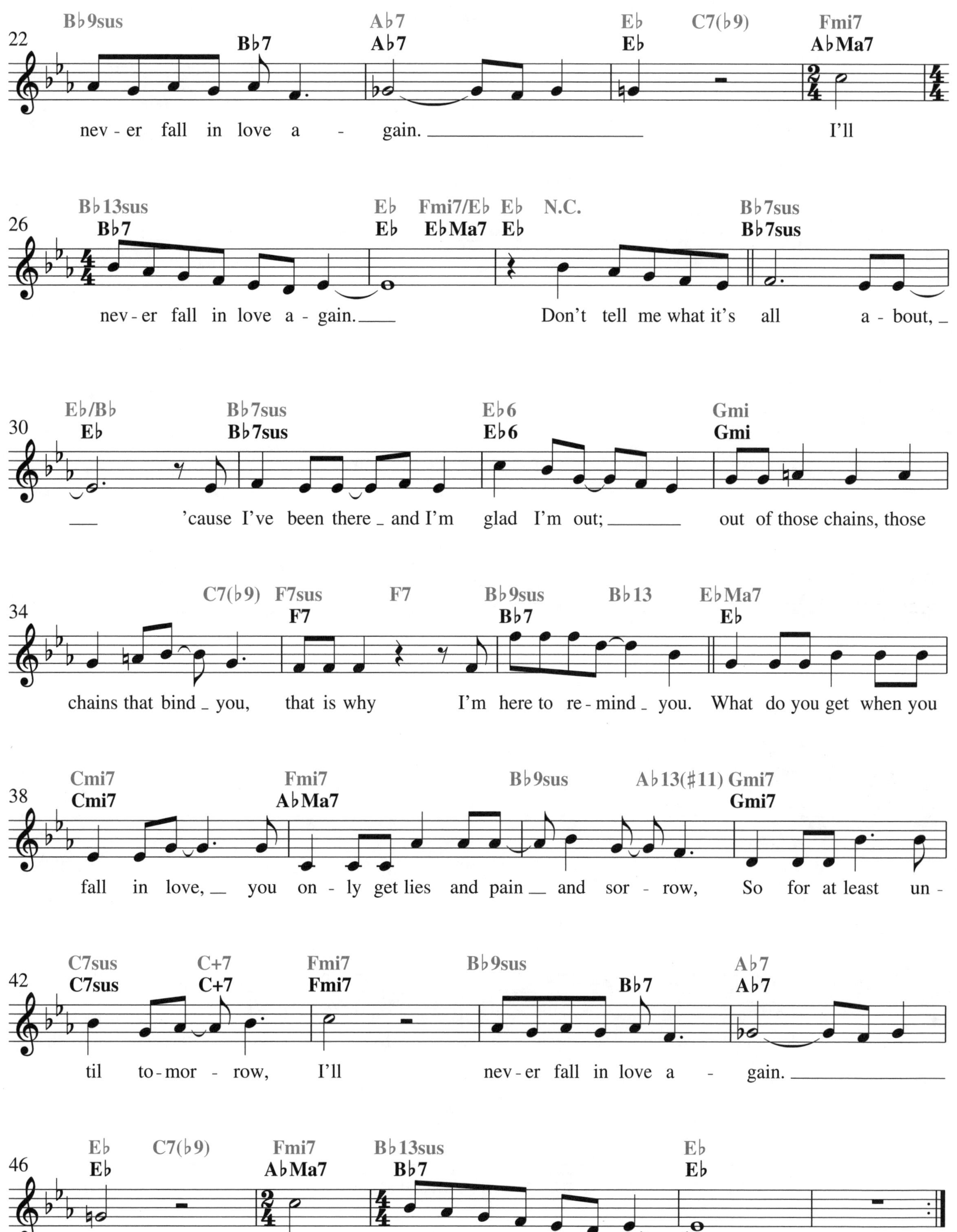
22
B♭9sus Bb7 A♭7 A♭7 E♭ E♭ C7(♭9) Fmi7 A♭Ma7
nev - er fall in love a - gain. I'll
26
B♭13sus B♭7 E♭ E♭ Fmi7/E♭ E♭Ma7 E♭ E♭ N.C. B♭7sus B♭7sus
nev - er fall in love a - gain. Don't tell me what it's all a - bout,
30
E♭/B♭ E♭ B♭7sus B♭7sus E♭6 E♭6 Gmi Gmi
'cause I've been there and I'm glad I'm out; out of those chains, those
34
C7(♭9) F7sus F7 F7 B♭9sus B♭7 B♭13 E♭Ma7 E♭
chains that bind you, that is why I'm here to re - mind you. What do you get when you
38
Cmi7 Cmi7 Fmi7 A♭Ma7 B♭9sus A♭13(♯11) Gmi7 Gmi7
fall in love, you on - ly get lies and pain and sor - row, So for at least un -
42
C7sus C7sus C+7 C+7 Fmi7 Fmi7 B♭9sus B♭7 A♭7 A♭7
til to - mor - row, I'll nev - er fall in love a - gain.
46
E♭ E♭ C7(♭9) Fmi7 A♭Ma7 B♭13sus B♭7 E♭ E♭
I'll nev - er fall in love a - gain.

I'M ALWAYS CHASING RAINBOWS

Words by JOSEPH McCARTHY
Music by HARRY CARROLL

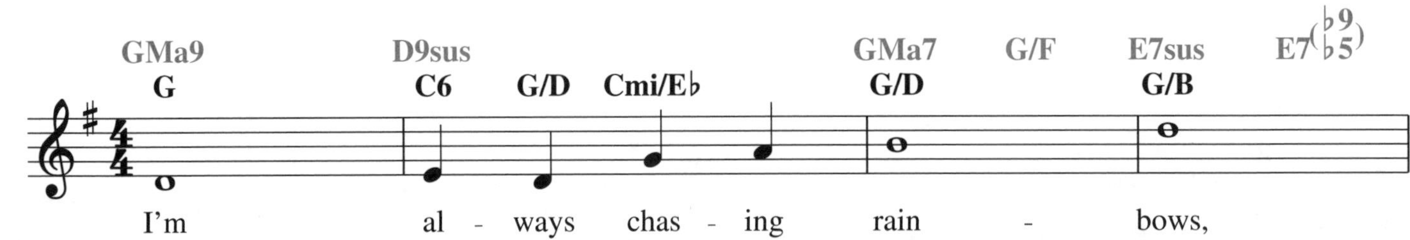

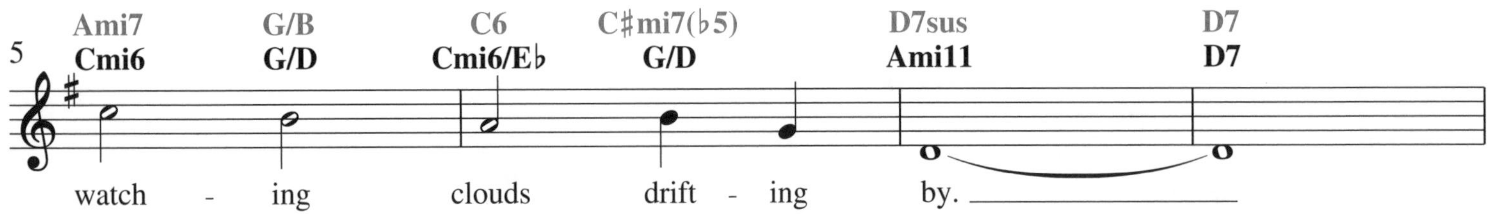

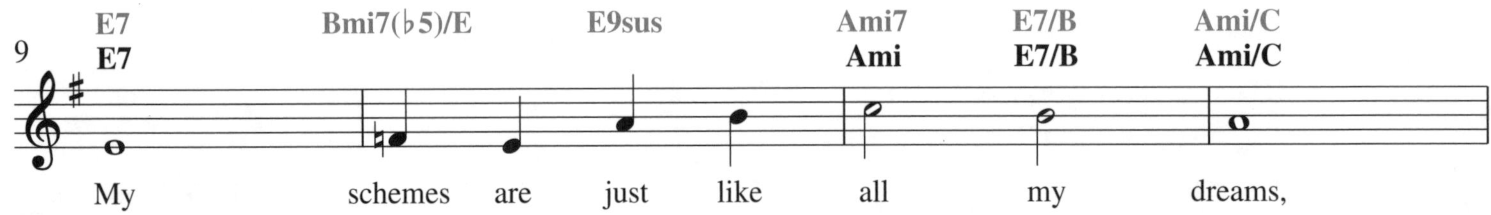

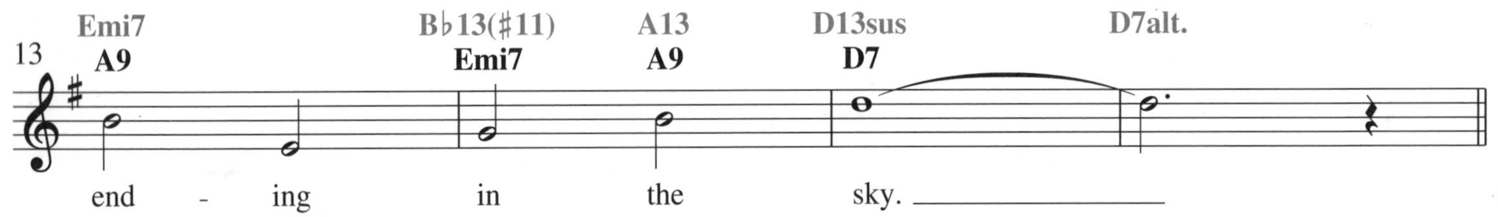

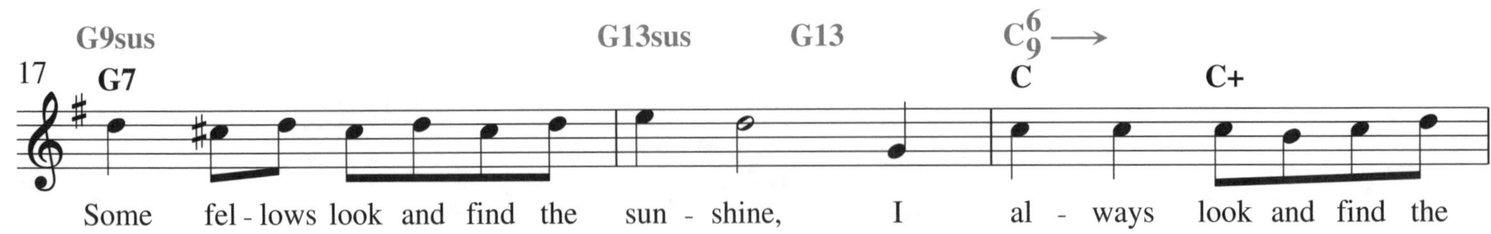

A13sus A13/E♭ D9sus D D9sus D7(♭9)
23
A7 A7/E♭ D7 (♭9)
nev - er e - ven make a gain. Be - lieve me,

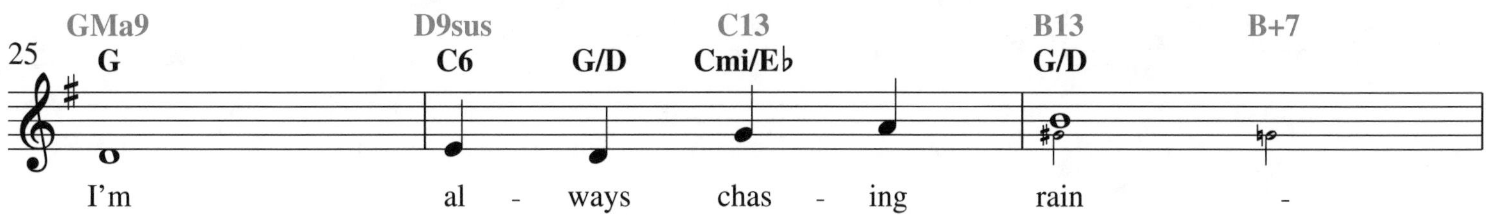
GMa9 D9sus C13 B13 B+7
25
G C6 G/D Cmi/E♭ G/D
I'm al - ways chas - ing rain -

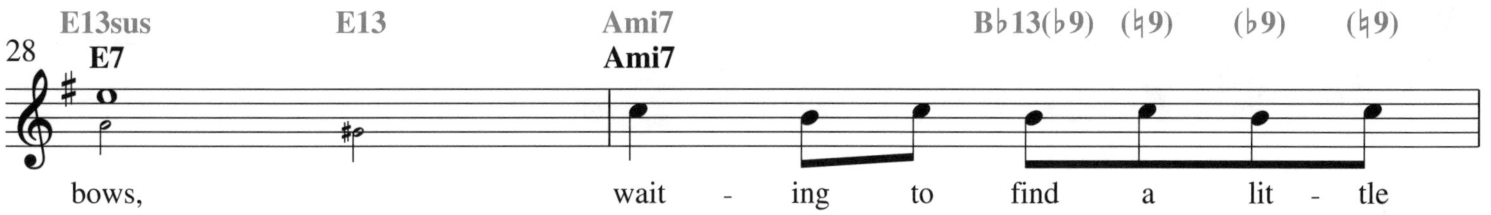
E13sus E13 Ami7 B♭13(♭9) (♮9) (♭9) (♮9)
28
E7 Ami7
bows, wait - ing to find a lit - tle

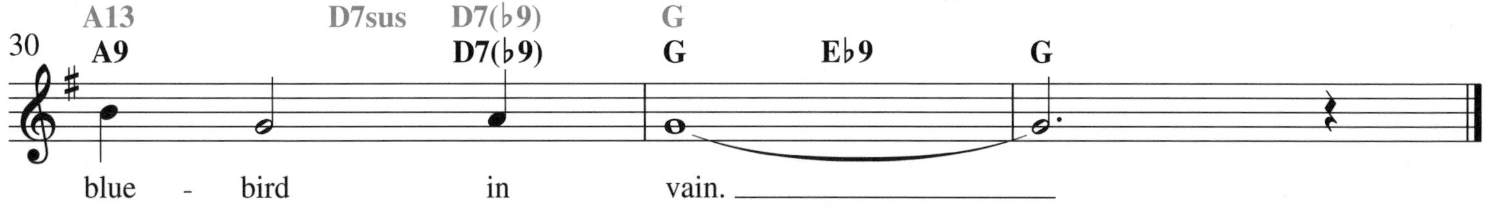
A13 D7sus D7(♭9) G
30
A9 D7(♭9) G E♭9 G
blue - bird in vain.

IF I WERE A BELL

from GUYS AND DOLLS

By FRANK LOESSER

C13sus C13sus(♭9) FMa7 Gmi11 Ami7 B♭13
18 C13sus C13sus(♭9) F6 C/E Fmi6
me with my qui - et up - bring - ing. Well sir,
now that we're fond - ly ca - ress - ing. Pal, if
Ami7(♭5) E♭9(♯11) D9sus D7(♭9)
21 F♯°7 E♭13(♯11) D7
all I can say is if I were a gate I'd be
I were a sal - ad I know I'd be splash - ing my
G9sus D♭9(♯11) C9sus C13(♭9) F9sus C♭9(♯11)
23 G9 B♭mi6/D♭ C13(♭9) F F/E♭
swing - ing. And if I were a watch I'd
dress - ing. Or if I were a sea - son
B♭$^{6}_{9}$ Bmi7 B♭13 Ami7 E♭13(♯11) D9sus D7(♭9)
26 B♭/D A♭°7 F/A E+7 E♭13 D9 D7(♭9)
start pop - ping my spring or if
I'd sure - ly be spring or if
G9sus G9 G♯°7 Ami7 A♭13 Gmi9 C9sus 1 F
29 G9sus G9(♭5) FMa7 Dmi7 B♭Ma7 C9 F
I were a bell I'd go ding dong ding dong ding.
I were a bell I'd go ding dong ding dong
32 A7/E E♭°7 2 F
F
Ask me ding.

IN THE MOOD

By JOE GARLAND

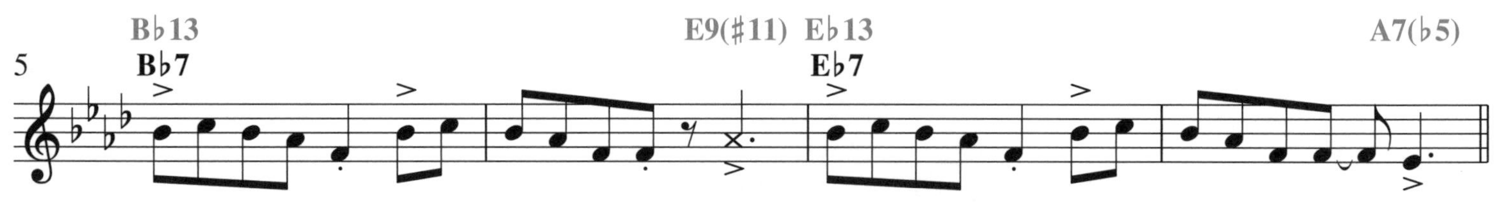

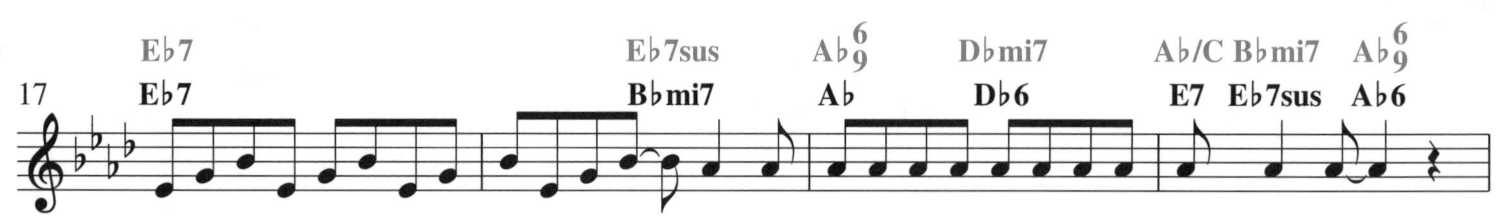

25
D♭7
D♭
A♭7
A♭
29
E♭7
E♭7
E♭7sus
B♭mi7
A♭6/9
A♭
D♭mi7
D♭6
A♭/C B♭mi7 A♭6/9
E7 E♭7sus A♭6
33
A♭6/9
A♭
F+7(♯9)
B°7
B♭mi7
B♭mi7
E♭13(♯11/♭9)
E♭13(♭9)
37
E♭13sus E♭13(♯11/♭9)
E♭11
E♭7
E♭°7
E7
41
45
E13sus
49
N.C.
(Ped. E♭) ⟶
A♭

IT'S BEEN A LONG, LONG TIME

Lyric by SAMMY CAHN
Music by JULE STYNE

LUSH LIFE

Words and Music by
BILLY STRAYHORN

Fmi7 Fmi6 Fmi13 A♭13 Gmi11 G♭13(♯11)
Fmi7 Fmi6 Fmi Gmi11 C7(♭9)
16
your si - ren song to tempt me to mad - ness, I
Fmi Fmi6 Fmi7 D7(♯11 ♯9) D♭Ma9 C/E
Fmi Fmi6 Fmi7 Fmi6 D♭Ma7/F E°7
19
thought for a - while that your poig-nant smile was tinged with the sad - ness
E♭mi7 A♭13 Cmi11 C♭9(♯11) B♭9sus B♭+7(♭9)
E♭mi7 A♭9 C♭9(♯11) B♭9 B♭7(♭9)
22
of a great love for me. Ah, yes I was
E♭mi7 A7(♭5) E♭mi11 D13(♯11)
E♭mi7 A7(♭5) E♭mi11 A♭7 A♭+7
25
wrong, a - gain I was wrong!
D♭Ma9 D13 D♭Ma9 D13 D♭Ma9 C7(♯11 ♯9) F+7(♯9)
D♭ D9 D♭ D9 D♭6 C7(♯11) B13(♭9)
29
Life is lone - ly a - gain, and on - ly last year ev - 'ry-thing seemed so
E E♭ D6/9 D♭Ma9 D13 D♭Ma9 D13
E E♭ D D♭ D9 D♭ D9
32
sure. Now life is aw - ful a - gain, a trough - ful of
D♭Ma9 G13(♭9) C13(♭9) F E E♭6/9 A♭Ma9 E♭+7(♯9)
D♭6 D♭9 C13(♭9) F E E♭ A♭6 E♭+7(♯9)
35
hearts could on - ly be a bore. A week in Pa - ris will

38
A♭Ma9 Emi9 A13(♭9) DMa7 G9sus C6 C♭7 B♭9sus A7(♯9) A♭9sus
A♭6 Emi9 A7(♭9) D Dmi7 C6 C♭7 B♭9 A7(♯9) A♭9
3
3
ease the bite of it. All I care is to smile in spite of it.
41
D♭Ma9 D13 D♭Ma9 D13 D♭Ma9 C7(♯11) F+7(♯9)
D♭ D9 D♭ D9 D♭6 C7(♯11) B13
3
3
3
I'll for - get you, I will, while yet you are still burn-ing in-side my
44
B♭13sus B♭13(♯11 ♭9) E♭mi11 G♭mi9 C♭13(♯11) A+7(♯9) A♭13sus A♭13(♯11 ♭9)
B♭13 B♭7(♭9) E♭mi11 G♭mi9 A+7(♯9) A♭13
brain. Ro - mance is mush, sti - fling those who strive._ I'll
47
D♭Ma9 G♭13sus G♭13(♯11 ♭9) C♭Ma9 B♭13sus B♭13(♯11 ♭9) E♭mi11 G♭mi9 C♭13(♯11)
D♭Ma9 D♭mi9 G♭13(♭9) C♭Ma9 Fmi11 B♭7(♭9) E♭mi11 G♭mi9
live a lush life in some small dive,_ and there I'll be, while I
50
A+7(♯9) A♭13sus EMa9 E♭6 DMa7 G9 D♭Ma9 D9 D♭Ma7
A+9 A♭13 E E♭6 DMa7 G9 D♭Ma9 D9 D♭Ma7
rot with the rest of those whose lives are lone - ly too.

IT'S SO NICE TO HAVE A MAN AROUND THE HOUSE

Lyric by JACK ELLIOTT
Music by HAROLD SPINA

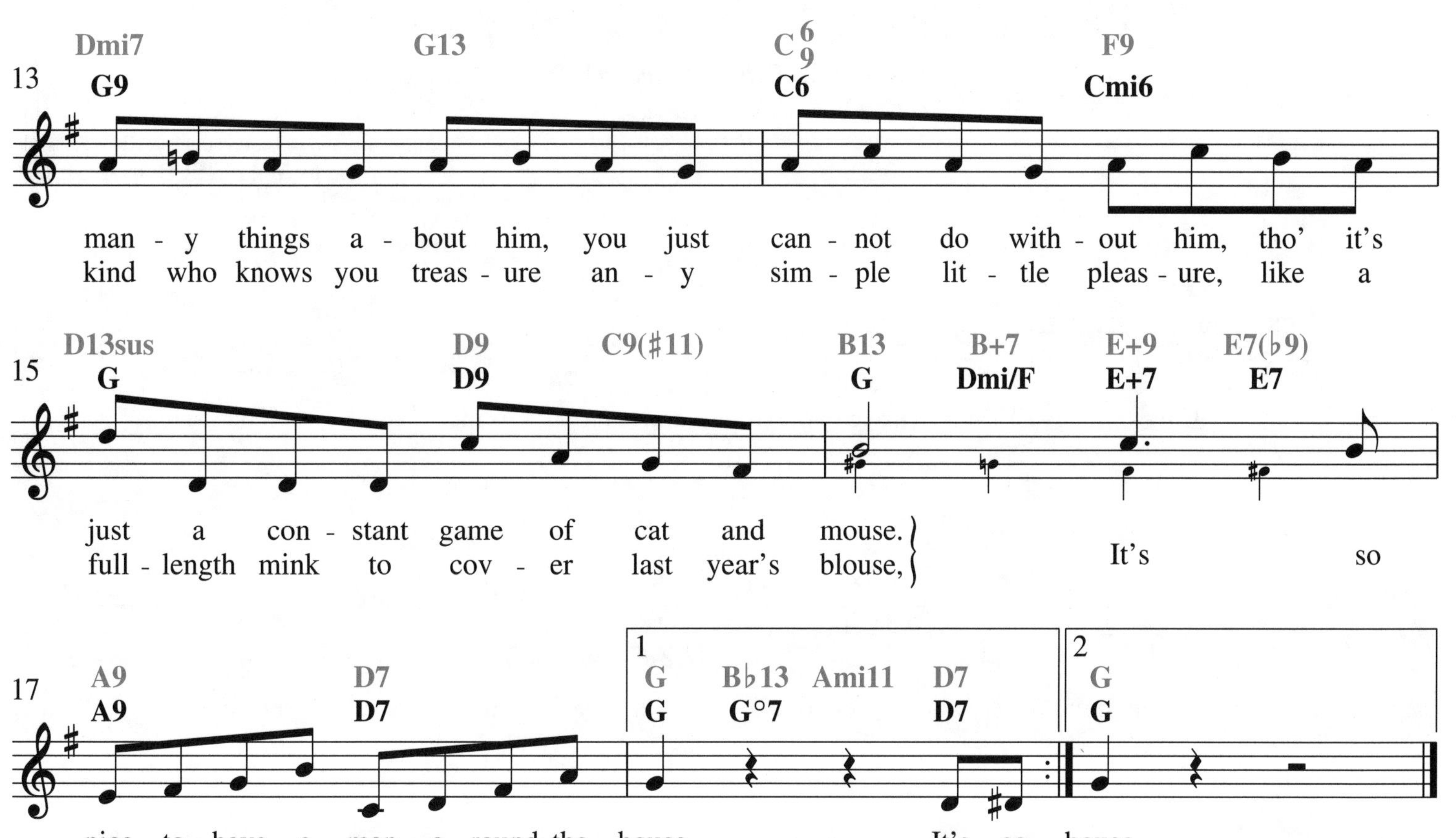
13
Dmi7 G13 C 6/9 F9
G9 C6 Cmi6
man - y things a - bout him, you just can - not do with - out him, tho' it's
kind who knows you treas - ure an - y sim - ple lit - tle pleas - ure, like a
15
D13sus D9 C9(♯11) B13 B+7 E+9 E7(♭9)
G D9 G Dmi/F E+7 E7
just a con - stant game of cat and mouse.
full - length mink to cov - er last year's blouse,
It's so
17
A9 D7 G B♭13 Ami11 D7 G
A9 D7 G G°7 D7 G
1 2
nice to have a man a - round the house. It's so house.

LOVE ME OR LEAVE ME

from LOVE ME OR LEAVE ME

Lyrics by GUS KAHN
Music by WALTER DONALDSON

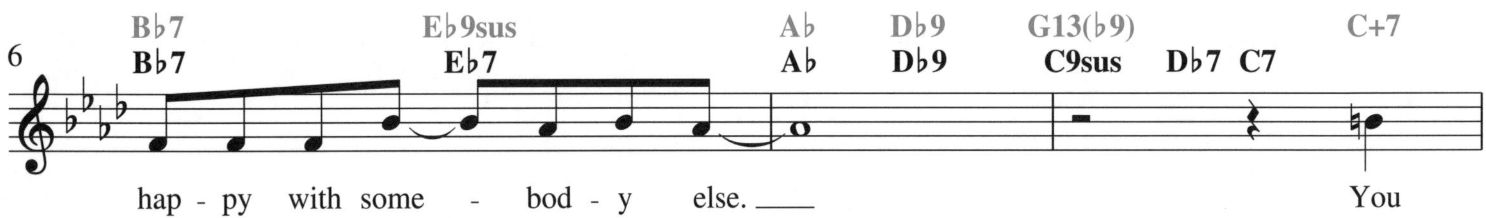

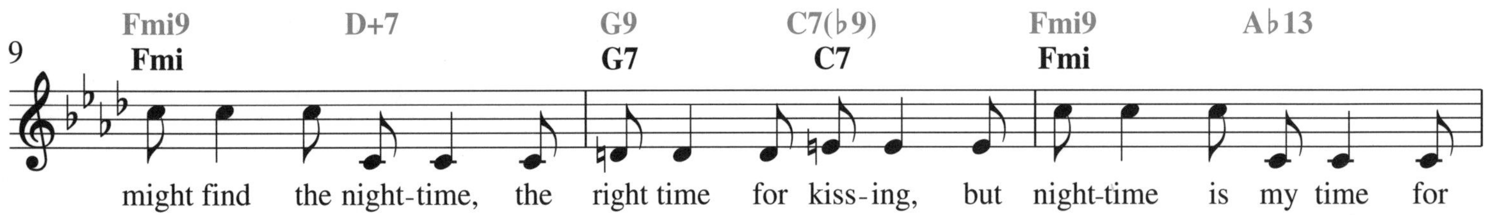

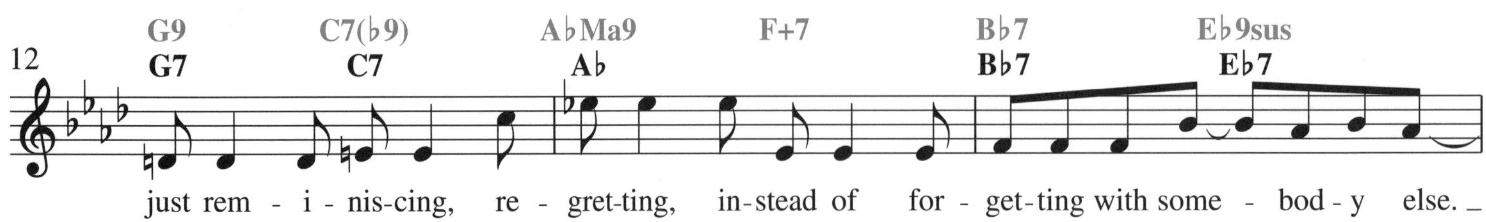

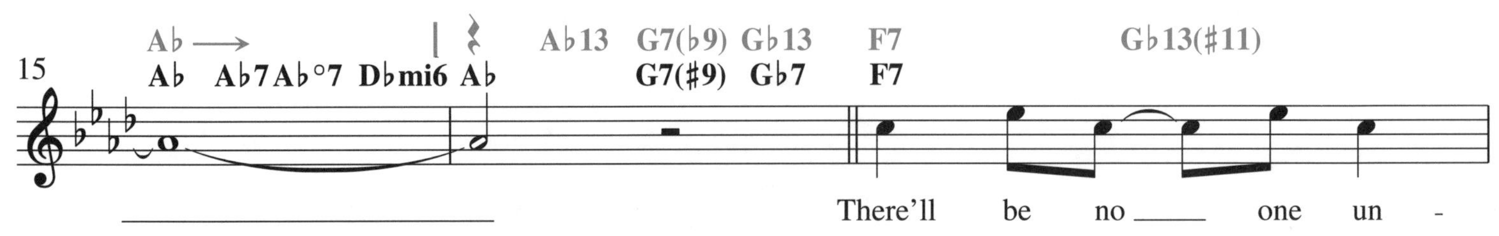

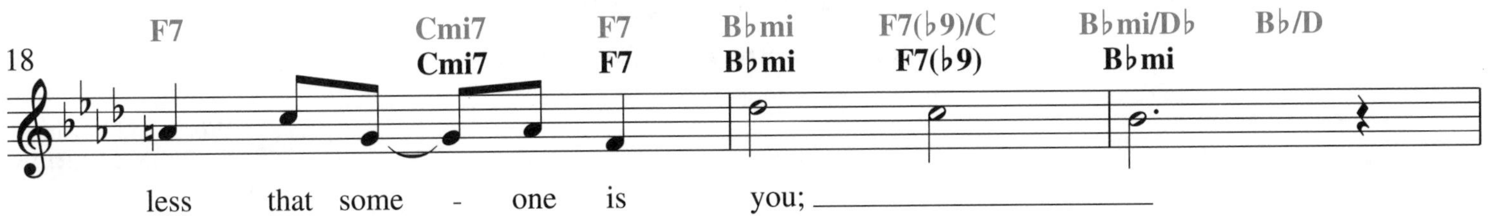
18
F7 Cmi7 F7 B♭mi F7(♭9)/C B♭mi/D♭ B♭/D
Cmi7 F7 B♭mi F7(♭9) B♭mi
less that some - one is you;

21
E♭7 E9(♯11) E♭7 B♭mi7 E♭7 Cmi7 Bmi7
E♭7 B♭mi7 E♭7 A♭/C B°7
I in - tend to be in - de - pen - dent - ly blue.

24
B♭mi7 Gmi7(♭5) C7(♭9) Fmi9 D+7 G9 C7(♭9)
B♭mi7 C7(♭9) Fmi G7 C7
I want your love, but I don't want to bor - row to

27
Fmi9 A♭13 G9 C7(♭9) A♭Ma9 B9
Fmi G7 C7 A♭
have it to - day, and to give back to - mor - row, for my love is your love, there's

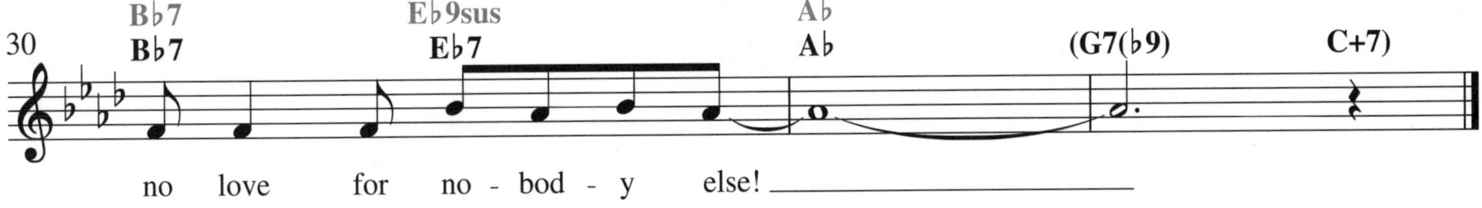
30
B♭7 E♭9sus A♭
B♭7 E♭7 A♭ (G7(♭9) C+7)
no love for no - bod - y else!

MARIE

from the Motion Picture THE AWAKENING

Words and Music by
IRVING BERLIN

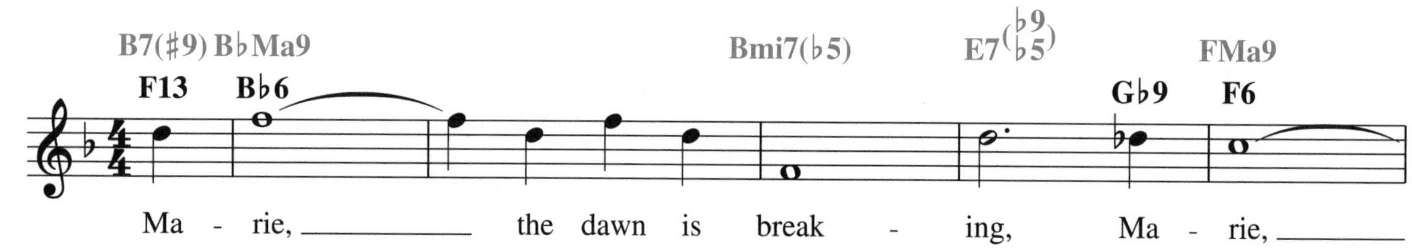
B7(♯9) B♭Ma9
F13
B♭6
Bmi7(♭5)
E7(♭9 ♭5)
G♭9
FMa9
F6
Ma - rie, the dawn is break - ing, Ma - rie,

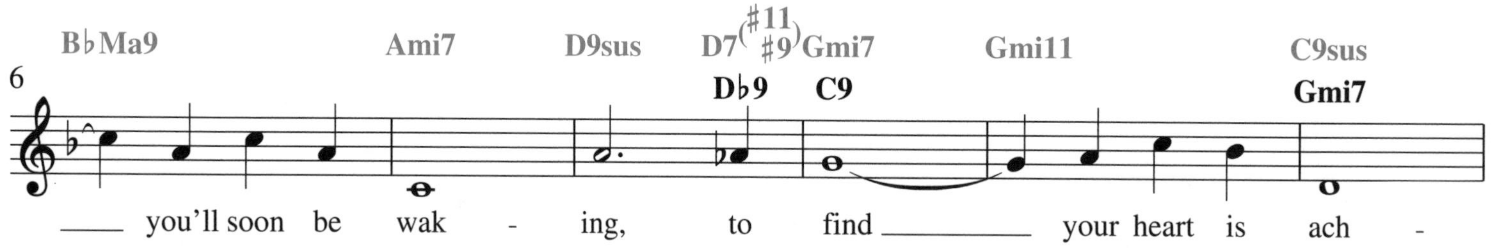
6
B♭Ma9
Ami7
D9sus
D7(♯11 ♯9)
D♭9
Gmi7
C9
Gmi11
C9sus
Gmi7
you'll soon be wak - ing, to find your heart is ach -

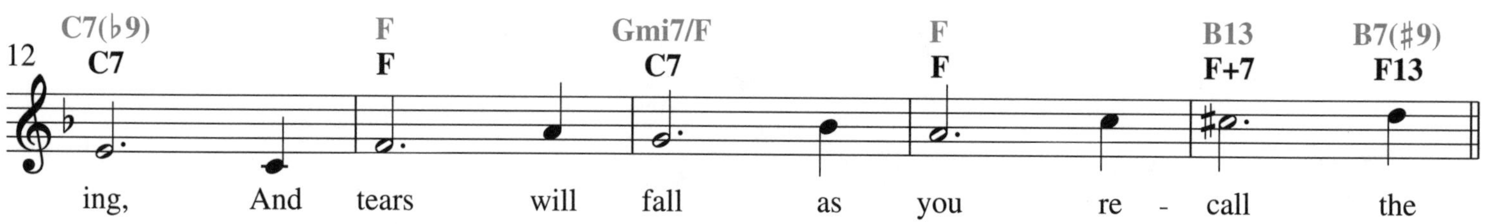
12
C7(♭9)
C7
F
F
Gmi7/F
C7
F
F
B13
F+7
B7(♯9)
F13
ing, And tears will fall as you re - call the

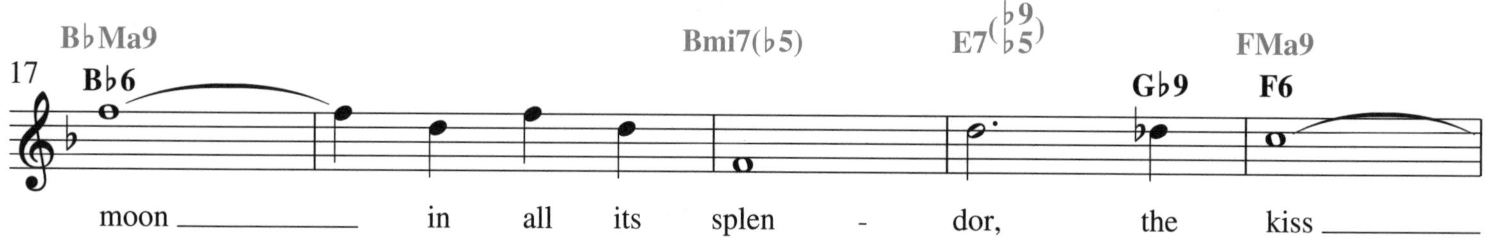
17
B♭Ma9
B♭6
Bmi7(♭5)
E7(♭9 ♭5)
G♭9
FMa9
F6
moon in all its splen - dor, the kiss

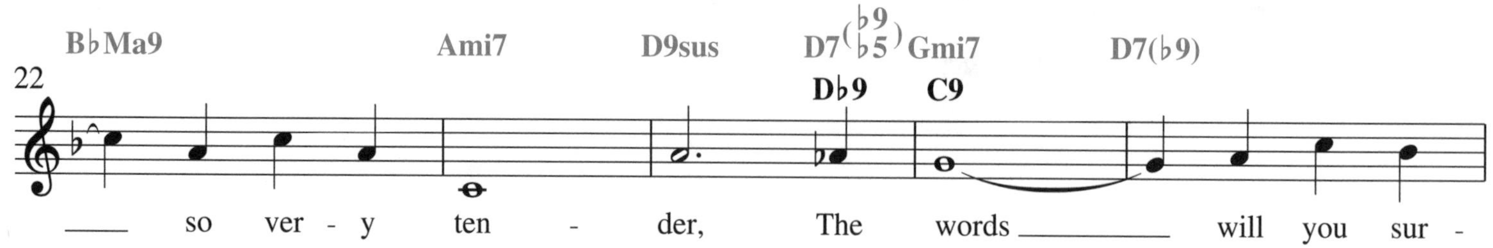
22
B♭Ma9
Ami7
D9sus
D7(♭9 ♭5)
D♭9
Gmi7
C9
D7(♭9)
so ver - y ten - der, The words will you sur -

27
Gmi7
Gmi7
C7(♭9)
C7
F
F
D7(♭9)
Gmi9
C9sus
C9
F
F
ren - der, to me Ma - rie.

MY IDEAL

from the Paramount Picture **PLAYBOY OF PARIS**

Words by LEO ROBIN
Music by RICHARD A. WHITING and NEWELL CHASE

(I'm Afraid)

THE MASQUERADE IS OVER

Words by HERB MAGIDSON
Music by ALLIE WRUBEL

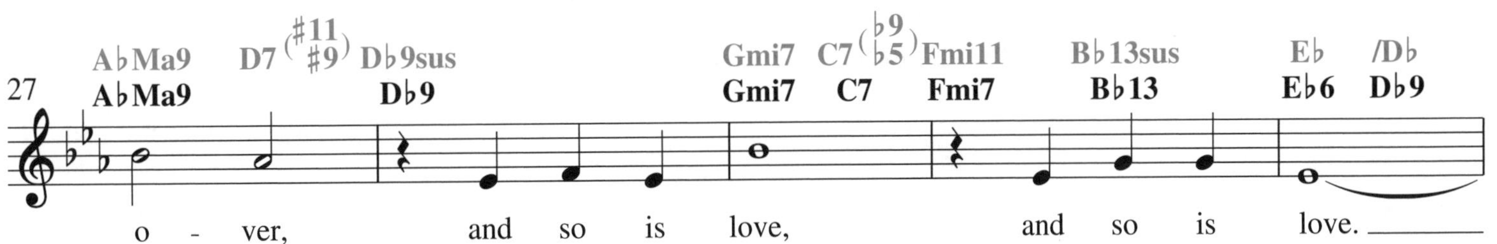
A♭Ma9 D7(♯11/♯9) D♭9sus Gmi7 C7(♭9/♭5) Fmi11 B♭13sus E♭ /D♭
27
A♭Ma9 D♭9 Gmi7 C7 Fmi7 B♭13 E♭6 D♭9
o - ver, and so is love, and so is love.

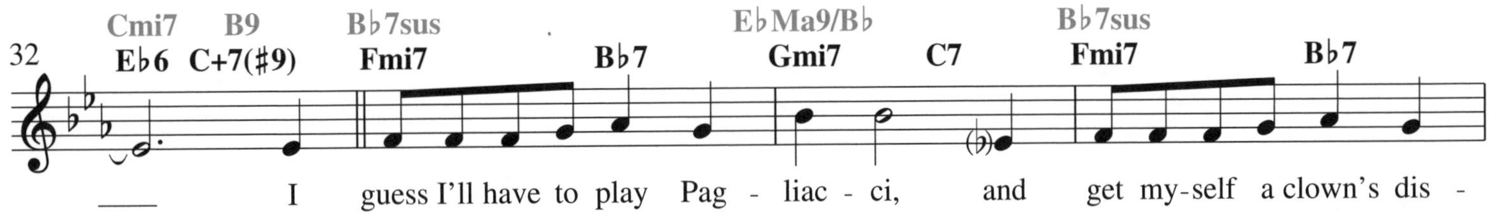
Cmi7 B9 B♭7sus E♭Ma9/B♭ B♭7sus
32
E♭6 C+7(♯9) Fmi7 B♭7 Gmi7 C7 Fmi7 B♭7
I guess I'll have to play Pag - liac - ci, and get my-self a clown's dis -

E♭Ma9/B♭ Ami7(♭5)/D D7(♭9/♭5) Gmi7 C9sus F13sus F13 B♭7sus B♭7
36
E♭Ma7 Ami7(♭5) D7 Gmi7 C9 Cmi11 F7 Fmi7 B♭7
guise; and learn to laugh like Pag - liac - ci, with tears in my eyes. You

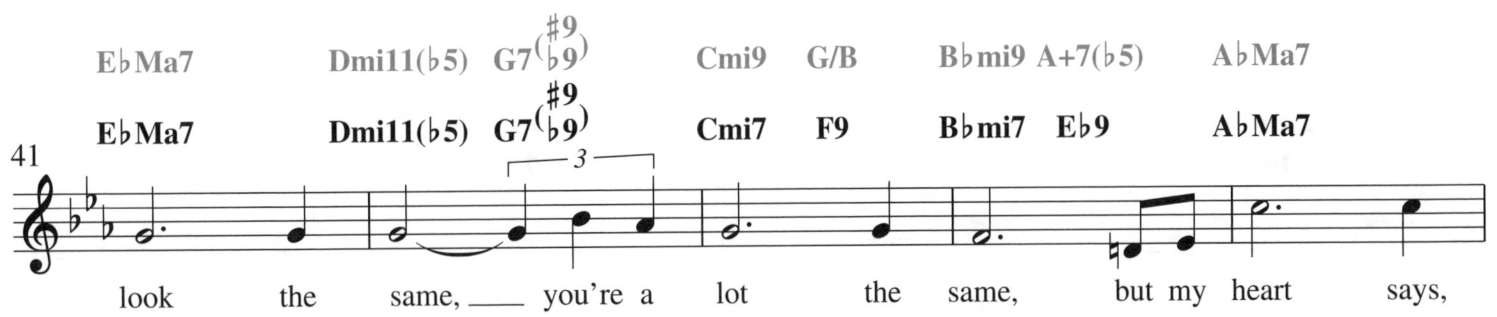
E♭Ma7 Dmi11(♭5) G7(♯9/♭9) Cmi9 G/B B♭mi9 A+7(♭5) A♭Ma7
41
E♭Ma7 Dmi11(♭5) G7(♯9/♭9) Cmi7 F9 B♭mi7 E♭9 A♭Ma7
look the same, you're a lot the same, but my heart says,

Gmi7(♭5) C7(♭9/♭5) F9 B9(♯11) B♭9sus B♭13(♯11/♭9) E♭Ma9 Cmi7 F7/B B♭mi11 A7(♯11/♭9)
46
Gmi7(♭5) C7 F7 Fmi7 B♭7 E♭Ma7 B♭mi11 E♭7
"No, no you're not the same." I'm a - fraid the mas-que-rade is

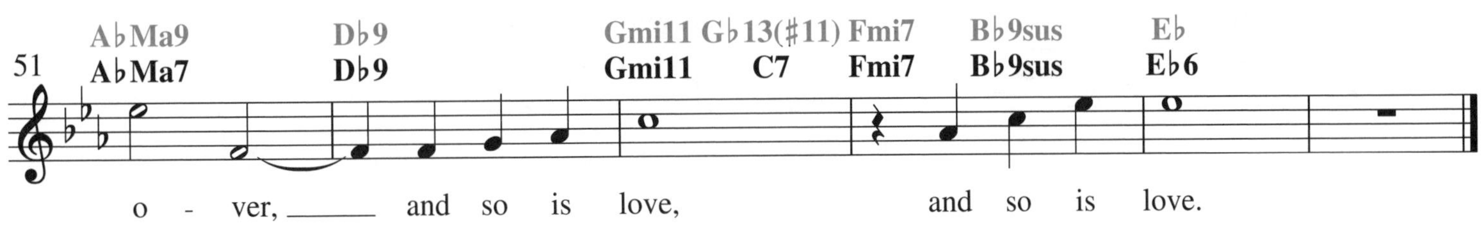
A♭Ma9 D♭9 Gmi11 G♭13(♯11) Fmi7 B♭9sus E♭
51
A♭Ma7 D♭9 Gmi11 C7 Fmi7 B♭9sus E♭6
o - ver, and so is love, and so is love.

MY SHINING HOUR

from the Motion Picture THE SKY'S THE LIMIT

Lyric by JOHNNY MERCER
Music by HAROLD ARLEN

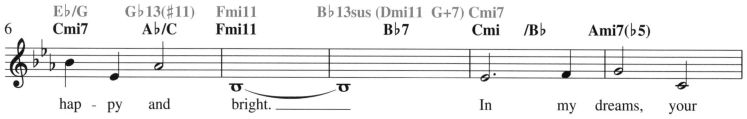

E♭Ma7 Fmi7/E♭ E♭Ma7 F13 F+9 B♭13sus B♭7 E♭Ma7 A♭13
E♭ E♭sus Cmi7 F9 B♭13(♭9) B♭7 E♭ E♭sus
This will be my shin - ing hour, calm and

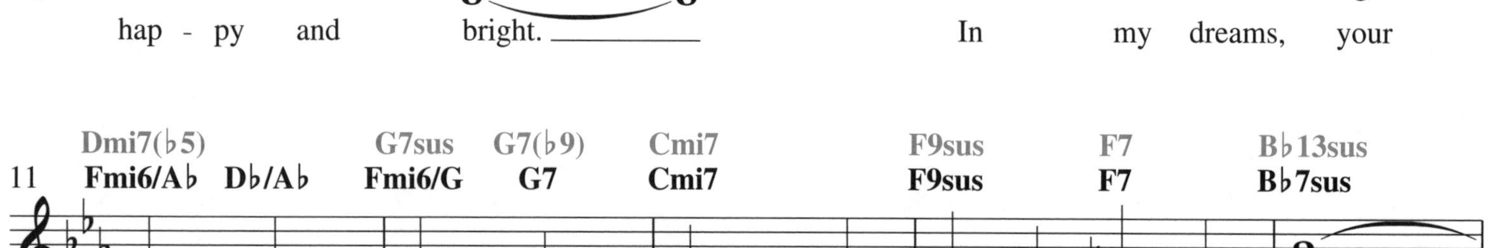
6
E♭/G G♭13(♯11) Fmi11 B♭13sus (Dmi11 G+7) Cmi7
Cmi7 A♭/C Fmi11 B♭7 Cmi /B♭ Ami7(♭5)
hap - py and bright. In my dreams, your

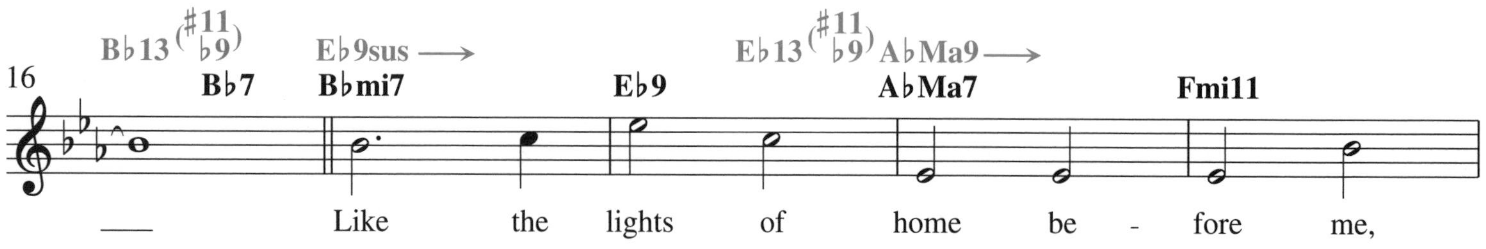
11
Dmi7(♭5) G7sus G7(♭9) Cmi7 F9sus F7 B♭13sus
Fmi6/A♭ D♭/A♭ Fmi6/G G7 Cmi7 F9sus F7 B♭7sus
face will flow - er, through the dark - ness of the night.

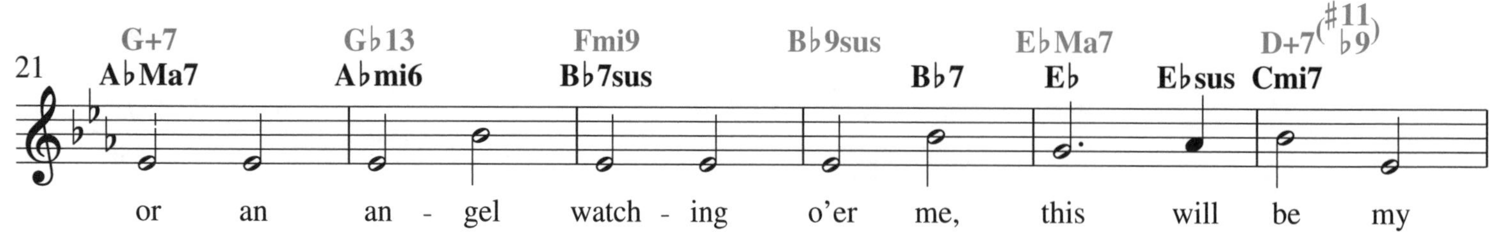
16
B♭13(♯11 ♭9) E♭9sus E♭13(♯11 ♭9) A♭Ma9
B♭7 B♭mi7 E♭9 A♭Ma7 Fmi11
Like the lights of home be - fore me,
21
G+7 G♭13 Fmi9 B♭9sus E♭Ma7 D+7(♯11 ♭9)
A♭Ma7 A♭mi6 B♭7sus B♭7 E♭ E♭sus Cmi7
or an an - gel watch - ing o'er me, this will be my

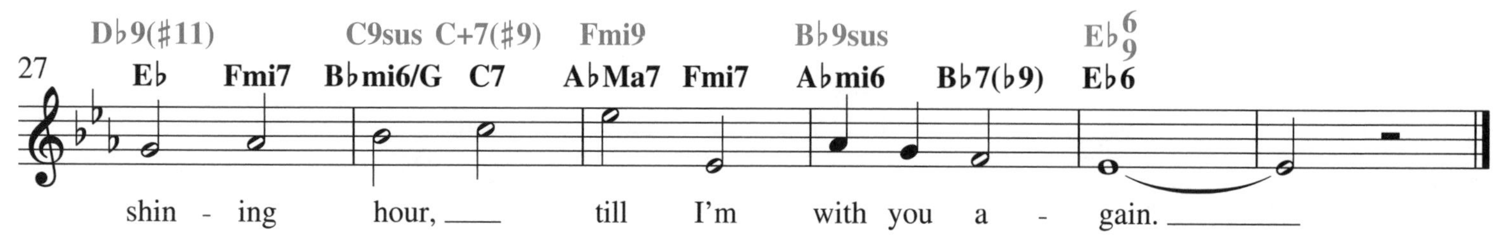
27
D♭9(♯11) C9sus C+7(♯9) Fmi9 B♭9sus E♭6/9
E♭ Fmi7 B♭mi6/G C7 A♭Ma7 Fmi7 A♭mi6 B♭7(♭9) E♭6
shin - ing hour, till I'm with you a - gain.

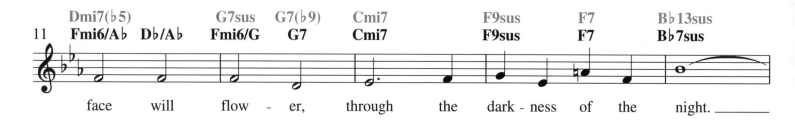

ONE FOR MY BABY

(And One More for the Road)

from the Motion Picture THE SKY'S THE LIMIT

Lyric by JOHNNY MERCER
Music by HAROLD ARLEN

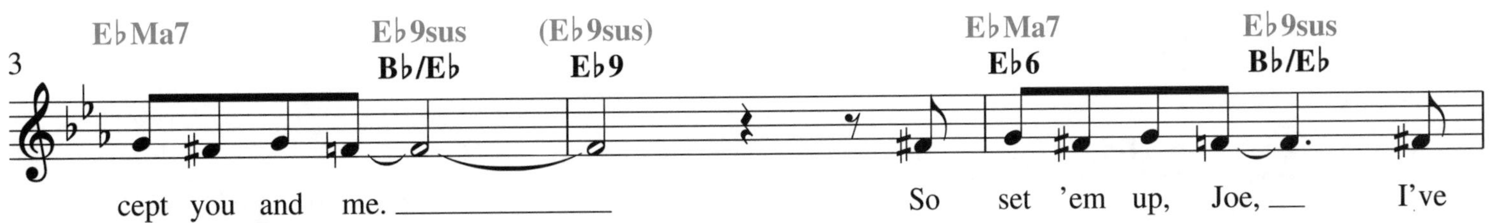

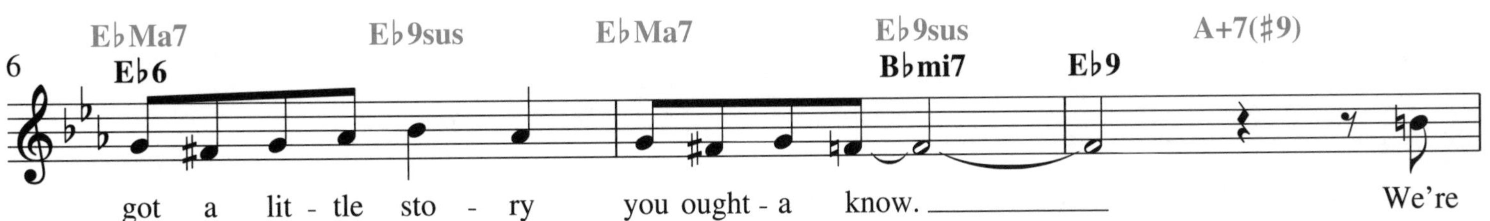

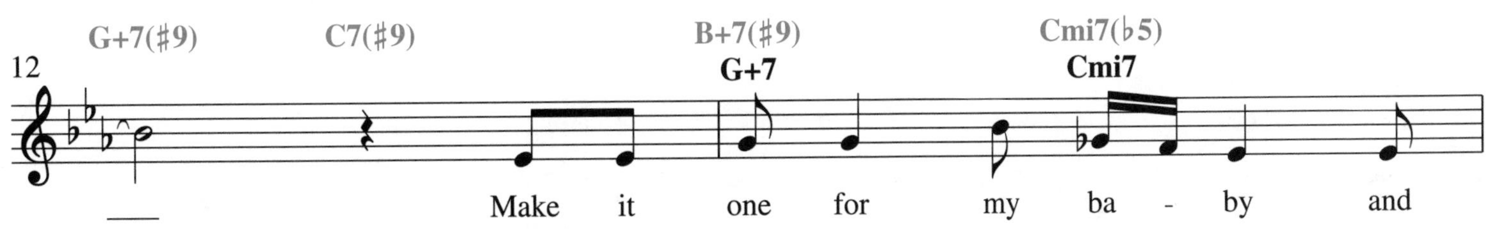

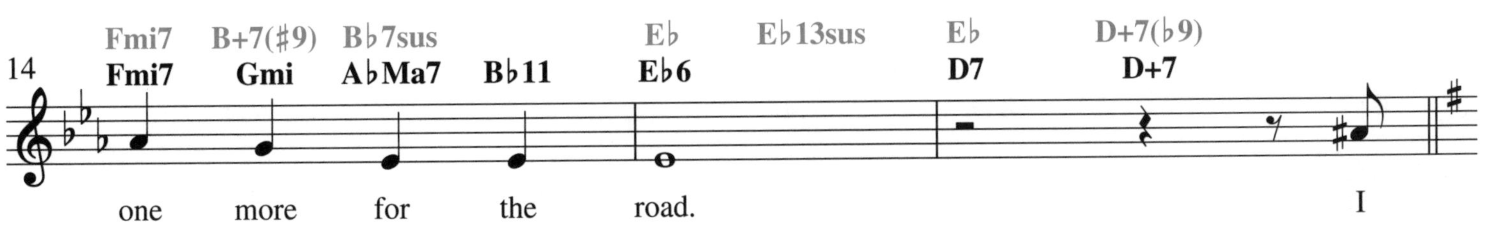

got the rou - tine, so drop an - oth - er nick - el in the ma - chine.
I'm feel - in' so bad, I wish you'd make the mu - sic
dream - y and sad. Could tell you a lot,
but you've got to be true to your code. Make it
one for my ba - by and one more got the road.
You'd nev - er know it, but Bud-dy, I'm a kind of po - et and I've
got-ta lot - ta things to say. And when I'm gloom - y you

38
C9sus
C9sus
C13
C9
Emi11
Gmi9
A13
E♭9(♯11)
sim - ply got - ta lis - ten to me, un - til it's talked a -
40
E♭mi9 A♭13sus A♭13
D+7
GMa7
G
F/G
D/G
GMa7
G
G9sus
way. Well, that's how it goes and Joe, I know you're get - ting
43
GMa7
F/G
D/G
(F/G)
G9
GMa7
G
F/G
D/G
anx - ious to close, so, thanks for the cheer, I
46
GMa7
G
G9sus
GMa7
G
F/G
Dmi7
G9
D♭+7(♯9)
hope you did - n't mind my bend - ing your ear. This
49
CMa7
C
C9sus
G/C
CMa7
C
F13
GMa7
G
C13
torch that I've found, must be drowned or it soon might ex - plode.
52
B+7(♯9)
E7(♯9)
E♭+7(♯9)
B+7
E7 (♯11 ♯9)
Emi7
Make it one for my ba - by and
54
Ami7
Ami7
E♭+9
G/B
D7sus
CMa7
D11
G
G
one more for the road.

OKLAHOMA

from OKLAHOMA!

Lyrics by OSCAR HAMMERSTEIN II
Music by RICHARD RODGERS

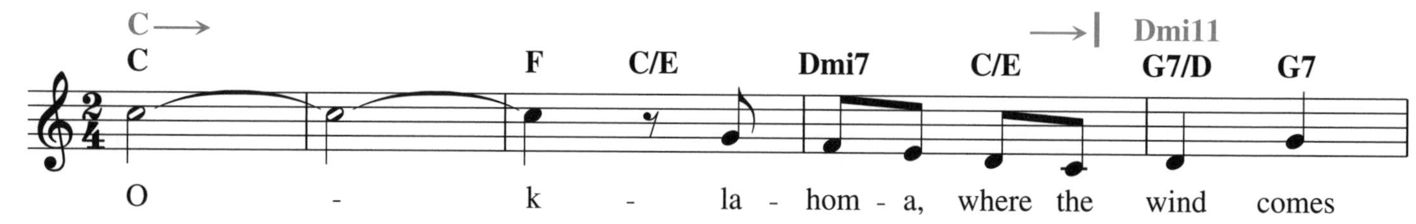

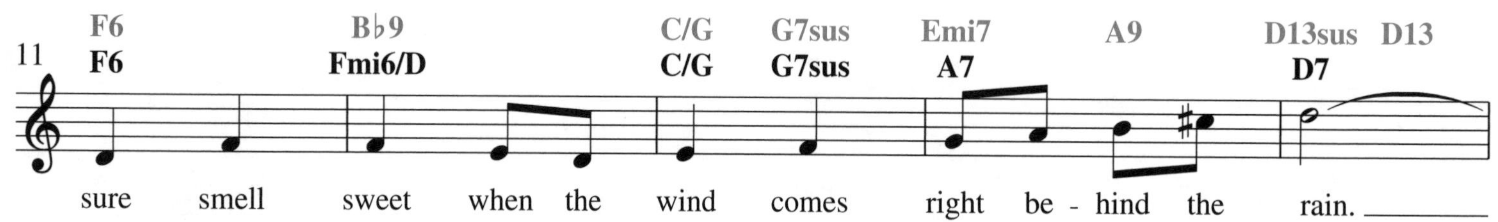

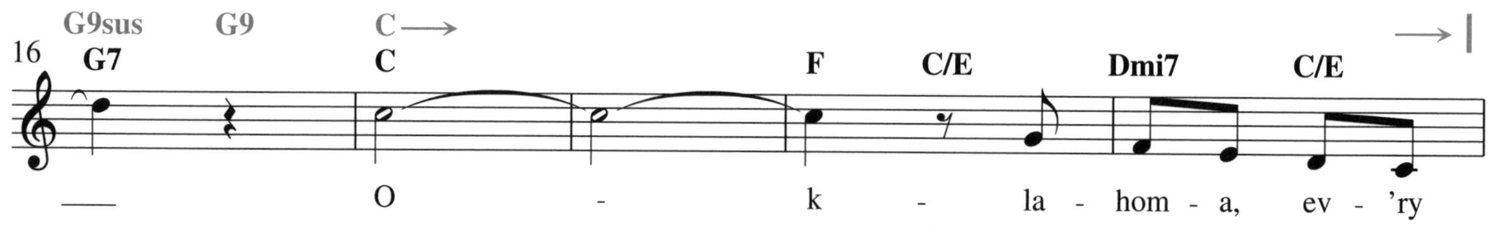

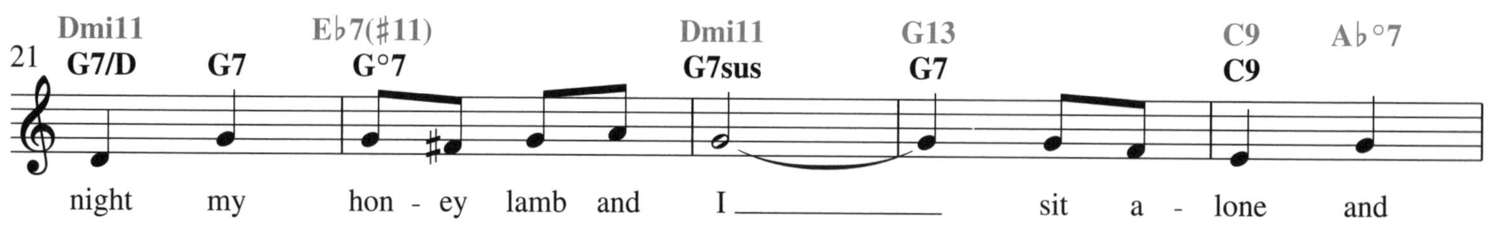

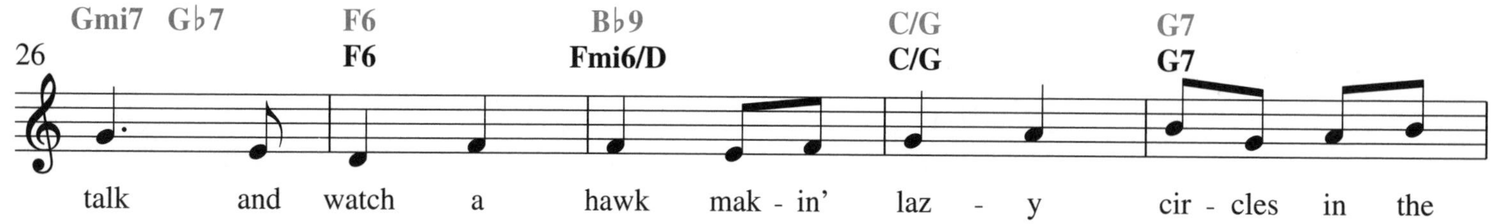

31
C Gmi11 G♭9(♯11) F C
C F C
sky. We know we be - long to the land

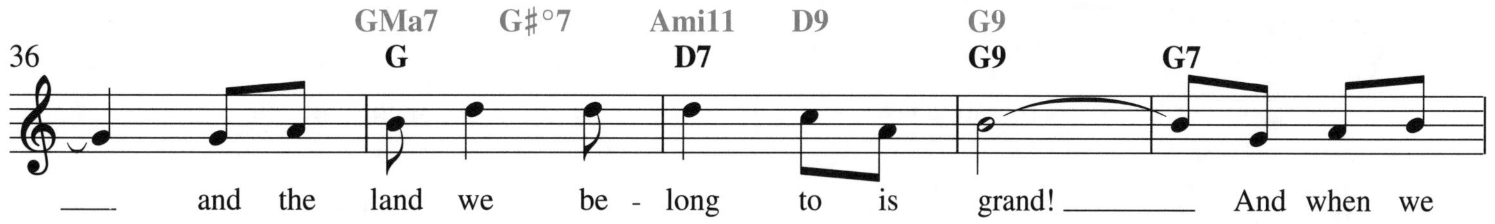
36
GMa7 G♯°7 Ami11 D9 G9
G D7 G9 G7
and the land we be - long to is grand! And when we

41
C D7
C F C/E Dmi7 C/E D7
say Yeeow! A - yip - i - o - ee - ay!

46
C/G E/G♯
G D7/F♯ Emi7 D9 C E7/G♯
We're on - ly say - in' you're do - in' fine, Ok - la -

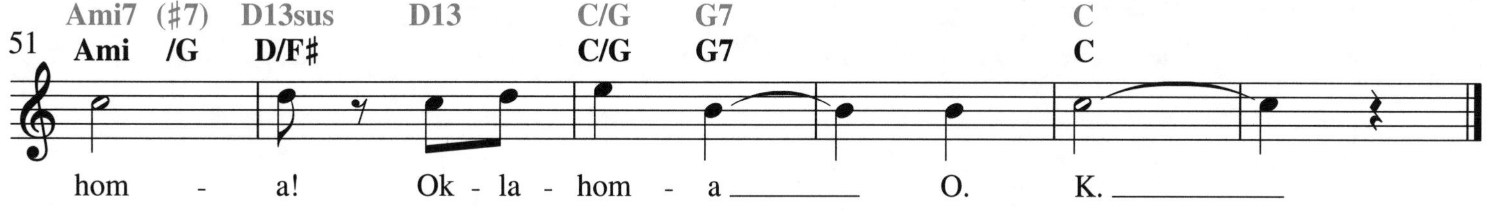
51
Ami7 (♯7) D13sus D13 C/G G7 C
Ami /G D/F♯ C/G G7 C
hom - a! Ok - la - hom - a O. K.

OLD CAPE COD

Words and Music by CLAIRE ROTHROCK,
MILT YAKUS and ALLEN JEFFREY

Fmi7 B♭13(♭9) E♭Ma7 A7(♭5)
19 Fmi7 B♭7(♭9) E♭Ma7 E♭7
miles of green be - neath the skies of blue;

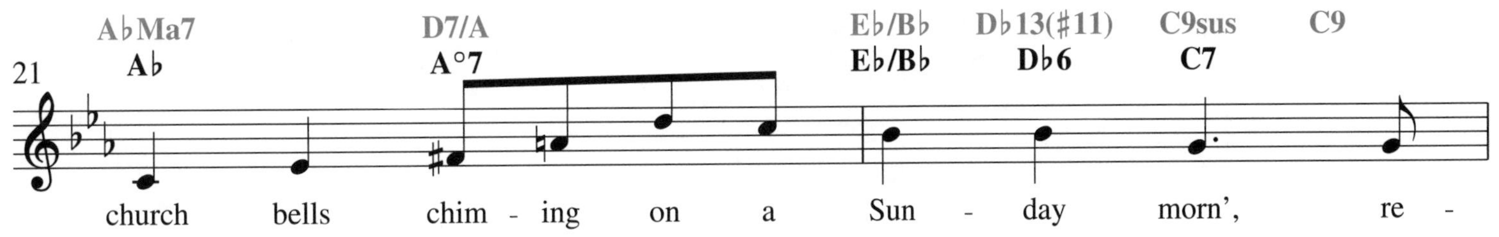
A♭Ma7 D7/A E♭/B♭ D♭13(♯11) C9sus C9
21 A♭ A°7 E♭/B♭ D♭6 C7
church bells chim - ing on a Sun - day morn', re -

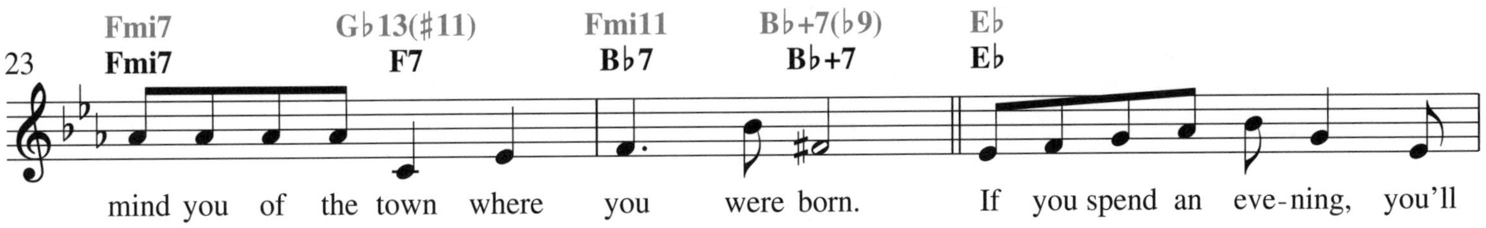
Fmi7 G♭13(♯11) Fmi11 B♭+7(♭9) E♭
23 Fmi7 F7 B♭7 B♭+7 E♭
mind you of the town where you were born. If you spend an eve-ning, you'll

E♭9sus A+7 A♭Ma7 D♭9(♯11)
26 B♭mi7 E♭9 A♭Ma7 D♭9(♯11)
want to stay, watch - ing the moon-light on Cape Cod Bay;

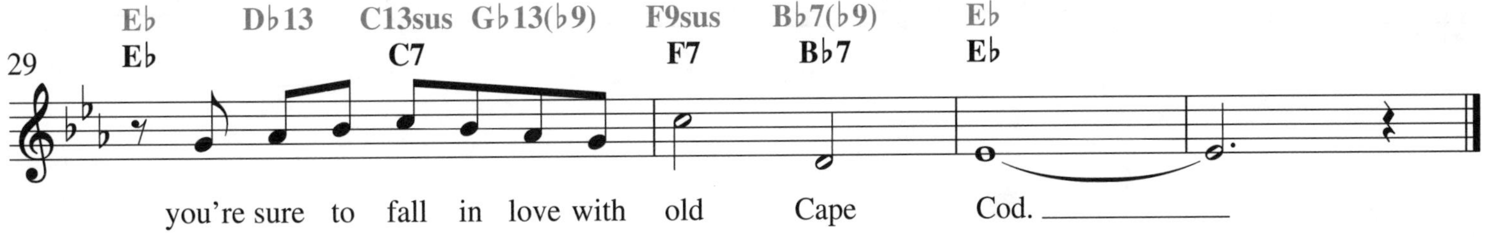
E♭ D♭13 C13sus G♭13(♭9) F9sus B♭7(♭9) E♭
29 E♭ C7 F7 B♭7 E♭
you're sure to fall in love with old Cape Cod.

ON A SLOW BOAT TO CHINA

By FRANK LOESSER

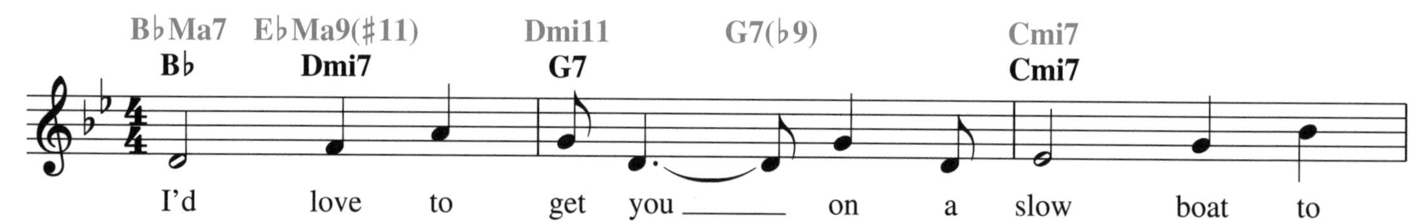

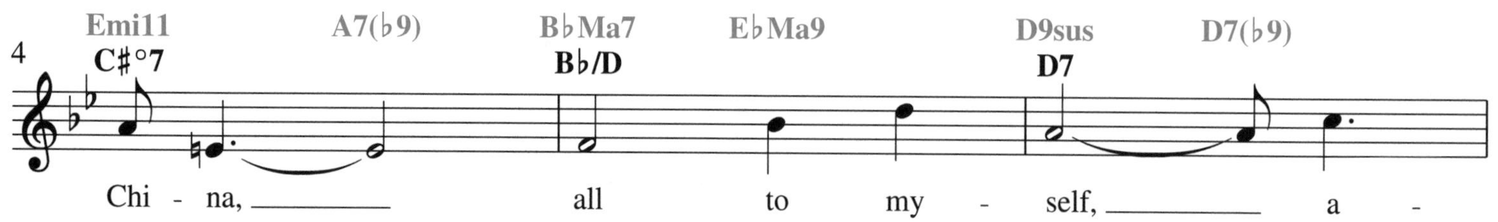

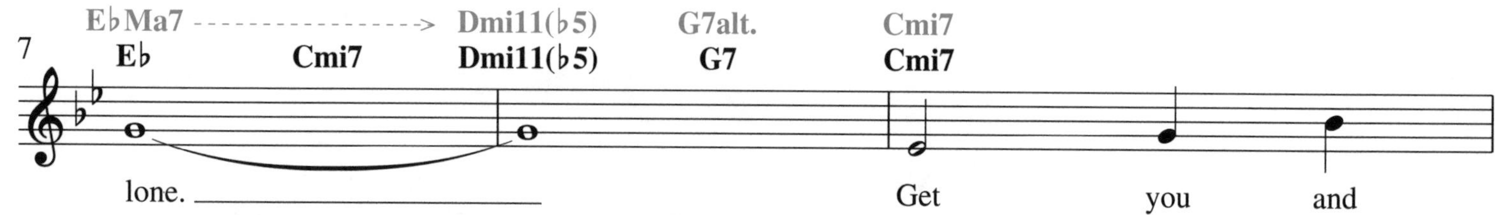

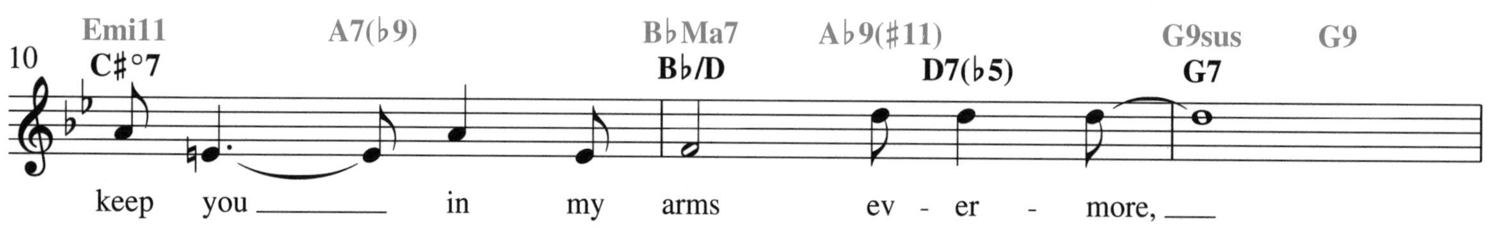

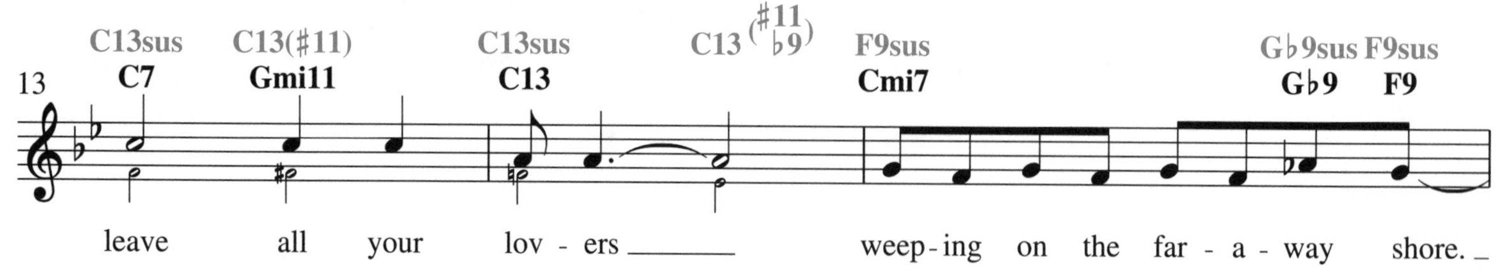

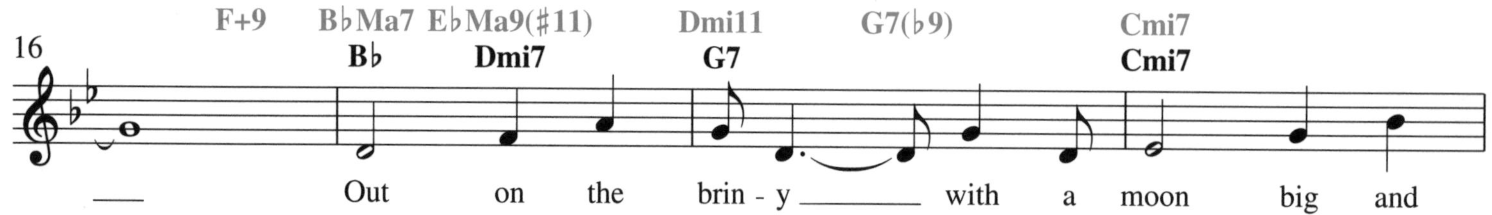

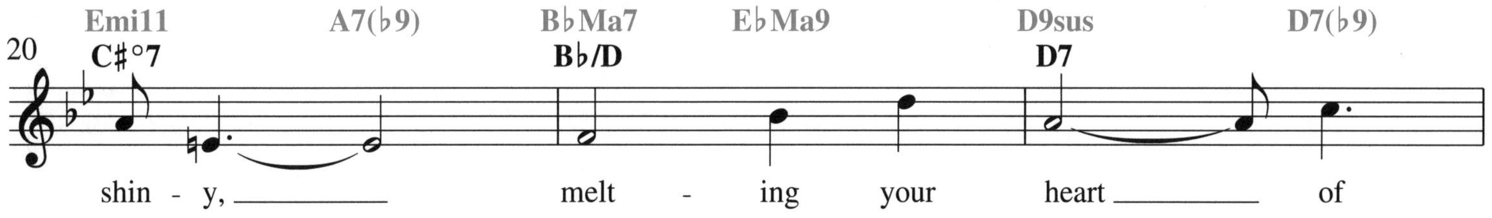
Emi11 A7(♭9) B♭Ma7 E♭Ma9 D9sus D7(♭9)
20
C♯°7 B♭/D D7
shin - y, melt - ing your heart of

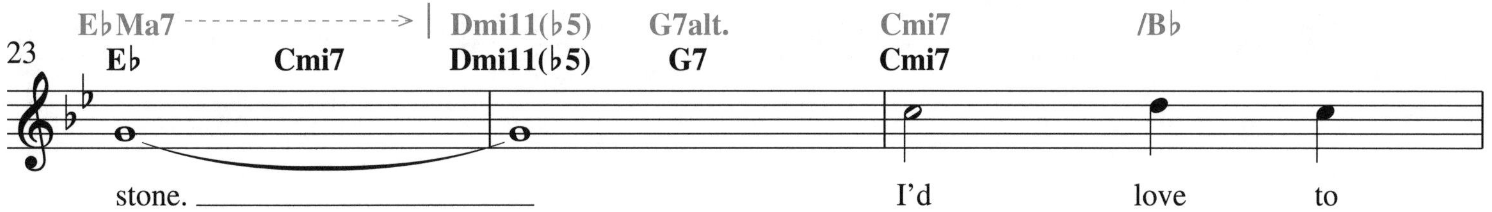
E♭Ma7 Dmi11(♭5) G7alt. Cmi7 /B♭
23
E♭ Cmi7 Dmi11(♭5) G7 Cmi7
stone. I'd love to

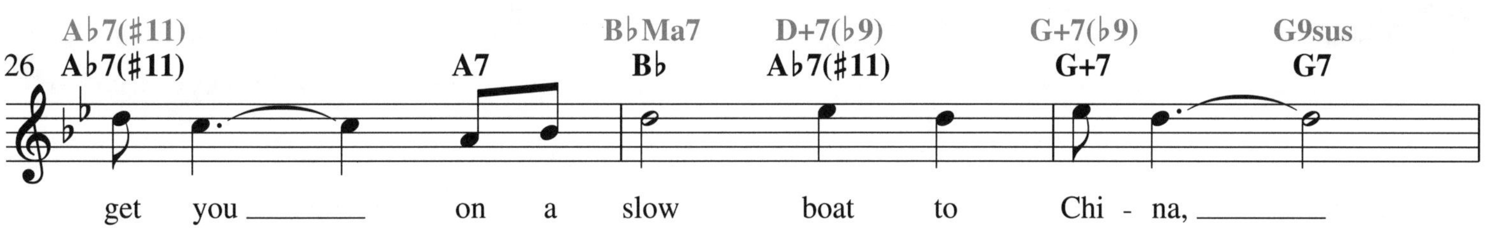
A♭7(♯11) B♭Ma7 D+7(♭9) G+7(♭9) G9sus
26
A♭7(♯11) A7 B♭ A♭7(♯11) G+7 G7
get you on a slow boat to Chi - na,

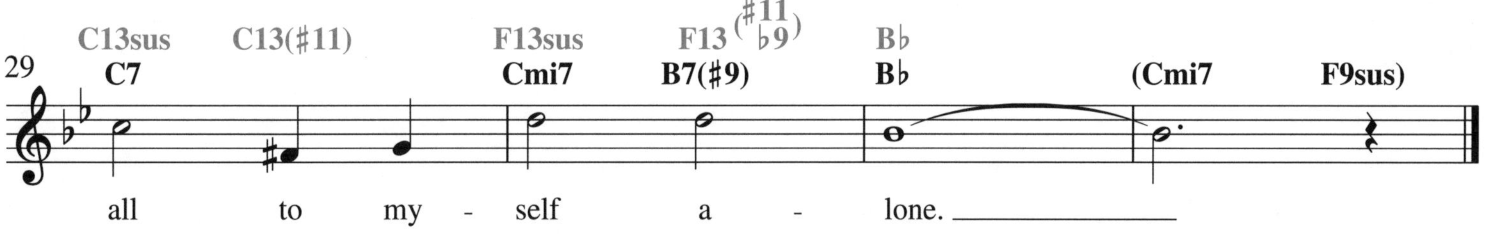
C13sus C13(♯11) F13sus F13(♯11 ♭9) B♭
29
C7 Cmi7 B7(♯9) B♭ (Cmi7 F9sus)
all to my - self a - lone.

PAPER DOLL

Words and Music by
JOHNNY S. BLACK

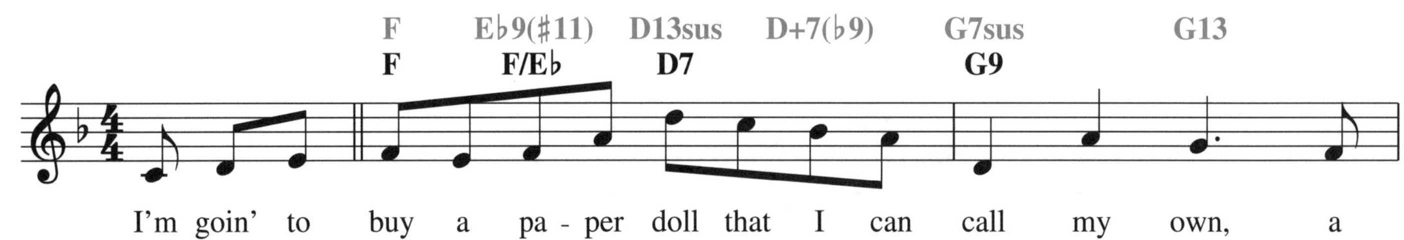
F Eb9(#11) D13sus D+7(b9) G7sus G13
F F/Eb D7 G9
I'm goin' to buy a pa - per doll that I can call my own, a

C7 /Bb Ami11 Ab7(#11) Gmi7 C/Bb F/A Ab°7
3
C7 E7 F6 FMa9 /A Fmi/Ab
doll that oth - er fel-lows can-not steal. And then the flir - ty, flir - ty guys with their

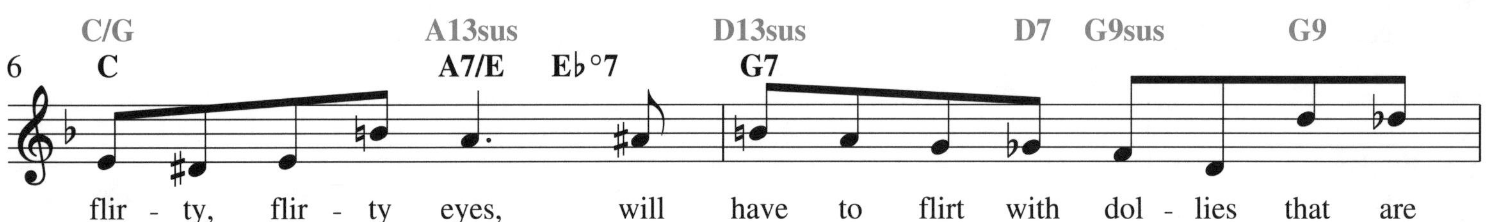
C/G A13sus D13sus D7 G9sus G9
6
C A7/E Eb°7 G7
flir - ty, flir - ty eyes, will have to flirt with dol - lies that are

C13sus C+7 F D+7(b9) G13 C7 FMa7 C13sus
8
C C°7 C7 F D+7 G7 C7 F
real. When I come home at night she will be wait - ing, she'll

F D+7(b9) Db9(#11) C9 /Bb A13 A+7 D9 Gmi7 G#°7
11
F D+7 G7 C7 A7 Dmi6/A A7 Bb B°7
be the tru - est doll in all this world. I'd rath - er have a pa - per doll to

F/A A9 D13sus D+7(b9) G9 Db9(#11) C13(#11 b9) F
14
F A7 D7 G7 Bbmi6/Db C13 F
call my own, than have a fick - le - mind - ed real live girl.

THE RAINBOW CONNECTION

from THE MUPPET MOVIE

By PAUL WILLIAMS
and KENNETH L. ASCHER

A(add2) F♯mi11 Bmi11 D/E E /D
A F♯mi11 Bmi7 D/E E
Why are there so man - y songs a - bout rain - bows, and
Who said that ev - 'ry wish would be heard and an - swered when
5
C♯mi7 F♯mi7 Bmi7 D/E
A E/G♯ F♯mi7 A/E D D/E
what's on the oth - er side?
wished on the morn - ing star.
9
A(add2) F♯mi11 Bmi11 D/E E /D
A E/F♯ F♯mi7 Bmi7 D/E E
Rain - bows are vi - sions, but on - ly il - lu - sions, and
Some - bod - y thought of that, and some - one be - lieved it;
13
C♯mi7 F♯mi7 A/E DMa7
A E/G♯ F♯mi7 A/E D
rain - bows have noth - ing to hide.
look what it's done so far.
17
DMa7
DMa7
So we've been told, and some choose to be - lieve it;
What's so a - maz - ing that keeps us star - gaz - ing
21
C♯mi7 F♯9sus F♯9
G♯mi/C♯
I know they're wrong; wait and see.
what do we think we might see?

25
Bmi7 E D/E E/D C♯mi7 E/F♯ F♯7
Bmi7 E D/E C♯mi7 E/F♯ F♯7
Some - day we'll find it,
Some - day we'll find it,
the Rain - bow Con - nec - tion; the
29
Bmi7 E13sus E7(♭9) A D/A
Bmi7 E13sus E7 A D/A
1
lov - ers, the dream - ers, and me.
33
A D/A A E/G♯
A D/A A E/G♯
2
me. All of us
37
F♯mi7 A/E D A/C♯
F♯mi7 A/E D A/C♯
un - der its spell; we know that it's prob - ab - ly
41
E9sus F9sus F13 B♭(add2)
E9sus F9sus F B♭
ma - gic. Have you been
45
Gmi11 Cmi11 E♭/F F /E♭ Dmi7
F/G Gmi7 Cmi7 E♭/F F B♭ F/A
half a - sleep and have you heard voic - es? I've heard them
49
Gmi7 Cmi7 E♭/F B♭(add2)
Gmi7 E♭ E♭/F F7sus B♭
call - ing my name. Is this the

53
Gmi11 Cmi11 Eb/F F /Eb Dmi7
F/G Gmi7 Cmi7 Eb/F F Bb F/A
sweet sound _ that calls the young sai - lors? The voice might be
57
Gmi7 Bb/F EbMa7 EbMa7
Gmi7 Eb EbMa7
one and the same. _ I've heard it
61
Dmi7
D9sus
too man - y times to ig - nore it. It's some - thing that
65
G9sus G9 Cmi7
Dmi9 Ami/D Cmi7
I'm s'posed to be. _ Some - day we'll
69
F Eb/F F/Eb Dmi7 F/G G7 Cmi7
F Eb/F Dmi7 F/G G7 Cmi7
find it, the Rain - bow Con - nec - tion; the lov - ers, _ the
73
F13sus F7(b9) Bb F/A Gmi7
F13sus F7 Bb F/A Gmi7
dreamers, _ and me. La da da dee da da
77
Bb/F Eb F7sus F7 Bb
Bb/F Eb F7sus F7 Bb
do la la da da da de da do. _

PERDIDO

By HARRY LENK, ERVIN DRAKE
and JUAN TIZOL

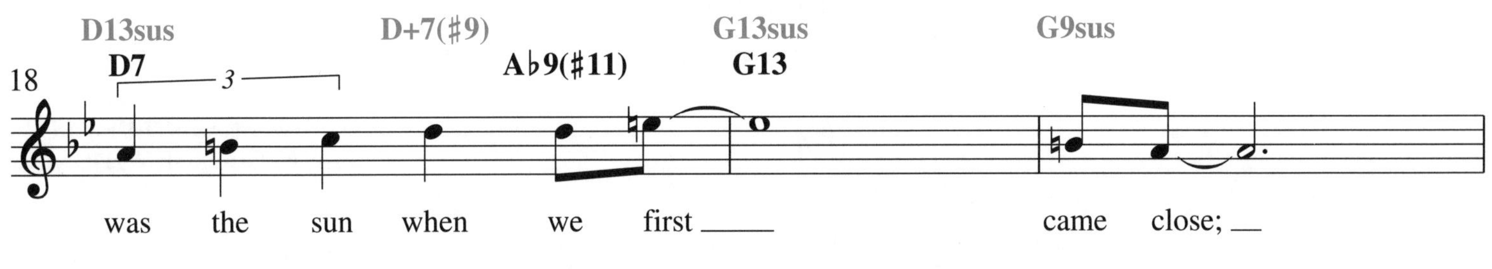
D13sus D+7(♯9) G13sus G9sus
18
D7 A♭9(♯11) G13
3
was the sun when we first ___ came close; __

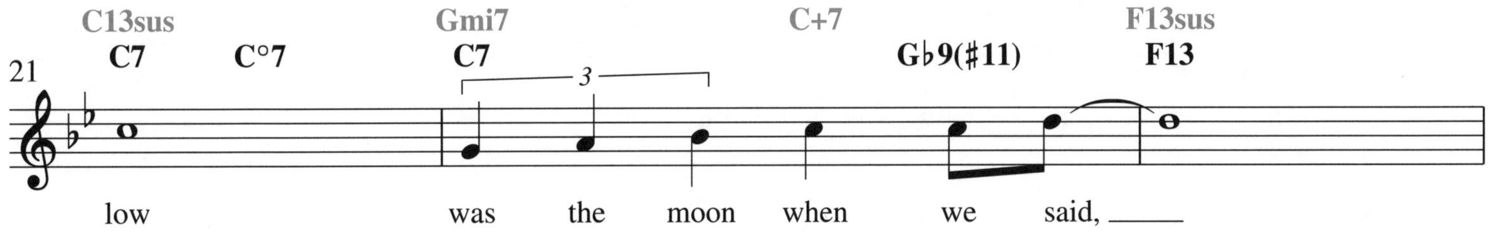
C13sus Gmi7 C+7 F13sus
21
C7 C°7 C7 G♭9(♯11) F13
3
low was the moon when we said, ___

F9sus Dmi11 G+7 Cmi11 F9sus
24
G9 G♭7(♭9) F9 F7
"A - dios!" __ Per - di - do ___ since then has my heart been per -

B♭ E♭Ma9 Dmi7 G9sus Cmi11
27
B♭6 F7
di - do ___ I know I must go to Tor - ri - do ___ that

F9sus F9 B♭
30
Cmi7 F9 B♭6
3
yearn - ing to lose per - di - do. ___

PICNIC

from the Columbia Technicolor Picture PICNIC

Words by STEVE ALLEN
Music by GEORGE W. DUNING

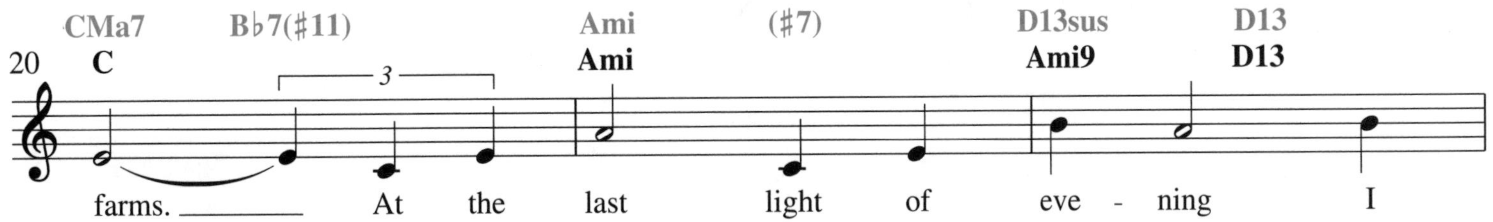
CMa7 B♭7(♯11) Ami (♯7) D13sus D13
20 C Ami Ami9 D13
3
farms. At the last light of eve - ning I

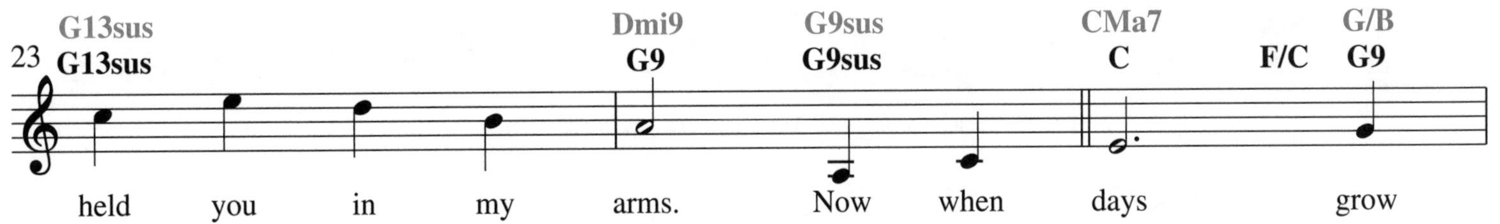
G13sus Dmi9 G9sus CMa7 G/B
23 G13sus G9 G9sus C F/C G9
held you in my arms. Now when days grow

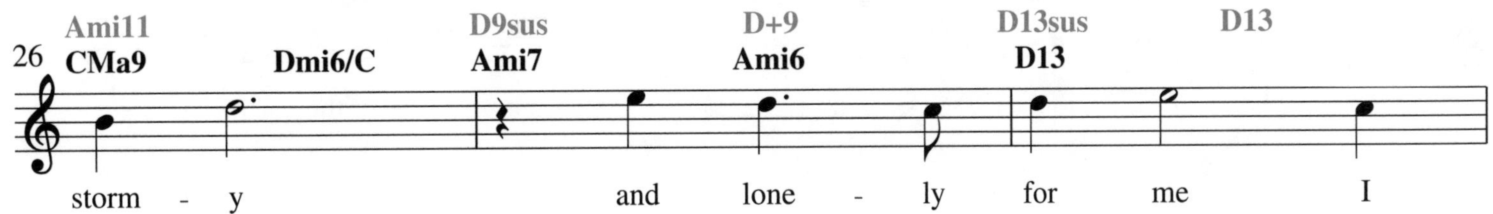
Ami11 D9sus D+9 D13sus D13
26 CMa9 Dmi6/C Ami7 Ami6 D13
storm - y and lone - ly for me I

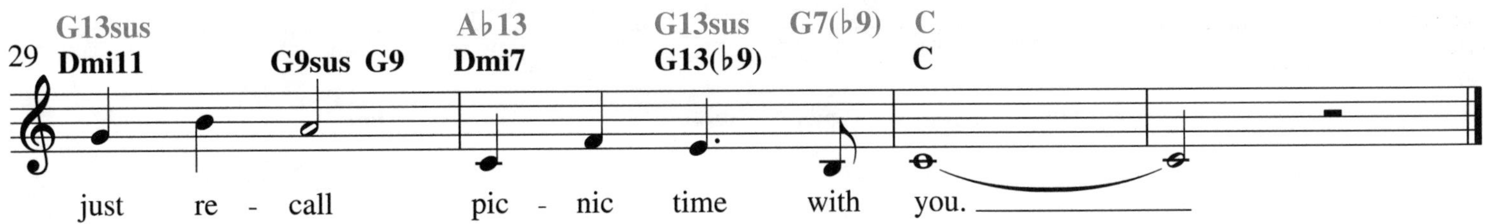
G13sus A♭13 G13sus G7(♭9) C
29 Dmi11 G9sus G9 Dmi7 G13(♭9) C
just re - call pic - nic time with you.

PUTTIN' ON THE RITZ

from the Motion Picture PUTTIN' ON THE RITZ

Words and Music by
IRVING BERLIN

Fmi /E Fmi/E♭ Fmi/D D♭Ma7 Fmi/C
Fmi
If you're blue and you don't know where to go to, why don't you

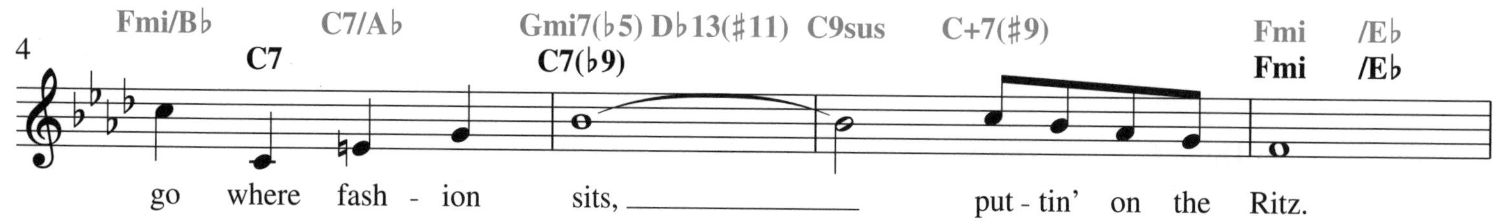
4
Fmi/B♭ C7/A♭ Gmi7(♭5) D♭13(♯11) C9sus C+7(♯9) Fmi /E♭
C7 C7(♭9) Fmi /E♭
go where fash - ion sits, put - tin' on the Ritz.

8
D♭9 C7 Fmi /E Fmi/E♭ Fmi/D
D♭9 C7 Fmi
Dif - f'rent types who wear a day coat, pants

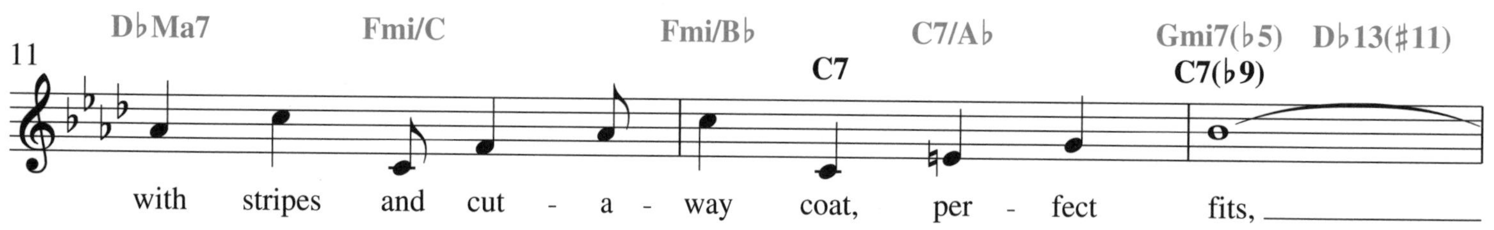
11
D♭Ma7 Fmi/C Fmi/B♭ C7/A♭ Gmi7(♭5) D♭13(♯11)
C7 C7(♭9)
with stripes and cut - a - way coat, per - fect fits,

14
C9sus C+7(♯9) Fmi Cmi11 B9(♯11) B♭mi7 G+7(♭9)
Fmi /E♭ D♭ F7/C B♭mi
put - tin' on the Ritz.
Stroll - ing up the
Dressed up like a

18
Cmi11 F+7 B♭mi E9(♯11) E♭9sus E♭7(♭9)
G♭9 F9 B♭mi6 E♭13 E♭+13
a - ve - nue so hap - py
mil - lion dol - lar troup - er.

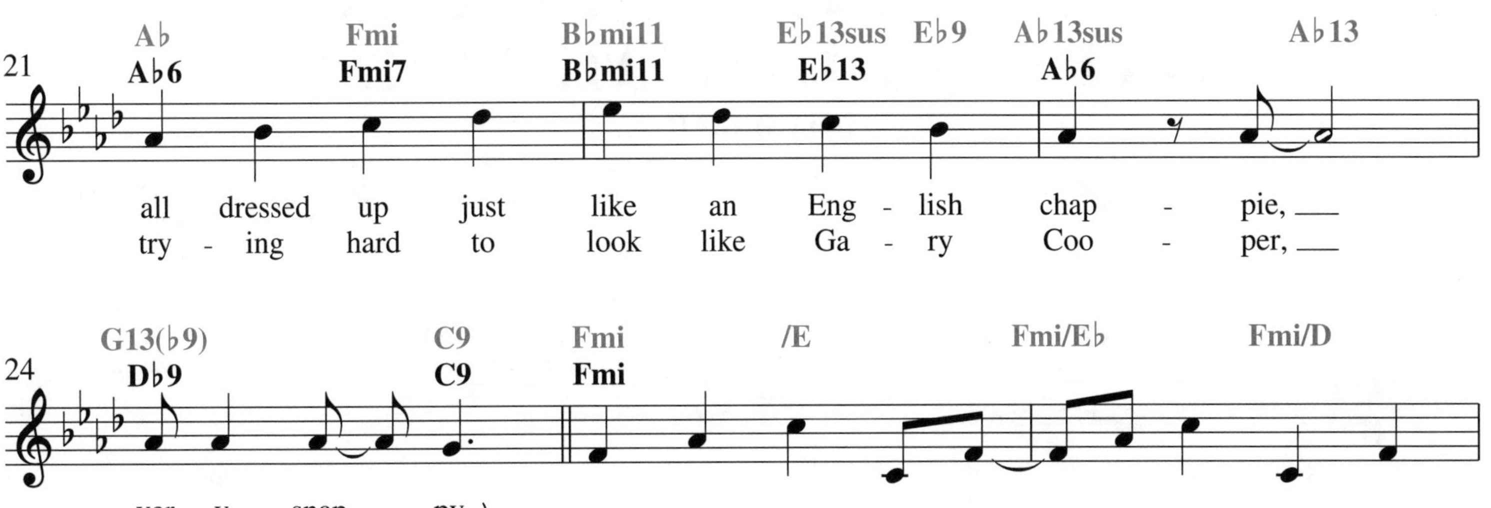
21
A♭ Fmi B♭mi11 E♭13sus E♭9 A♭13sus A♭13
A♭6 Fmi7 B♭mi11 E♭13 A♭6
all dressed up just like an Eng - lish chap - pie,
try - ing hard to look like Ga - ry Coo - per,
24
G13(♭9) C9 Fmi /E Fmi/E♭ Fmi/D
D♭9 C9 Fmi
ver - y snap - py.
su - per du - per.
Come let's mix where Rock - e - fel - lers walk

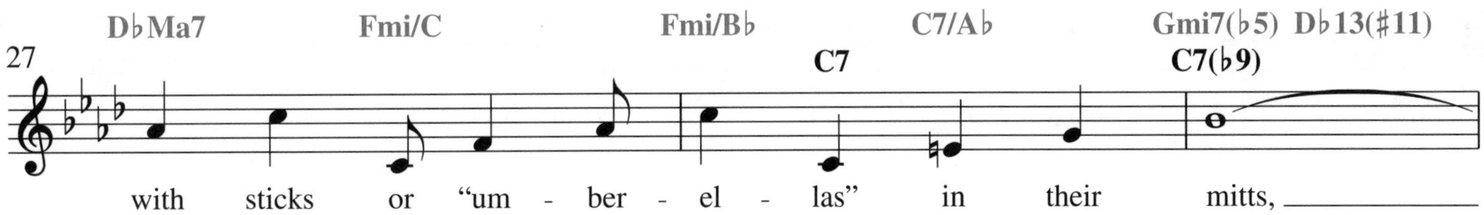
27
D♭Ma7 Fmi/C Fmi/B♭ C7/A♭ Gmi7(♭5) D♭13(♯11)
C7 C7(♭9)
with sticks or "um - ber - el - las" in their mitts,

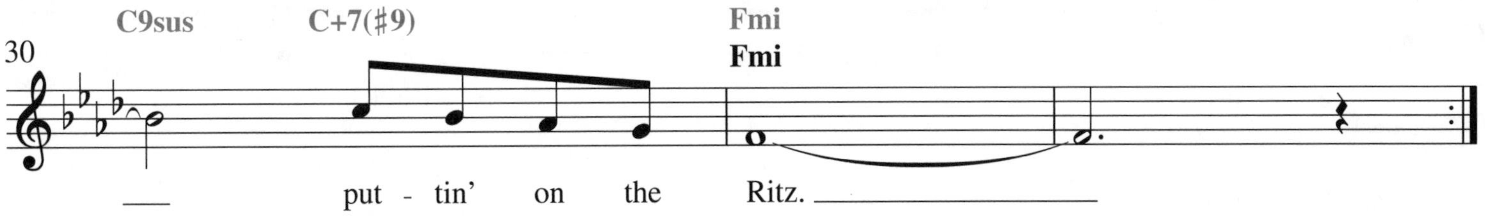
30
C9sus C+7(♯9) Fmi
Fmi
put - tin' on the Ritz.

ROCK-A-BYE YOUR BABY WITH A DIXIE MELODY

from SINBAD

Words by SAM M. LEWIS and JOE YOUNG
Music by JEAN SCHWARTZ

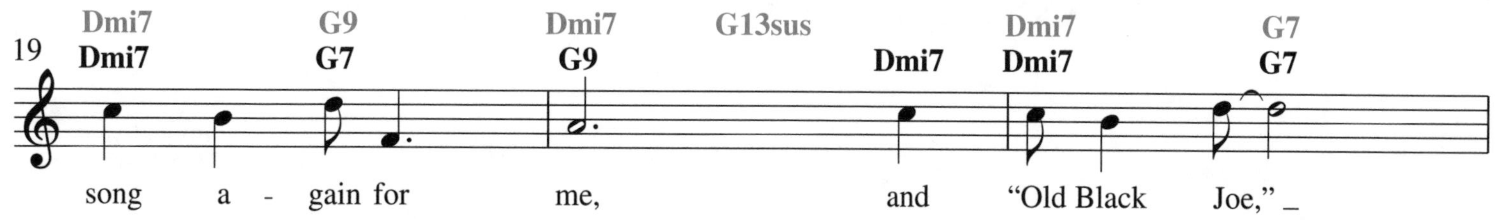
19
Dmi7 G9 Dmi7 G13sus Dmi7 G7
Dmi7 G7 G9 Dmi7 Dmi7 G7
song a - gain for me, and "Old Black Joe," _

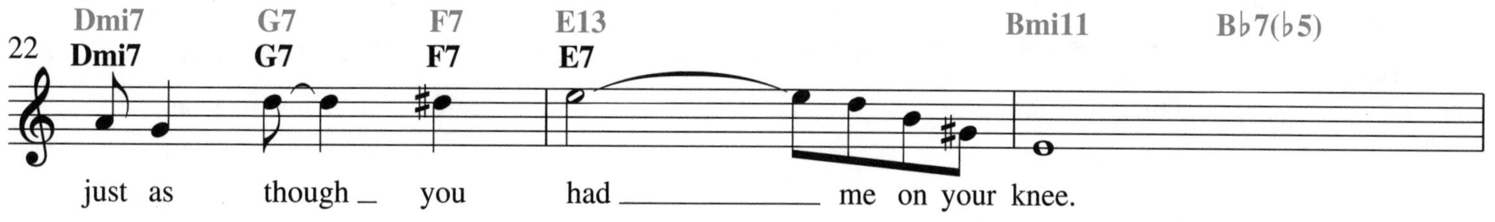
22
Dmi7 G7 F7 E13 Bmi11 B♭7(♭5)
Dmi7 G7 F7 E7
just as though _ you had _______ me on your knee.

25
A+7 B♭9 A7
A+7 A+7 A7
A mil - lion ba - by kiss - es I'll de - liv - er

27
D13sus D13 Ami7 D13(♯11 ♭9) G+9 CMa7 F13
D13 E♭°7 C/E C G7/B A°7
the min-ute that you sing the "Swan - ee Riv - er," rock - a - bye your

30
Emi7 Ami7 D9 G7sus G13(♯11 ♭9) C
C/G E7/G♯ Ami D9 Fmi G13 C
rock - a - bye ba - by with a Dix - ie mel - o - dy.

ROCKIN' CHAIR

Words and Music by
HOAGY CARMICHAEL

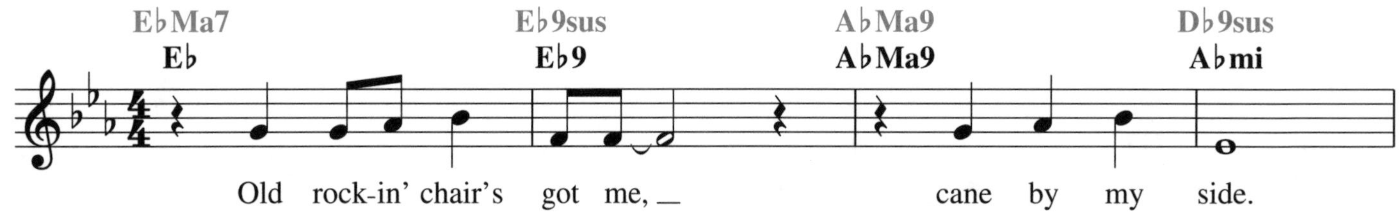
E♭Ma7 E♭9sus A♭Ma9 D♭9sus
E♭ E♭9 A♭Ma9 A♭mi
Old rock-in' chair's got me, cane by my side.

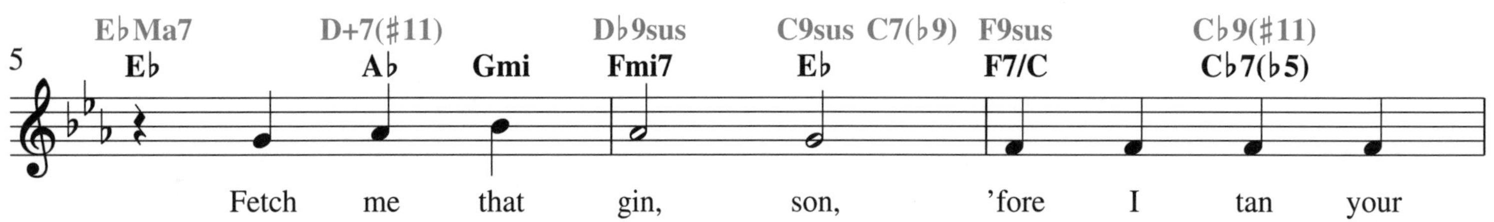
5
E♭Ma7 D+7(♯11) D♭9sus C9sus C7(♭9) F9sus C♭9(♯11)
E♭ A♭ Gmi Fmi7 E♭ F7/C C♭7(♭5)
Fetch me that gin, son, 'fore I tan your

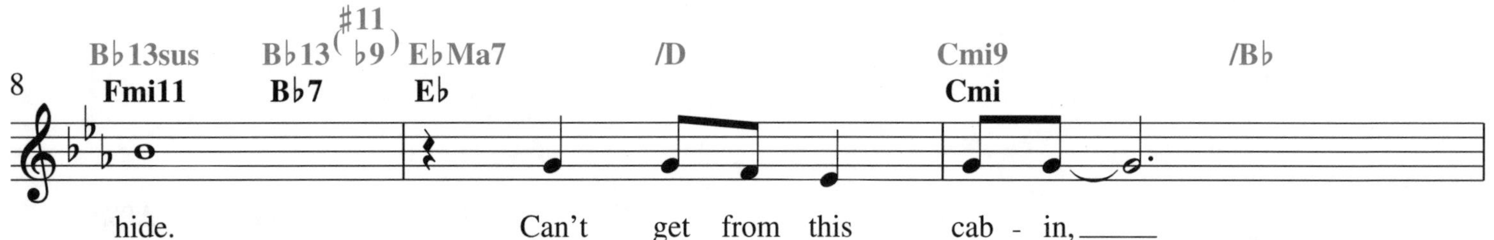
8
B♭13sus B♭13(♯11 ♭9) E♭Ma7 /D Cmi9 /B♭
Fmi11 B♭7 E♭ Cmi
hide. Can't get from this cab - in,

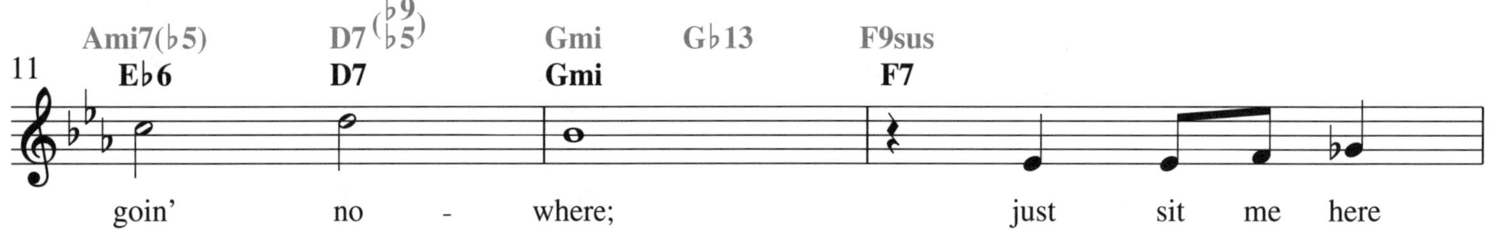
11
Ami7(♭5) D7(♭9 ♭5) Gmi G♭13 F9sus
E♭6 D7 Gmi F7
goin' no - where; just sit me here

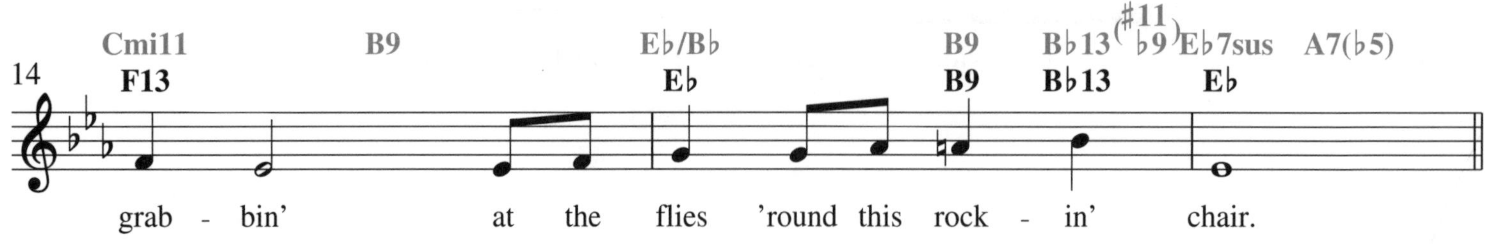
14
Cmi11 B9 E♭/B♭ B9 B♭13(♯11 ♭9) E♭7sus A7(♭5)
F13 E♭ B9 B♭13 E♭
grab - bin' at the flies 'round this rock - in' chair.

17
A♭9 E♭Ma9
A♭9 E♭ E♭Ma7
My dear old Aunt Har - ri - et in heav - en she

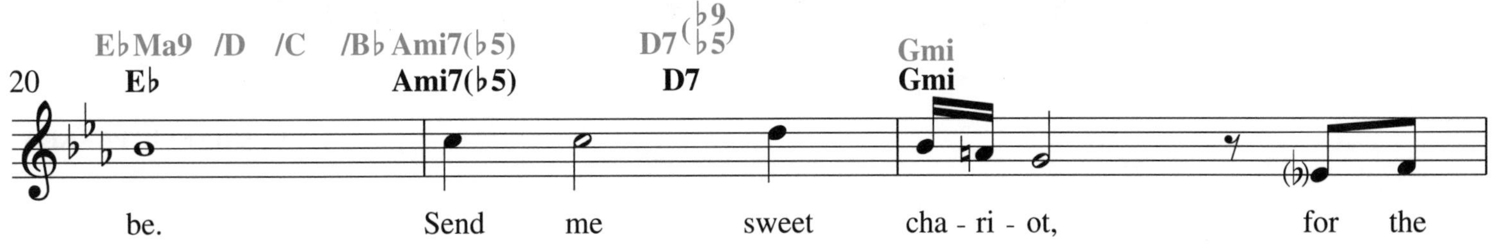
E♭Ma9 /D /C /B♭ Ami7(♭5) D7(♭9 ♭5) Gmi
20
E♭ Ami7(♭5) D7 Gmi
be. Send me sweet cha - ri - ot, for the

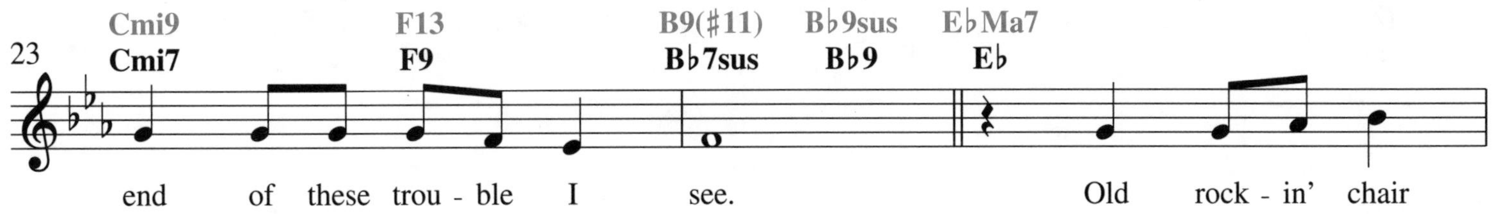
Cmi9 F13 B9(♯11) B♭9sus E♭Ma7
23
Cmi7 F9 B♭7sus B♭9 E♭
end of these trou - ble I see. Old rock - in' chair

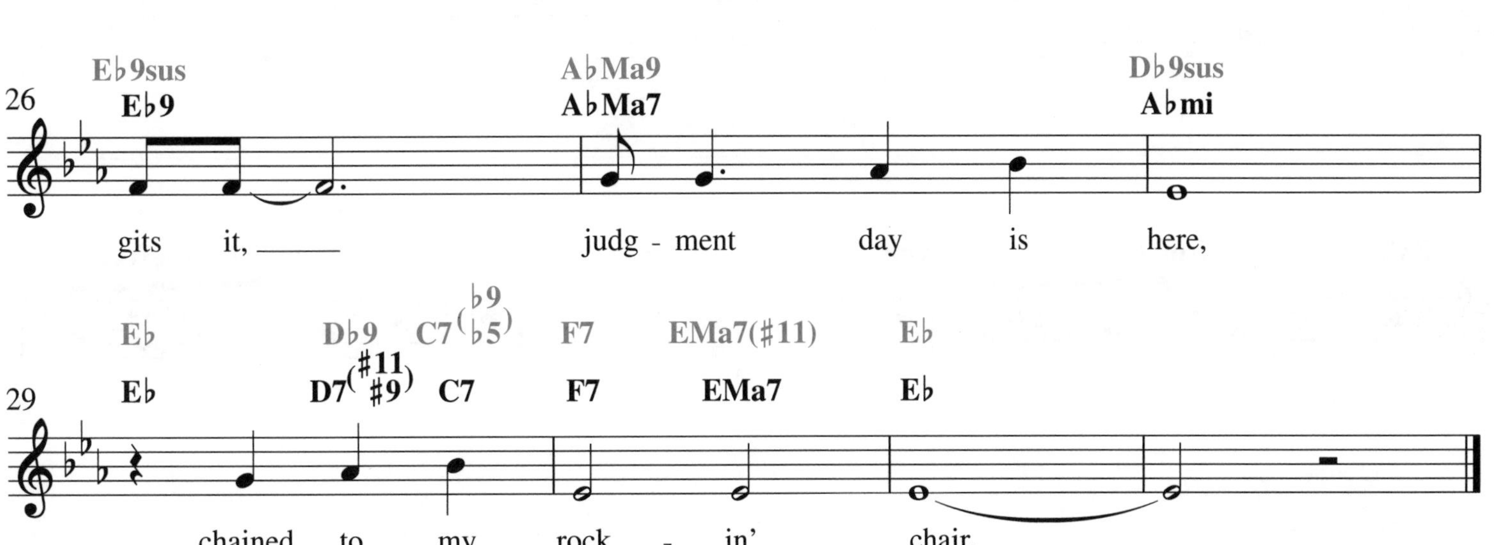
E♭9sus A♭Ma9 D♭9sus
26
E♭9 A♭Ma7 A♭mi
gits it, judg - ment day is here,
E♭ D♭9 C7(♭9 ♭5) F7 EMa7(♯11) E♭
29
E♭ D7(♯11 ♯9) C7 F7 EMa7 E♭
chained to my rock - in' chair.

SCRAPPLE FROM THE APPLE

By CHARLIE PARKER

Gmi7
19
Gmi7
C13
C7
Gmi7
Gmi7
3

C13(♭9)
22
C13(♭9)
FMa7
FMa7
3
Gmi7
Gmi7
C7
G♭7
3

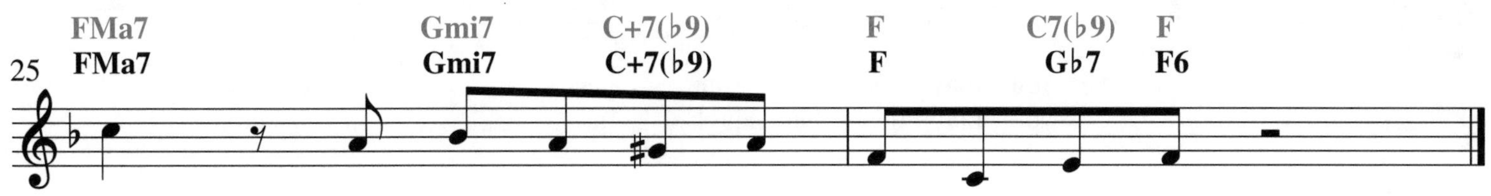
FMa7
25
FMa7
Gmi7
Gmi7
C+7(♭9)
C+7(♭9)
F
F
C7(♭9)
G♭7
F
F6

SOME ENCHANTED EVENING

from SOUTH PACIFIC

Lyrics by OSCAR HAMMERSTEIN II
Music by RICHARD RODGERS

21
G7sus CMa7/G Ami11 A♭7(♯11) G13sus G7alt.
G7sus G7 C Ami11 D7 G A°/G B♭°/G G7sus C°/C
Fools give you rea - sons, wise men nev - er try.
25
CMa9 C Dmi11 G7
C Dmi11 G7
Some en-chant-ed eve - ning when you find your true love,
29
CMa9 E+7(♯9) FMa7 Emi7
C E+ FMa7 F6
when you feel her call you a - cross a crowd - ed room,
32
Dmi7 A7(♭9) Dmi7 /C Bmi7(♭5) E+7(♯9)
Ami7/E Dmi7 G7 Dmi7 E7(♯9)
then fly to her side and make her your
35
Ami /G F♯mi7(♭5) G/F C/E E♭°7 Dmi7 G9sus
Ami C7/G F CMa7/E Dmi7 G9sus G7
own, or all through your life you may dream all a -
39
C G7sus CMa7/G G7sus C/G
C G7sus G7 CMa9 C Dmi7 G7 C6
lone. Once you have found her, nev - er let her go.
43
G7sus CMa7/G G9sus C
G7sus G7 CMa9 C G9sus C
Once you have found her, nev - er let her go!

SOMEBODY LOVES ME

from SHE LOVES ME

Words by B.G. DeSYLVA and BALLARD MacDONALD
Music by GEORGE GERSHWIN
French Version by EMELIA RENAUD

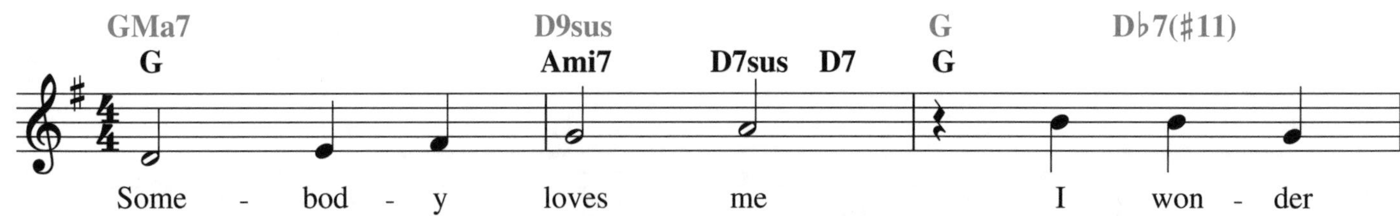

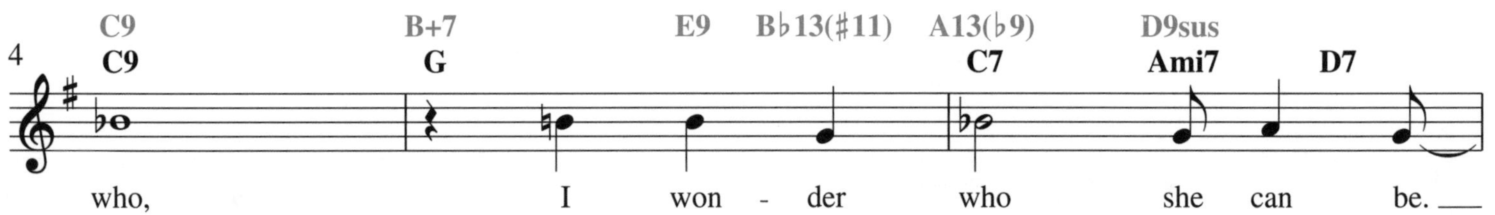

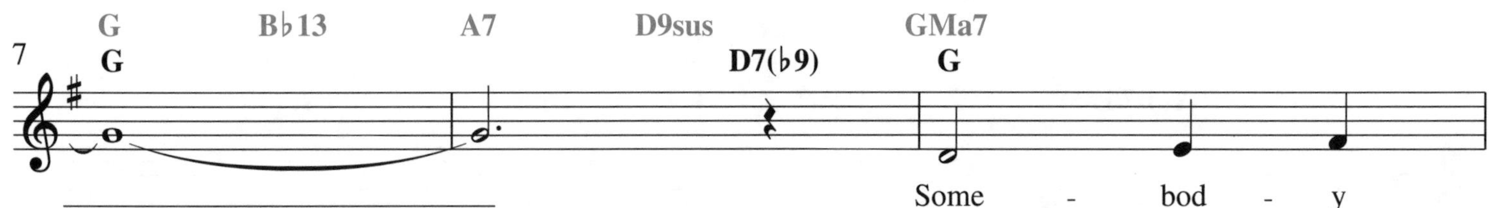

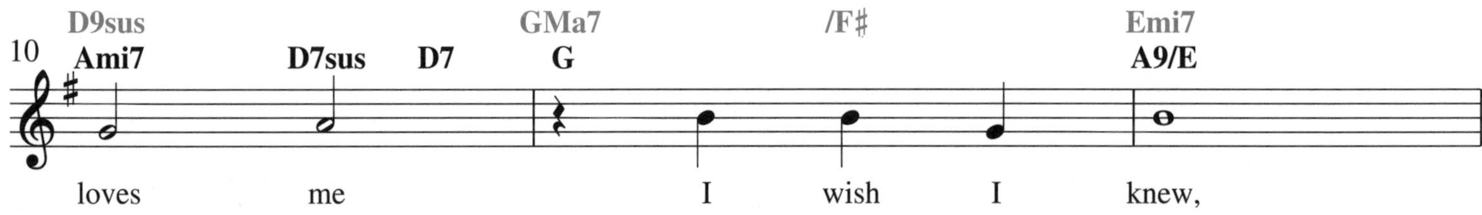

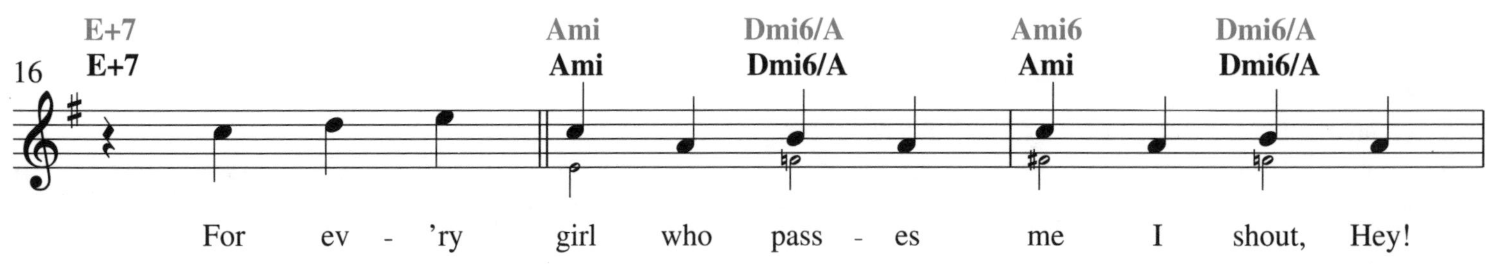

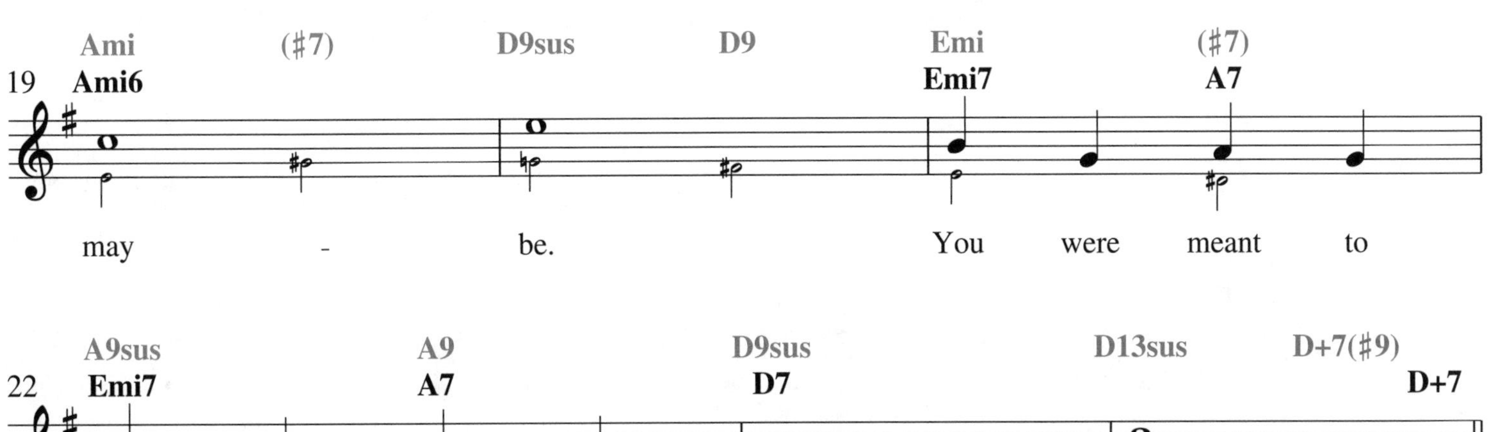
Ami
(♯7)
D9sus
D9
Emi
(♯7)
19
Ami6
Emi7
A7
may - be. You were meant to

A9sus
A9
D9sus
D13sus
D+7(♯9)
22
Emi7
A7
D7
D+7
be my lov - ing ba - by.

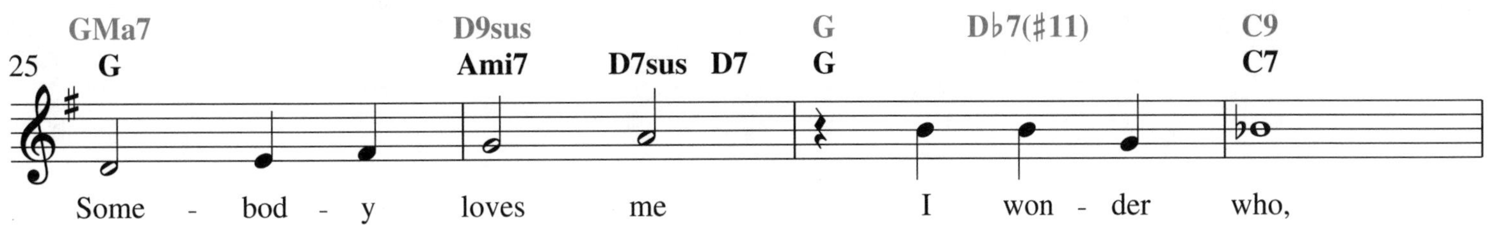
GMa7
D9sus
G
D♭7(♯11)
C9
25
G
Ami7
D7sus
D7
G
C7
Some - bod - y loves me I won - der who,

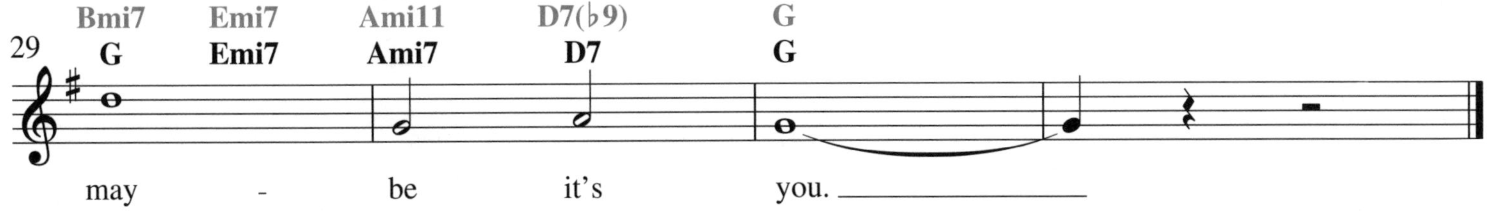
Bmi7
Emi7
Ami11
D7(♭9)
G
29
G
Emi7
Ami7
D7
G
may - be it's you.

SOMEWHERE ALONG THE WAY

Words by SAMMY GALLOP
Music by KURT ADAMS

E♭ G+7
E♭ G+7
3 3
I used to walk with you a - long the av - e - nue,

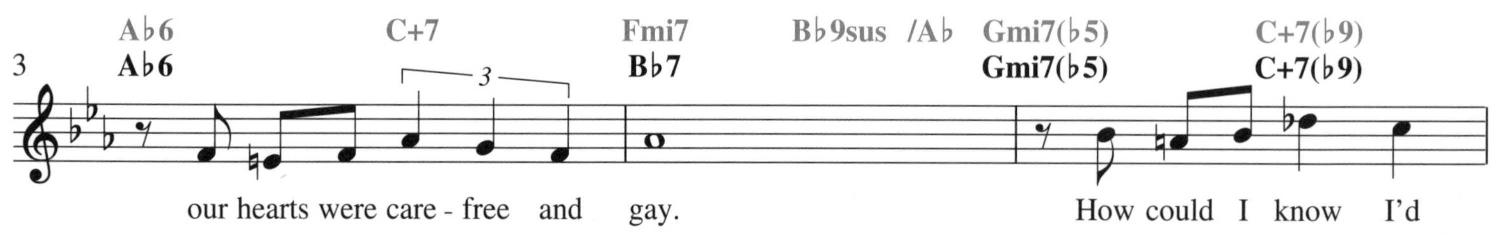
A♭6 C+7 Fmi7 B♭9sus /A♭ Gmi7(♭5) C+7(♭9)
3 A♭6 B♭7 Gmi7(♭5) C+7(♭9)
3
our hearts were care - free and gay. How could I know I'd

F7sus B9(♯11) B♭7sus B♭13 Gmi7 G♭9 Fmi11 E7(♭9)
6 F7 B♭7sus B♭13 E♭ B♭7
lose you, some-where a - long the way.

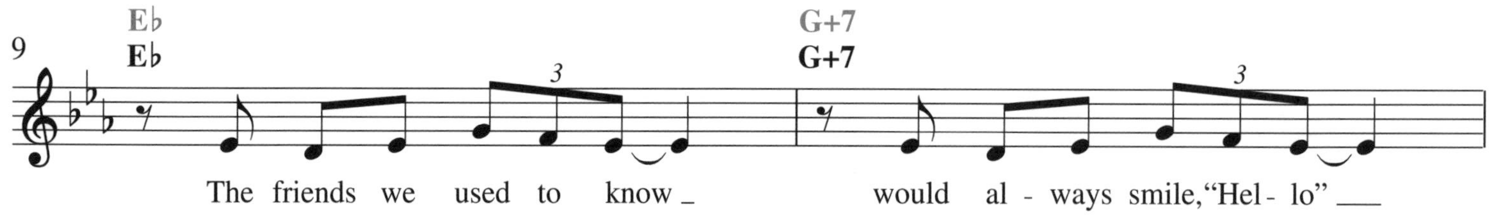
E♭ G+7
9 E♭ G+7
3 3
The friends we used to know would al - ways smile, "Hel - lo"

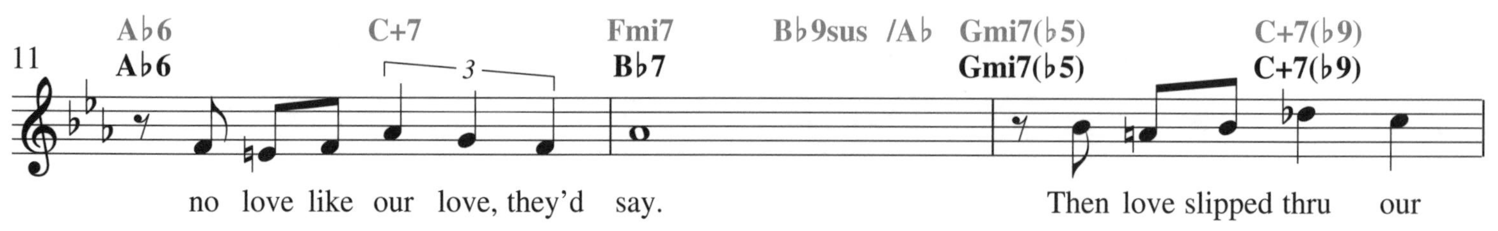
A♭6 C+7 Fmi7 B♭9sus /A♭ Gmi7(♭5) C+7(♭9)
11 A♭6 B♭7 Gmi7(♭5) C+7(♭9)
3
no love like our love, they'd say. Then love slipped thru our

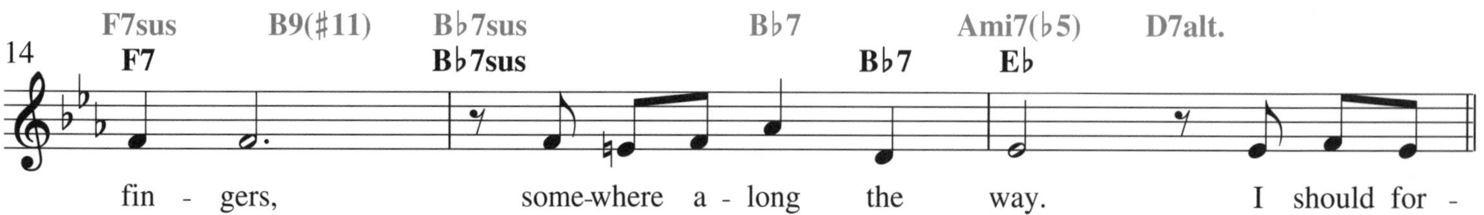
F7sus B9(♯11) B♭7sus B♭7 Ami7(♭5) D7alt.
14 F7 B♭7sus B♭7 E♭
fin - gers, some-where a - long the way. I should for -

17
GMa9 Emi7 Ami9 D7(♭9 ♭5) Bmi7 B♭13
GMa9 Emi7 Ami9 D7 GMa9
get, ___ but with the lone - li - ness of night, _ I start re - mem - ber - ing

20
Ami11 A♭13(♯11) GMa9 Emi7 Ami9 D7(♭9 ♭5)
Ami11 D7alt. GMa9 Emi7 Ami9 D7
ev - 'ry - thing. _ You're gone, and yet ___ there's still a feel - ing deep in - side _ that you will

23
GMa9 D/F♯ Fmi13 E9(♯11) E♭
GMa9 B♭7 E♭
al - ways be, part of me. So now I look for you, _

26
G+7 A♭6 C+7 Fmi7 B♭7sus/A♭
G+7 A♭6 B♭7
a - long the av - e - nue, _ And as I wan - der I pray,

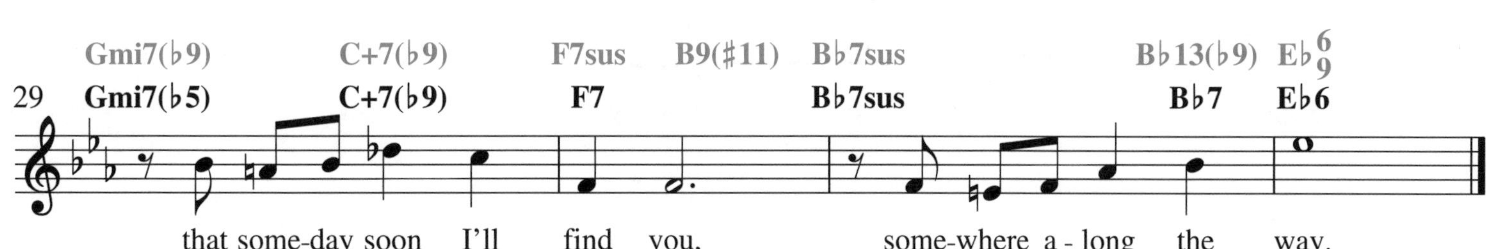
29
Gmi7(♭9) C+7(♭9) F7sus B9(♯11) B♭7sus B♭13(♭9) E♭6/9
Gmi7(♭5) C+7(♭9) F7 B♭7sus B♭7 E♭6
that some-day soon I'll find you, some-where a - long the way.

THE SOUND OF MUSIC

from THE SOUND OF MUSIC

Lyrics by OSCAR HAMMERSTEIN II
Music by RICHARD RODGERS

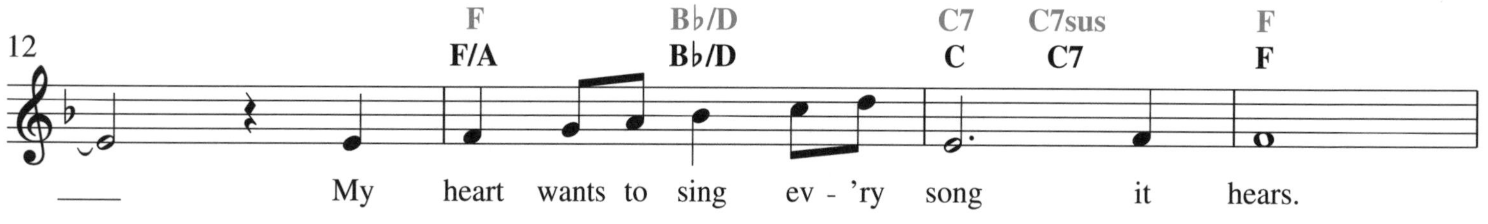

22
F/A Dmi7 G13sus D♭9(♯11) C7sus
F/A G7/D D♭7(♯11) C F/A
chime that flies from a church on a breeze, to
25
B♭ C/B♭ F/A B♭ C/B♭
B♭ B♭°7 F/A B♭ B♭°7
laugh like a brook when it trips and falls o - ver stones on its
28
F/A A+(♯9) Dmi7 Bmi7(♭5) Ami9 G9sus G7
F Dmi Dmi6 Ami Dmi7 G7
way, to sing through the night like a lark who is learn - ing to
32
C13sus C+7 F6 FMa9 E/F
C C7 F6 FMa9 E/F
pray. I go to the hills when my heart is lone - ly.
36
FMa9 B♭/D
FMa9 B♭/D
I know I will hear what I've heard be - fore.
40
B♭mi/D♭ F/C F9sus F7(♭9) B♭Ma9
B♭mi/D♭ F/C Ami/C B♭Ma9
My heart will be blessed with the sound of mu - sic
44
E♭13 C9 A♭°7 Gmi6 C7(♭9) F
Gmi7 C6 C7 F
and I'll sing once more.

SPRING WILL BE A LITTLE LATE THIS YEAR

from the Motion Picture CHRISTMAS HOLIDAY

By FRANK LOESSER

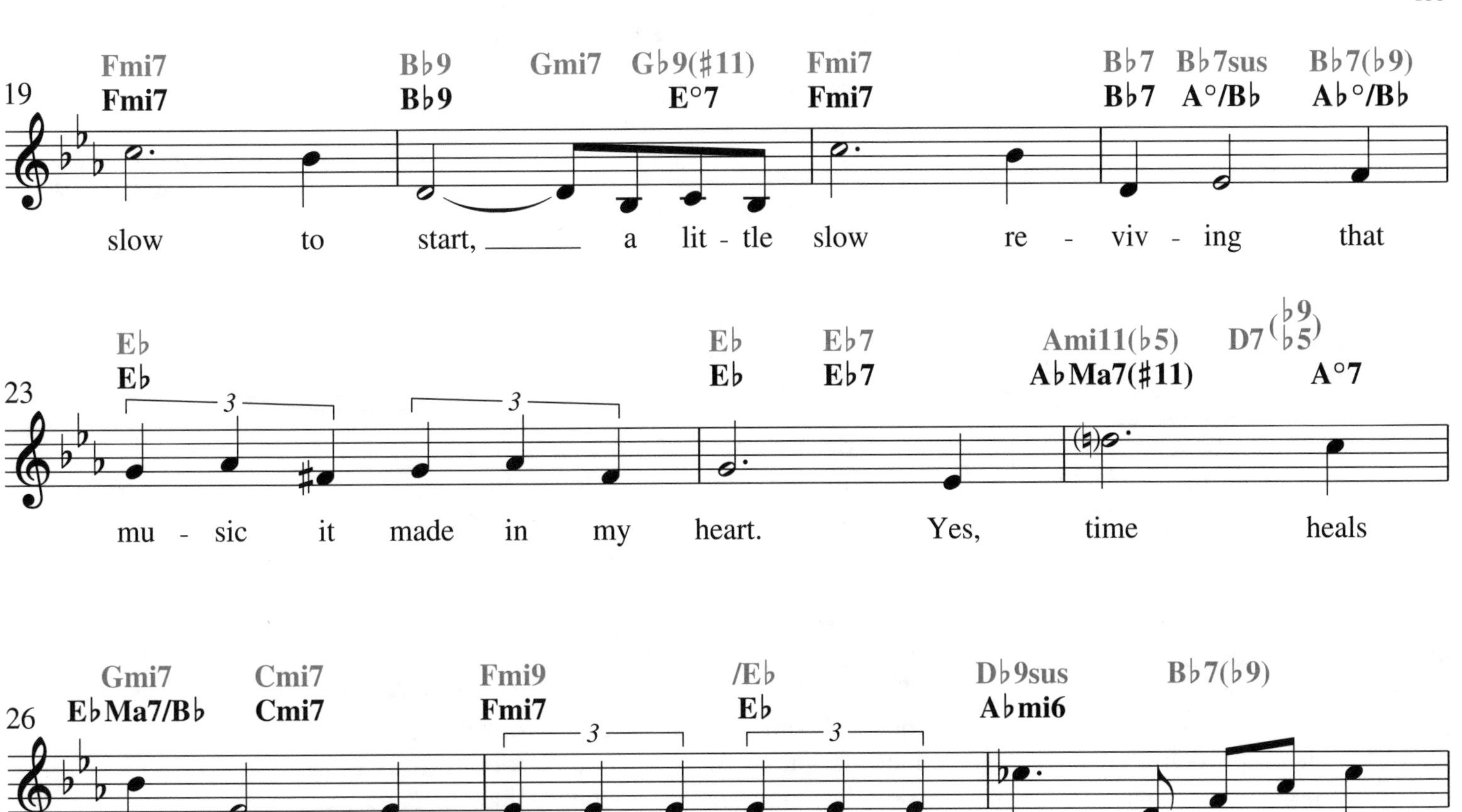
19
Fmi7 Bb9 Gmi7 Gb9(#11) Fmi7 Bb7 Bb7sus Bb7(b9)
Fmi7 Bb9 E°7 Fmi7 Bb7 A°/Bb Ab°/Bb
slow to start, a lit - tle slow re - viv - ing that
23
Eb Eb Eb7 Ami11(b5) D7(b9 b5)
Eb Eb Eb7 AbMa7(#11) A°7
mu - sic it made in my heart. Yes, time heals
26
Gmi7 Cmi7 Fmi9 /Eb Db9sus Bb7(b9)
EbMa7/Bb Cmi7 Fmi7 Eb Abmi6
all things, so I need - n't cling to this fear. It's mere - ly that

29
EbMa7 Ab9 Gmi11 Gb9(#11) Fmi7 Bb7(b9) Eb
Eb Bb+7 Eb6 E°7 Fmi7 Bb7(b9) Eb
spring will be a lit - tle late this year.

ST. LOUIS BLUES

from BIRTH OF THE BLUES

Words and Music by
W.C. HANDY

Gmi9 E+7(#11 #9) Ami7(♭5) E♭9(#11) D9sus D7(♭9)
25
Gmi Cmi C#°7 D7
wom - an wid her dia - mon' rings pulls dat
Cai - ro make St. Lou - is by ma - self git to
crap game he knows a pow'-ful lot but when
Ami7(♭5) E♭13(#11) D7sus D7(♭9) Gmi E+7(#9) A7(♭5) D9sus
29
Gmi
man 'roun by her a - pron strings 'twant for
Cai - ro find ma ole friend Jeff, gwine to
work-time comes he's on de dot gwine to
Gmi9 E+7(#11 #9) Ami7(♭5) E♭9(#11) D9sus D7(♭9)
33
Gmi Cmi7 C#°7 D7
pow - der an' for store bought hair de
pin ma' self close to his side If Ah
ask him for a cold ten spot what it
Ami7(♭5) E♭13(#11) D7sus D7(♭9) Gmi A13 D13sus
37
Gmi A7/E D7
man I love would not gone no - where. Got de
flag his train I sho' can ride. I
takes to git it he's cer - t'n - ly got. A
G13 ⟶ G13 E♭7 Dmi11 D♭9(#11)
41
G G6 G G6 G G6 G G6 G C/G G C/G G C/G G
St. Lou - is Blues jes as blue as Ah can be dat
loves dat man lak a school boy loves his pie lak a
black head-ed gal make a freight train jump the track said a
C13 G13 Ami7 G/B E+7(#9)
45
C13 G C/G G C/G G C/G G
man got a heart lak a rock cast in the sea or
Ken - tuck - y Col' - nel loves his mint and rye I'll
black head-ed gal make a freight train jump the track but a
Ami11 B♭9 Ami11 D+7(#9) G
49
G/D D7 G
else he would-n't have gone so far from me.
love ma ba - by till the day Ah die.
red - head wom - an makes a preach - er ball the Jack.

STAR DUST

Words by MITCHELL PARISH
Music by HOAGY CARMICHAEL

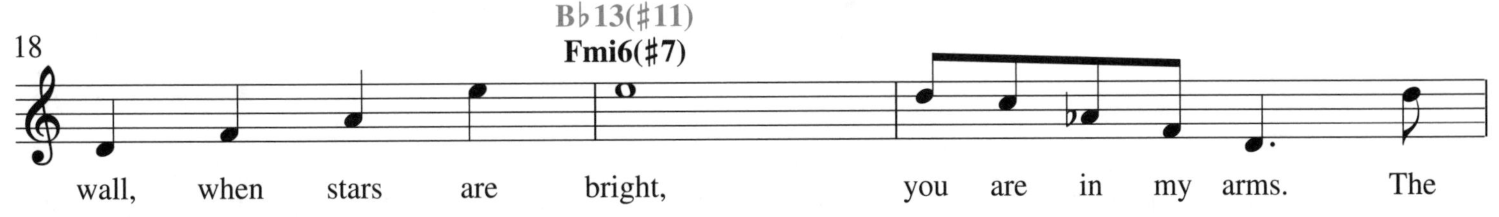
18
B♭13(♯11)
Fmi6(♯7)
wall, when stars are bright, you are in my arms. The

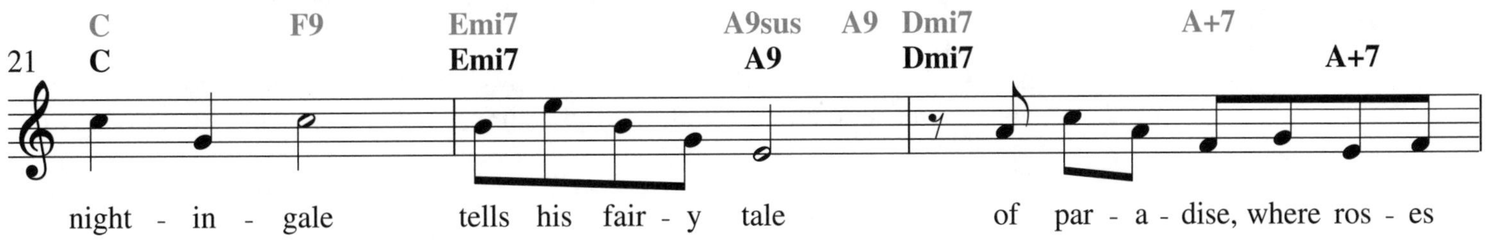
21
C F9 Emi7 A9sus A9 Dmi7 A+7
C Emi7 A9 Dmi7 A+7
night - in - gale tells his fair - y tale of par - a - dise, where ros - es

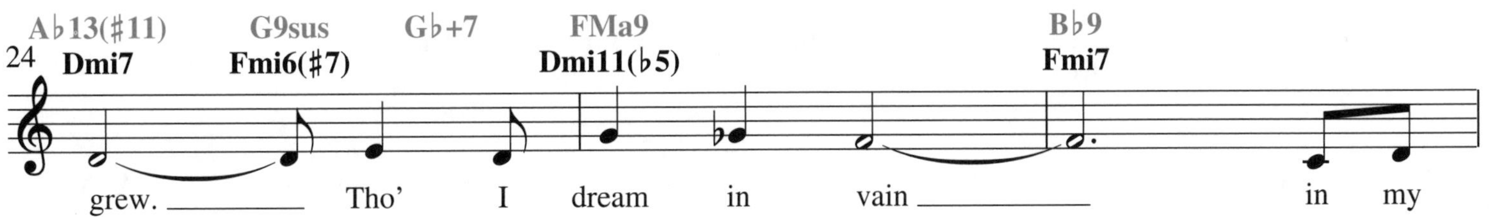
24
A♭13(♯11) G9sus G♭+7 FMa9 B♭9
Dmi7 Fmi6(♯7) Dmi11(♭5) Fmi7
grew. Tho' I dream in vain in my

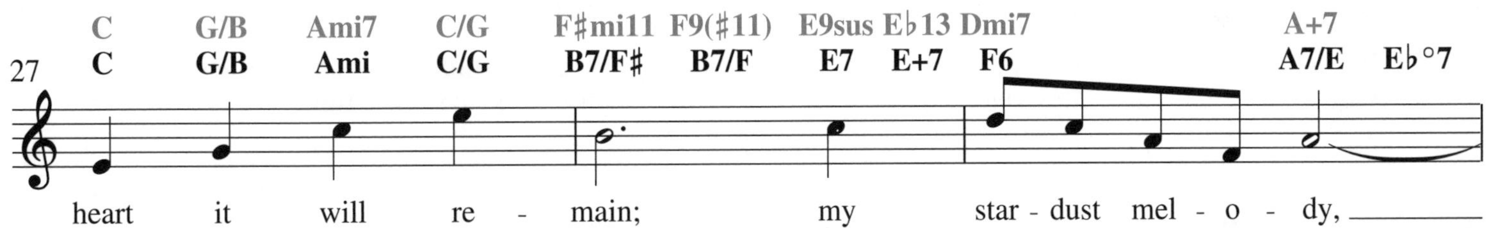
27
C G/B Ami7 C/G F♯mi11 F9(♯11) E9sus E♭13 Dmi7 A+7
C G/B Ami C/G B7/F♯ B7/F E7 E+7 F6 A7/E E♭°7
heart it will re - main; my star - dust mel - o - dy,

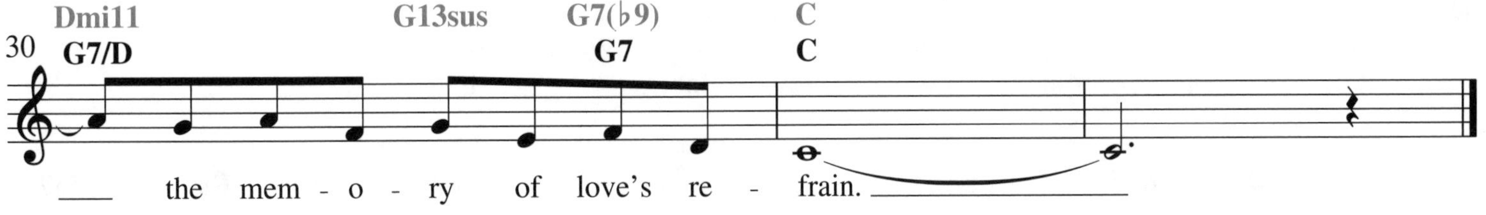
30
Dmi11 G13sus G7(♭9) C
G7/D G7 C
the mem - o - ry of love's re - frain.

A STRING OF PEARLS

from THE GLENN MILLER STORY

Music by
JERRY GRAY

(I Stayed)

TOO LONG AT THE FAIR

Words and Music by
BILLY BARNES

SUNRISE SERENADE

Lyric by JACK LAWRENCE
Music by FRANKIE CARLE

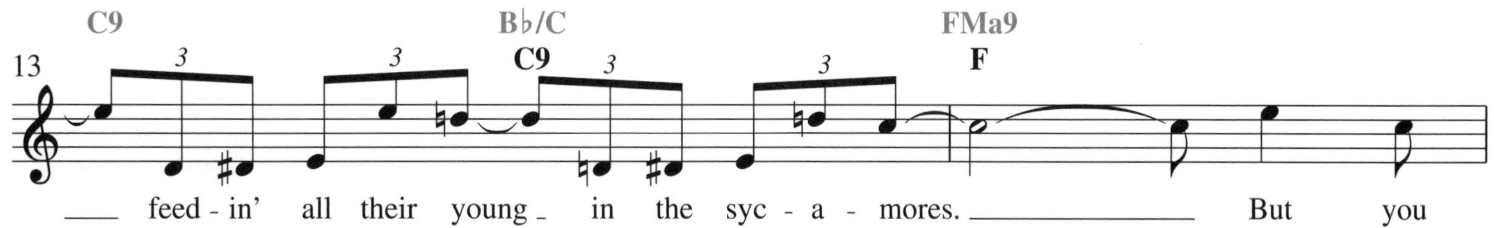
C9 Bb/C FMa9
13
C9 F
feed - in' all their young in the syc - a - mores. But you

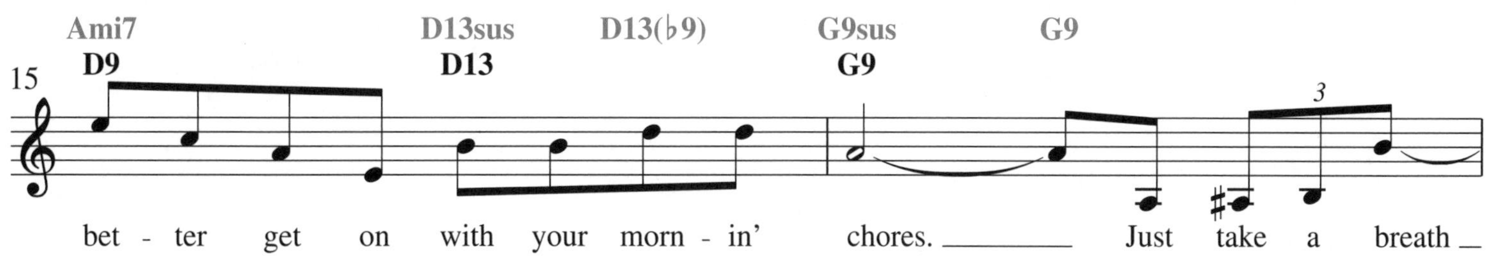
Ami7 D13sus D13(b9) G9sus G9
15
D9 D13 G9
bet - ter get on with your morn - in' chores. Just take a breath

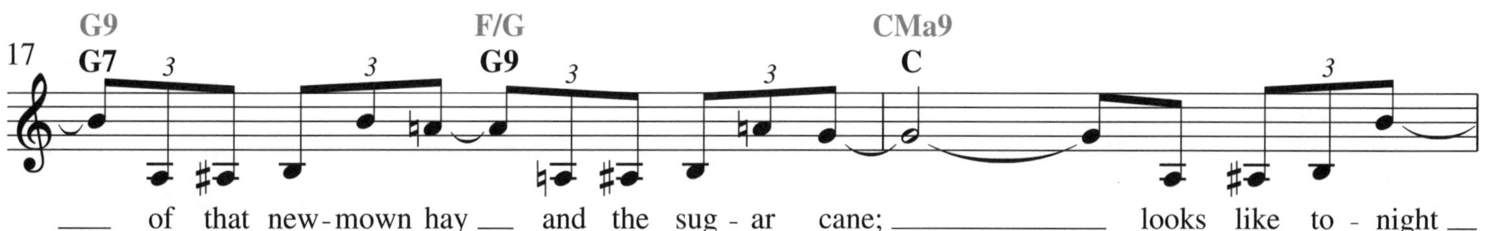
G9 F/G CMa9
17
G7 G9 C
of that new-mown hay and the sug - ar cane; looks like to - night

G9 F/G CMa9 Ami7 /G
19
G7 G9 C
there should be a moon down in lov - er's lane. There you

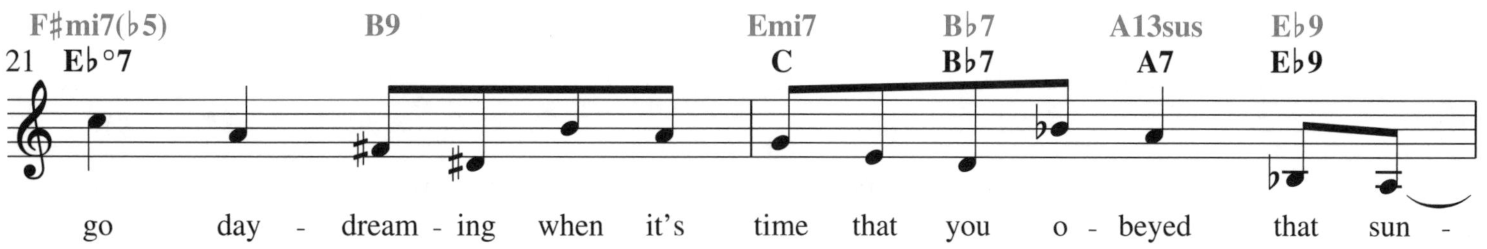
F#mi7(b5) B9 Emi7 Bb7 A13sus Eb9
21
Eb°7 C Bb7 A7 Eb9
go day - dream - ing when it's time that you o - beyed that sun -

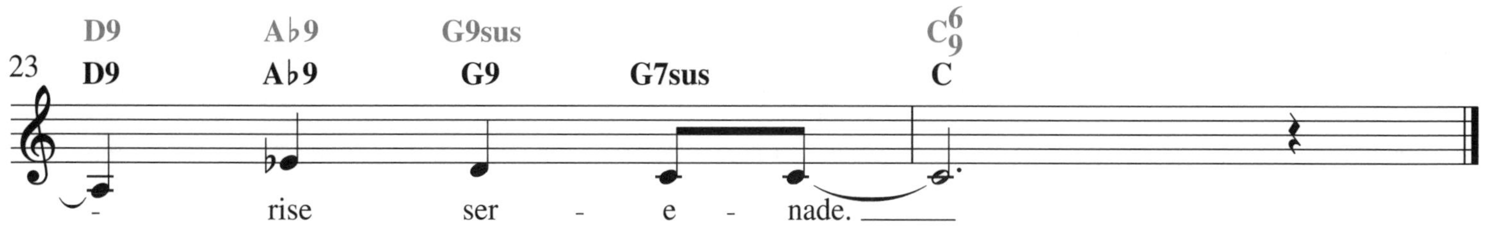
D9 Ab9 G9sus C6/9
23
D9 Ab9 G9 G7sus C
- rise ser - e - nade.

SWANEE

Words by IRVING CAESAR
Music by GEORGE GERSHWIN

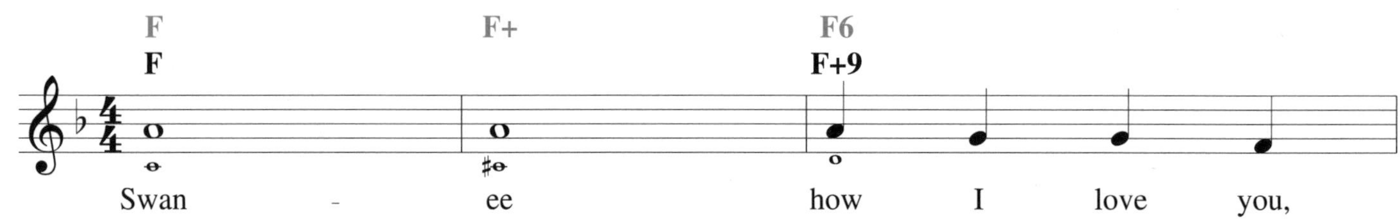

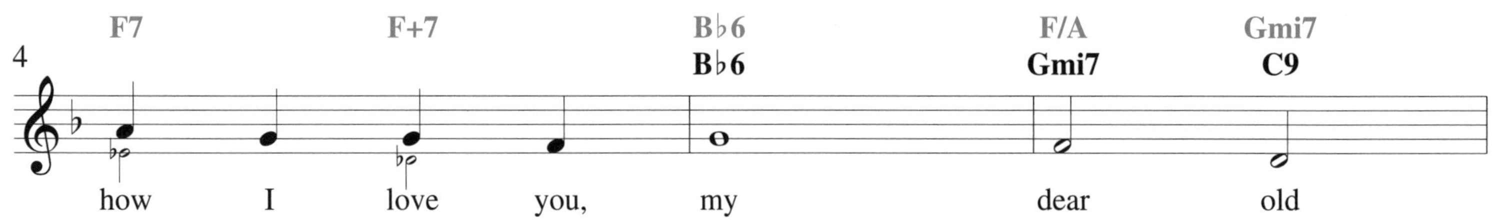

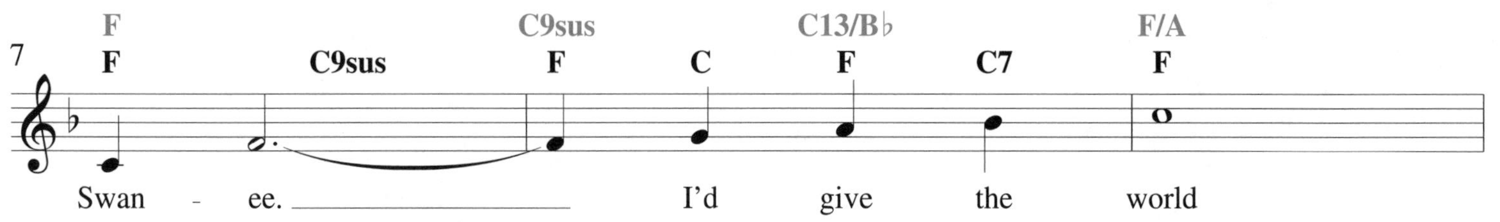

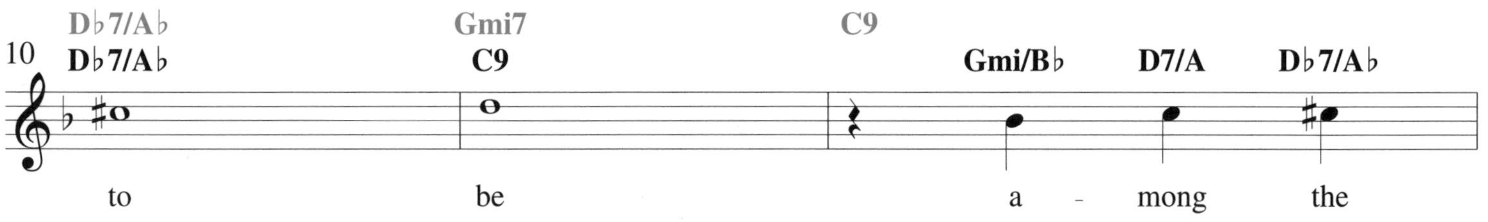

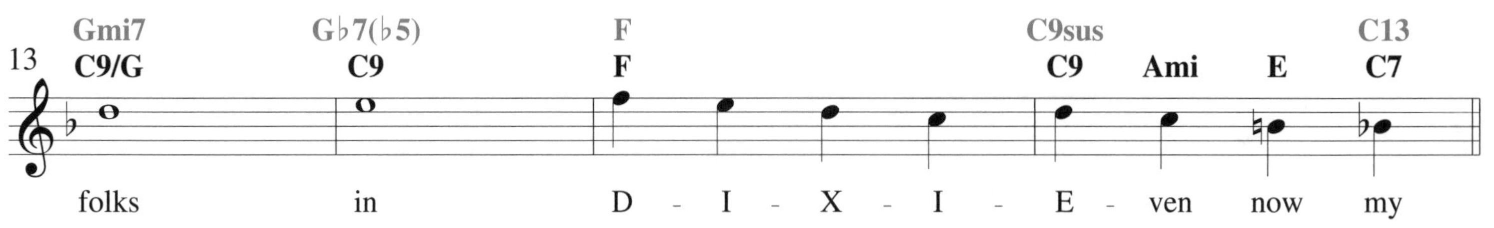

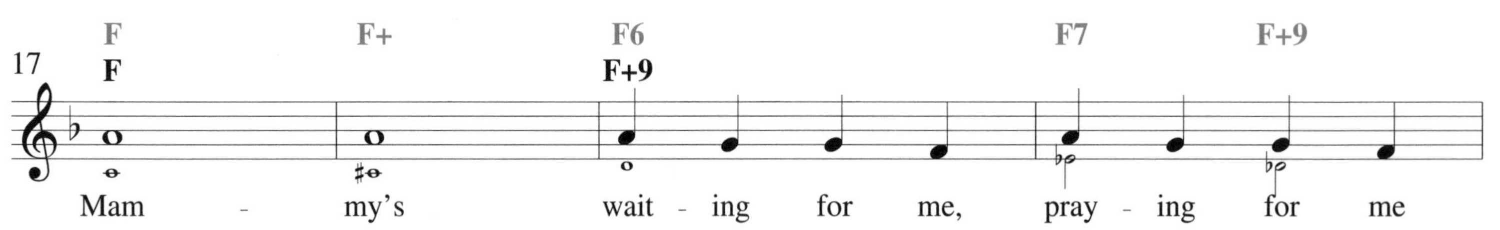

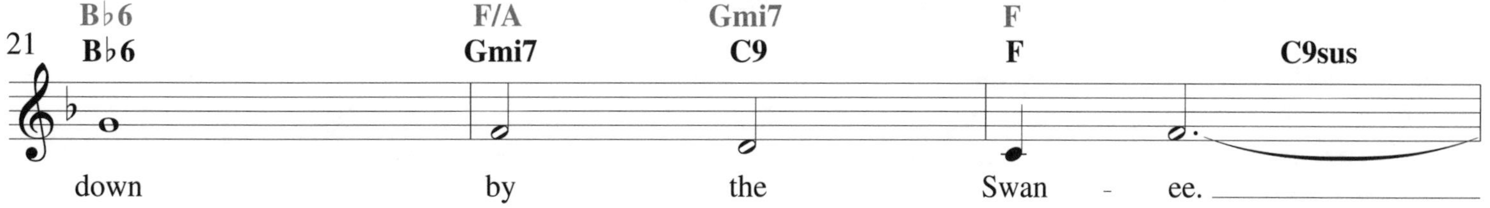
21
B♭6 F/A Gmi7 F
B♭6 Gmi7 C9 F C9sus
down by the Swan - ee.

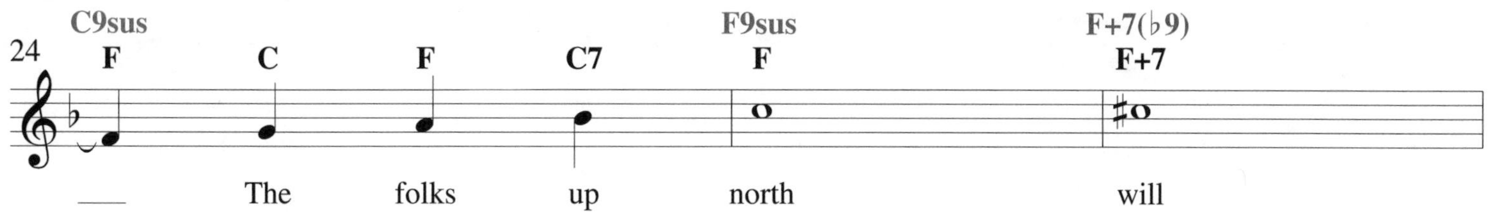
24
C9sus F9sus F+7(♭9)
F C F C7 F F+7
The folks up north will

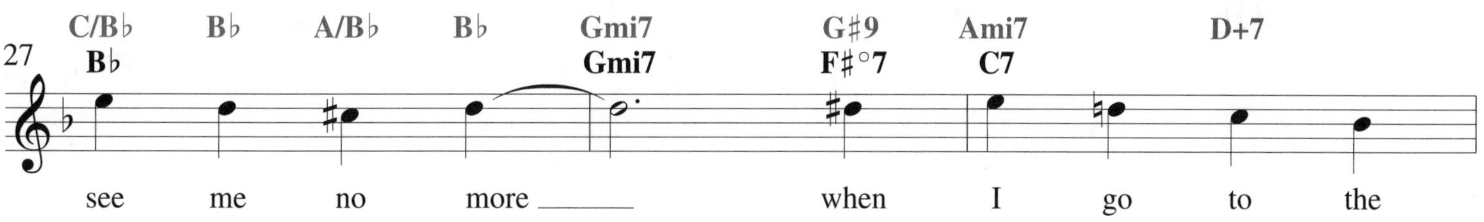
27
C/B♭ B♭ A/B♭ B♭ Gmi7 G♯9 Ami7 D+7
B♭ Gmi7 F♯°7 C7
see me no more when I go to the

30
G13 C7(♭9) F
C13 F
Swan - ee shore.

TAKE FIVE

By PAUL DESMOND

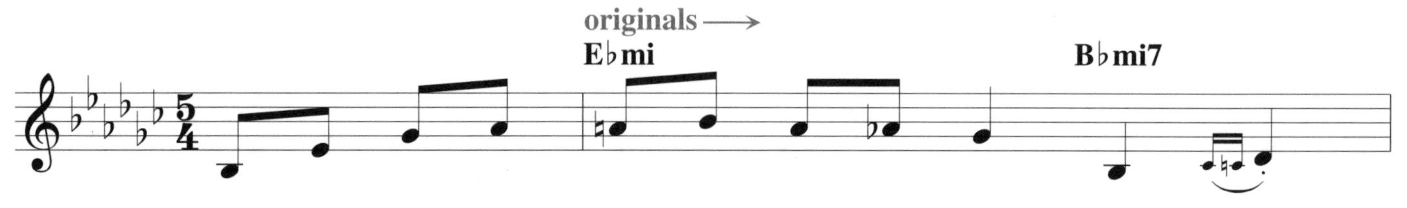

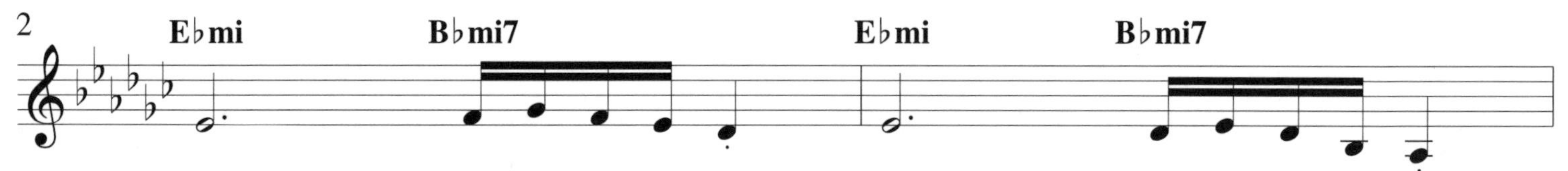

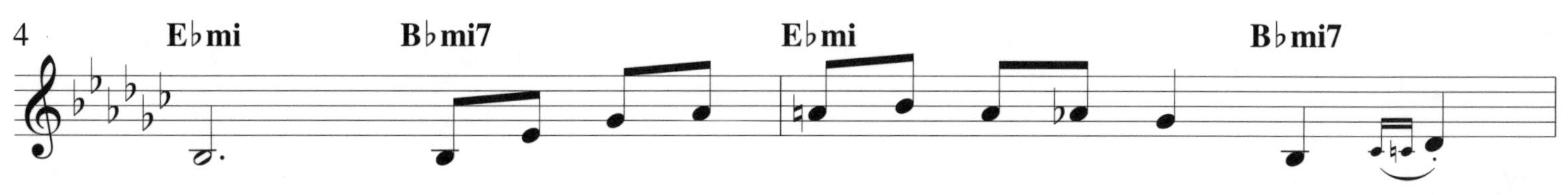

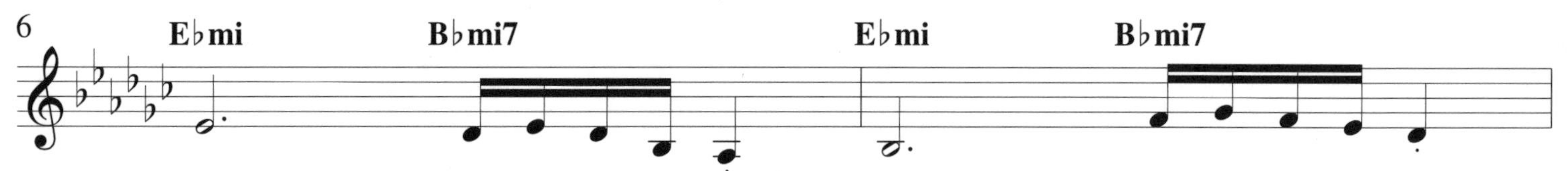

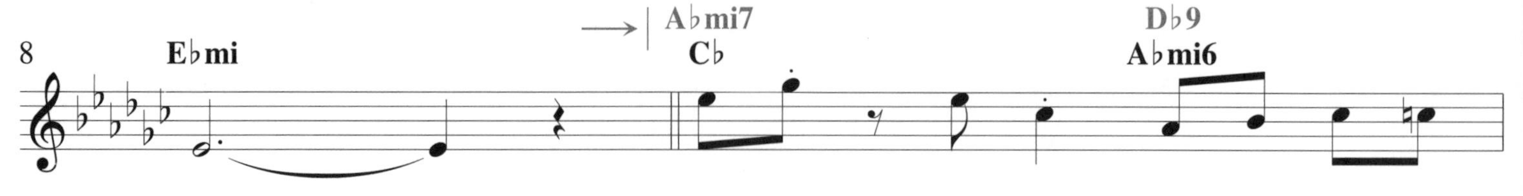

G♭Ma7 E♭7sus E♭7 A♭mi7 D♭9
12
G♭Ma7 C♭ A♭mi6

B♭mi7 E♭mi7 A♭mi7 D♭7 /C♭
14
B♭mi7 E♭mi7 A♭mi7 D♭7

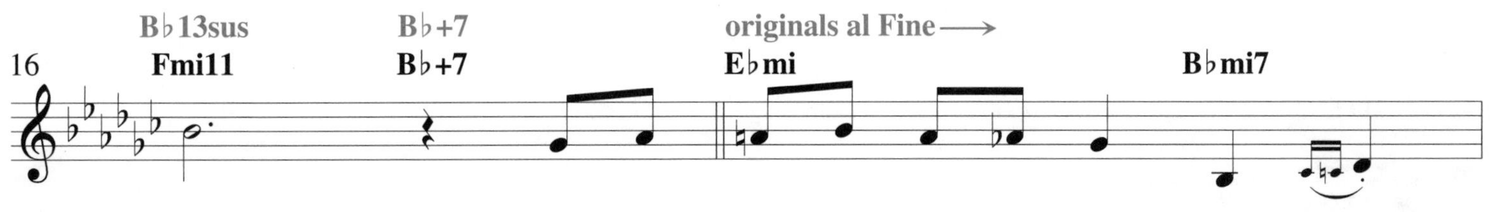
B♭13sus B♭+7 originals al Fine ⟶
16
Fmi11 B♭+7 E♭mi B♭mi7

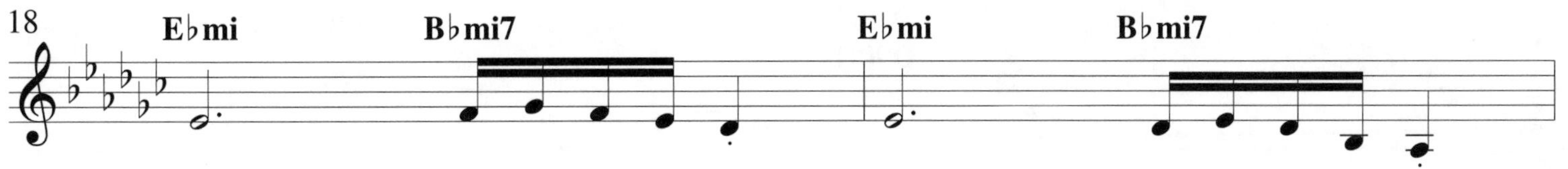
18
E♭mi B♭mi7 E♭mi B♭mi7

20
E♭mi B♭mi7 E♭mi B♭mi7

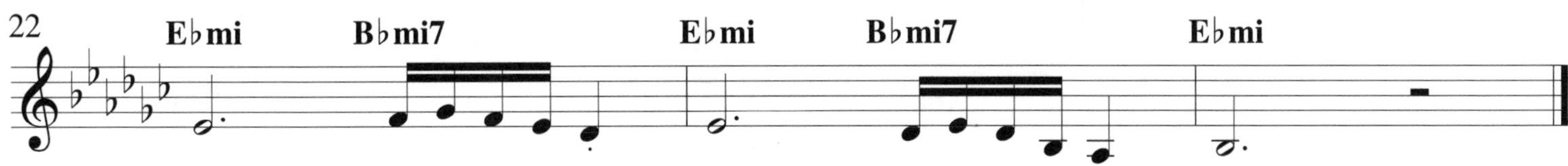
22
E♭mi B♭mi7 E♭mi B♭mi7 E♭mi

TAKE THE "A" TRAIN

Words and Music by
BILLY STRAYHORN

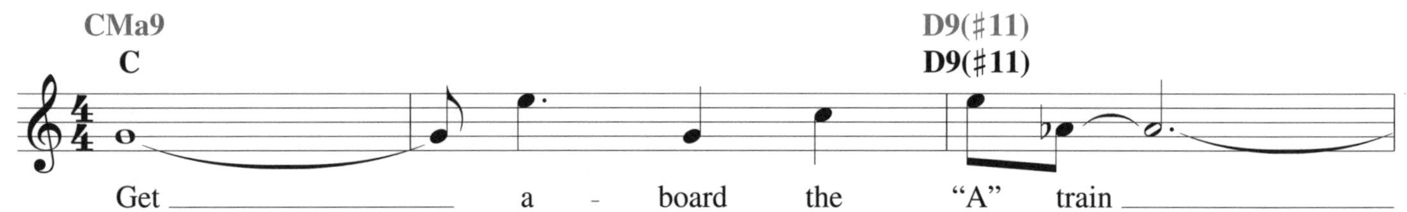

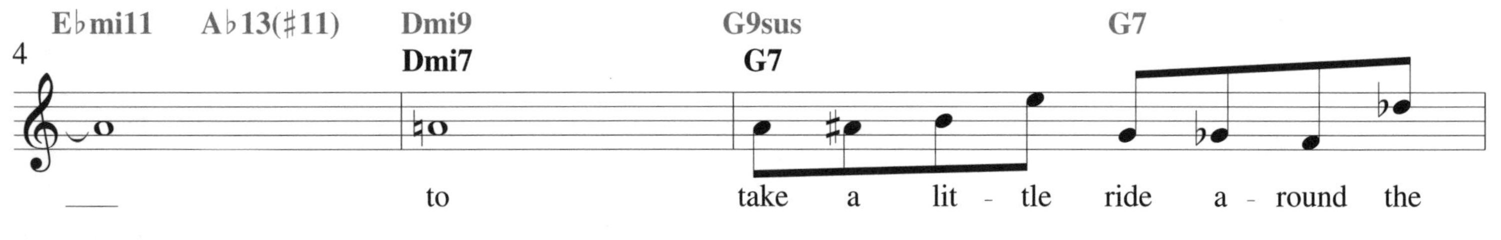

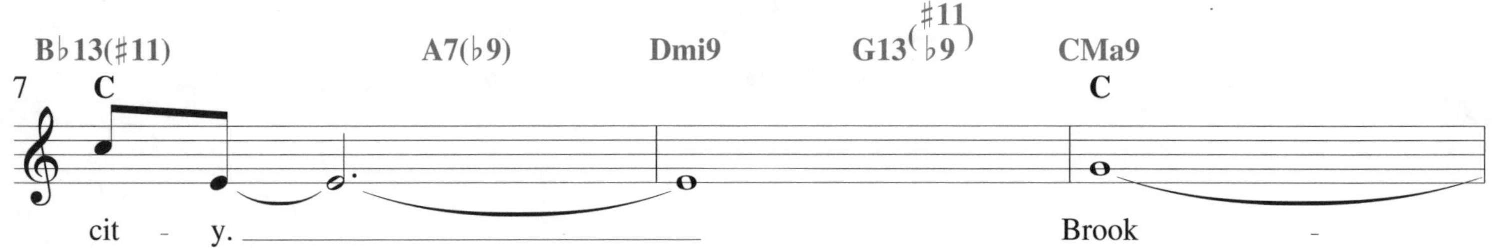

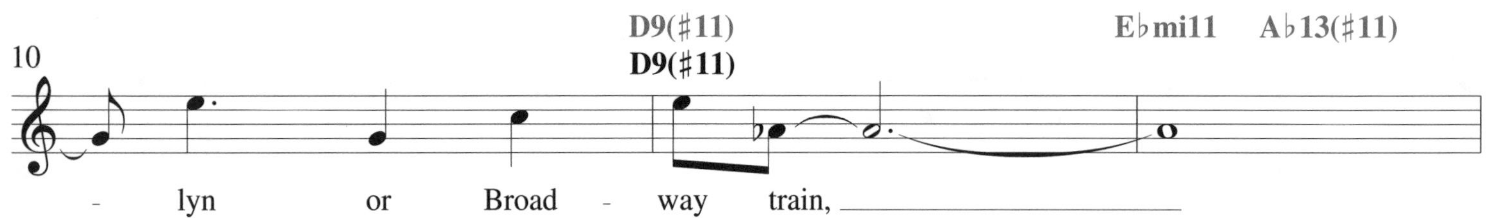

FMa9
Emi11
E♭9(♯11)
D9sus
D9
19
rid - ing.
That's where

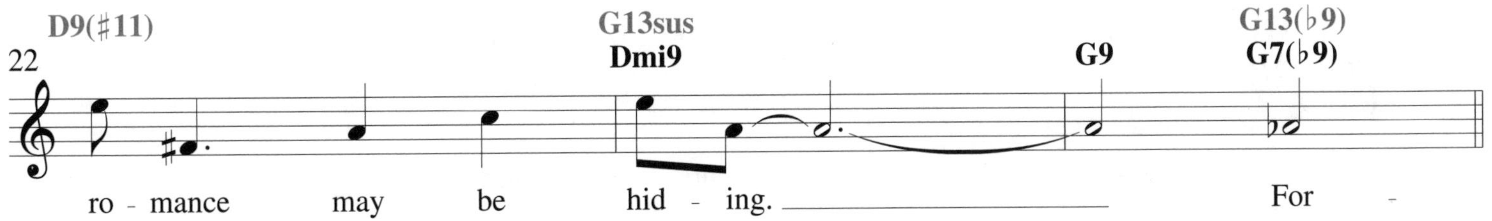
D9(♯11)
G13sus
Dmi9
G9
G13(♭9)
G7(♭9)
22
ro - mance may be hid - ing.
For -

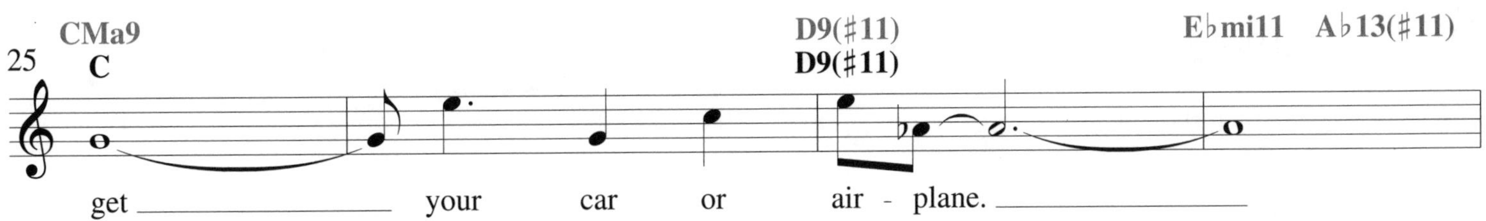
CMa9
C
D9(♯11)
D9(♯11)
E♭mi11
A♭13(♯11)
25
get your car or air - plane.

Dmi9
Dmi7
G9sus
G7
G7
C
C
29
You'll fine that it - 'll pay to take the "A" train.

THANK HEAVEN FOR LITTLE GIRLS

from GIGI

Words by ALAN JAY LERNER
Music by FREDERICK LOEWE

41
C♯/D D7 D9sus D13(♯11 ♭9) G
C♯/A D7 Ami7 D13(♭9) G
heav - en for lit - tle girls.

THANKS FOR THE MEMORY

from the Paramount Picture BIG BROADCAST OF 1938

Words and Music by LEO ROBIN
and RALPH RAINGER

18
A♭6/9 A♭Ma7 B♭mi7 /E♭ E♭13(♯11 ♭9) A♭6/9 A♭Ma7
A♭ E♭9 A♭
Man - y's the time that we feast - ed and man - y's the time that we
We said good - bye with a high - ball; then I got as "high" as a
21
A°7 D7(♭9) CMa7 Ami7 /G D/F♯ Fmi6
A°7 C/G Ami Dmi Fmi6/C G13
fast - ed. Oh, well, it was swell while it last - ed; we
stee - ple. But we were in - tel - li - gent peo - ple; no
24
Emi7 Ami7 E♭mi11 A♭13(♯11) D/F♯ Gmi11 C13(♭9)
Gmi7 B♭mi6/D♭ C7 C+ D♭°7 C13
did have fun and no harm done. And thanks for the
tears, no fuss, hur - ray for us. So thanks for the
27
F6 C+9 F6 F♯°7 C7/G F/A
F6 F♯°7 C7/G F/A
mem - o - ry of sun-burns at the shore, nights in Sing - a - pore. You
mem - o - ry and strict - ly en-tre-nous, dar - ling, how are you? And
30
D♯°7 C/E
D♯°7 C7/E
1
D/F♯ Gmi7 A♭13 Gmi7 C9sus C13(♯11 ♭9)
F♯°7 Gmi7 A°7 B♭6 C13
might have been a head-ache but you nev - er were a bore, so thank you so
how are all the lit - tle dreams that
33
F
F
2
D/F♯ Gmi7 E/G♯ F/A
F♯°7 Gmi7 G♯°7 F/A
much. nev - er did come true? Awf - 'ly glad I met you, chee-ri -
36
A♭mi11 D♭13 Gmi7 C9sus C13(♯11 ♭9) F
D♭7/A♭ Gmi7 C13 F
o and too-dle - oo and thank you so much!

THAT OLD FEELING

Words and Music by LEW BROWN
and SAMMY FAIN

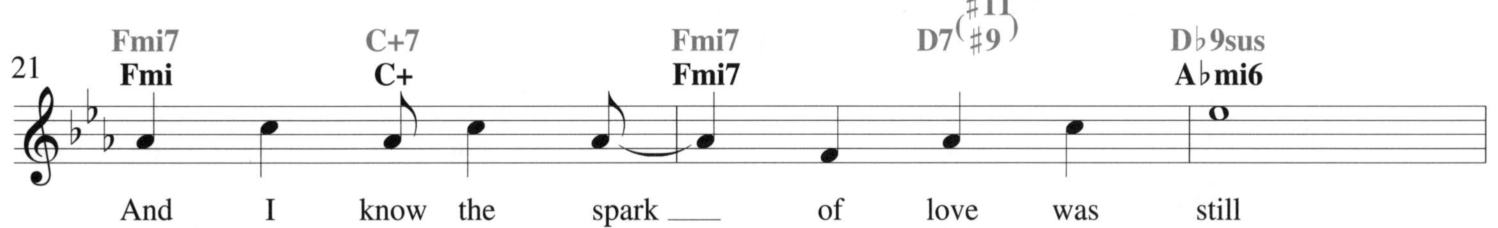
21
Fmi7 C+7 Fmi7 D7(#11 #9) D♭9sus
Fmi C+ Fmi7 A♭mi6
And I know the spark ___ of love was still

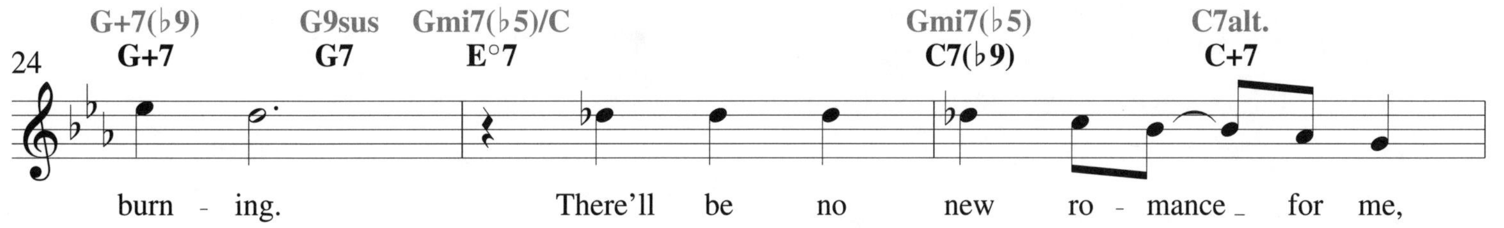
24
G+7(♭9) G9sus Gmi7(♭5)/C Gmi7(♭5) C7alt.
G+7 G7 E°7 C7(♭9) C+7
burn - ing. There'll be no new ro - mance _ for me,

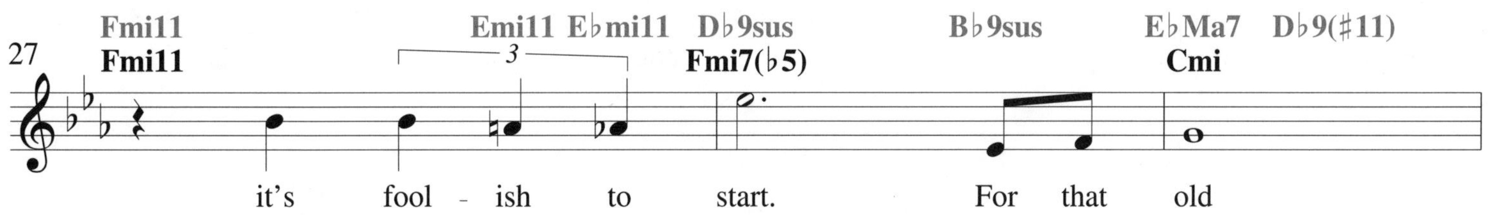
27
Fmi11 Emi11 E♭mi11 D♭9sus B♭9sus E♭Ma7 D♭9(#11)
Fmi11 Fmi7(♭5) Cmi
3
it's fool - ish to start. For that old

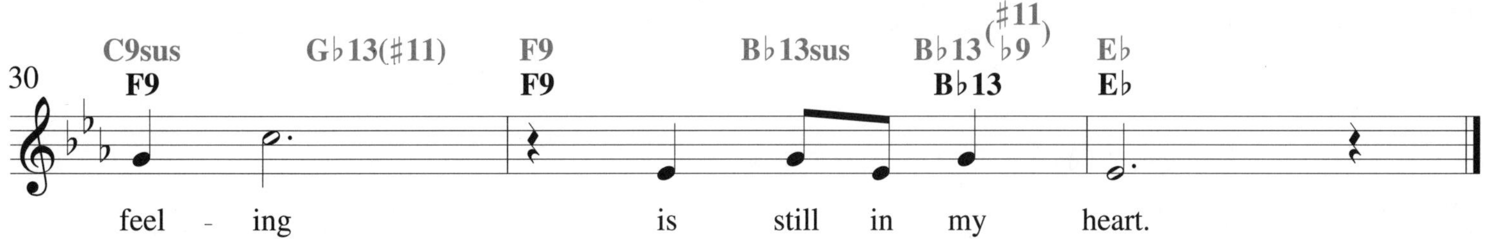
30
C9sus G♭13(#11) F9 B♭13sus B♭13(#11 ♭9) E♭
F9 F9 B♭13 E♭
feel - ing is still in my heart.

THEM THERE EYES

Words and Music by MACEO PINKARD,
WILLIAM TRACEY and DORIS TAUBER

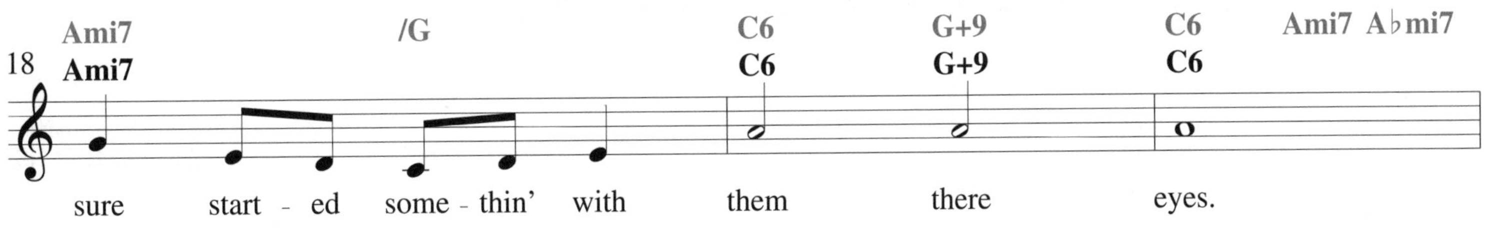
18
Ami7 /G C6 G+9 C6 Ami7 A♭mi7
Ami7 C6 G+9 C6
sure start - ed some - thin' with them there eyes.

21
Gmi11 C13sus C7(♭9) F6 C+9
C11 Cmi7(♭5) C7 F6
You'd bet - ter watch them if you're wise.

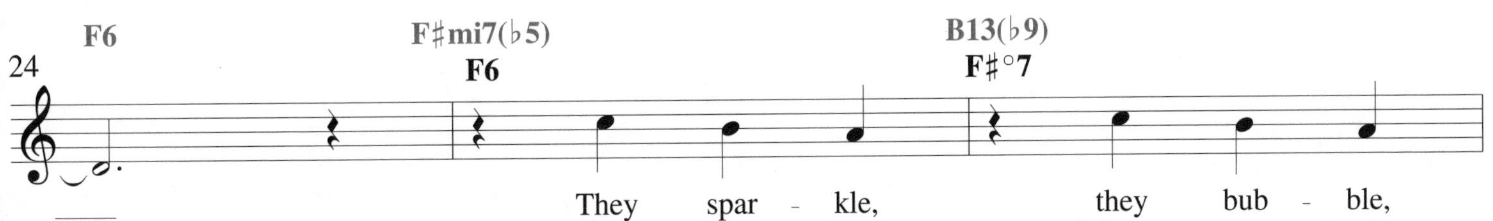
24
F6 F♯mi7(♭5) B13(♭9)
F6 F♯°7
They spar - kle, they bub - ble,

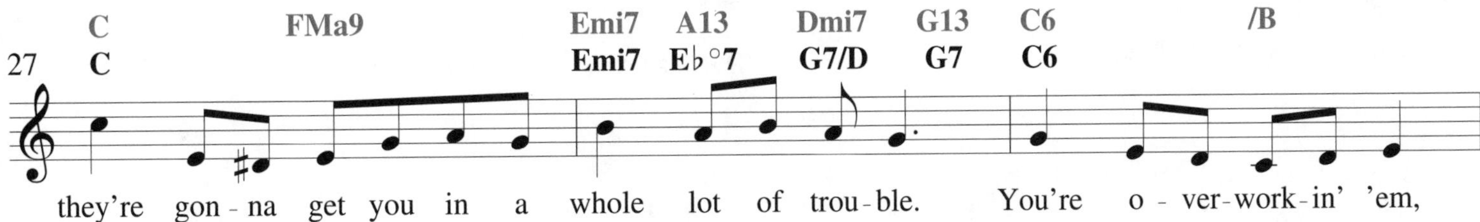
27
C FMa9 Emi7 A13 Dmi7 G13 C6 /B
C Emi7 E♭°7 G7/D G7 C6
they're gon - na get you in a whole lot of trou - ble. You're o - ver - work - in' 'em,

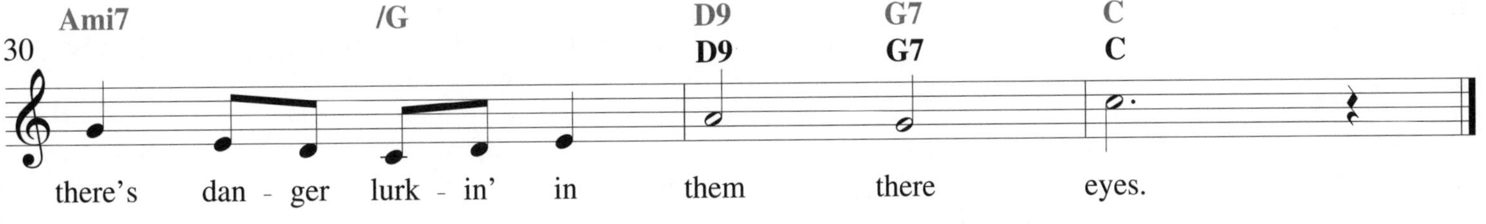
30
Ami7 /G D9 G7 C
D9 G7 C
there's dan - ger lurk - in' in them there eyes.

THERE! I'VE SAID IT AGAIN

By DAVE MANN
and REDD EVANS

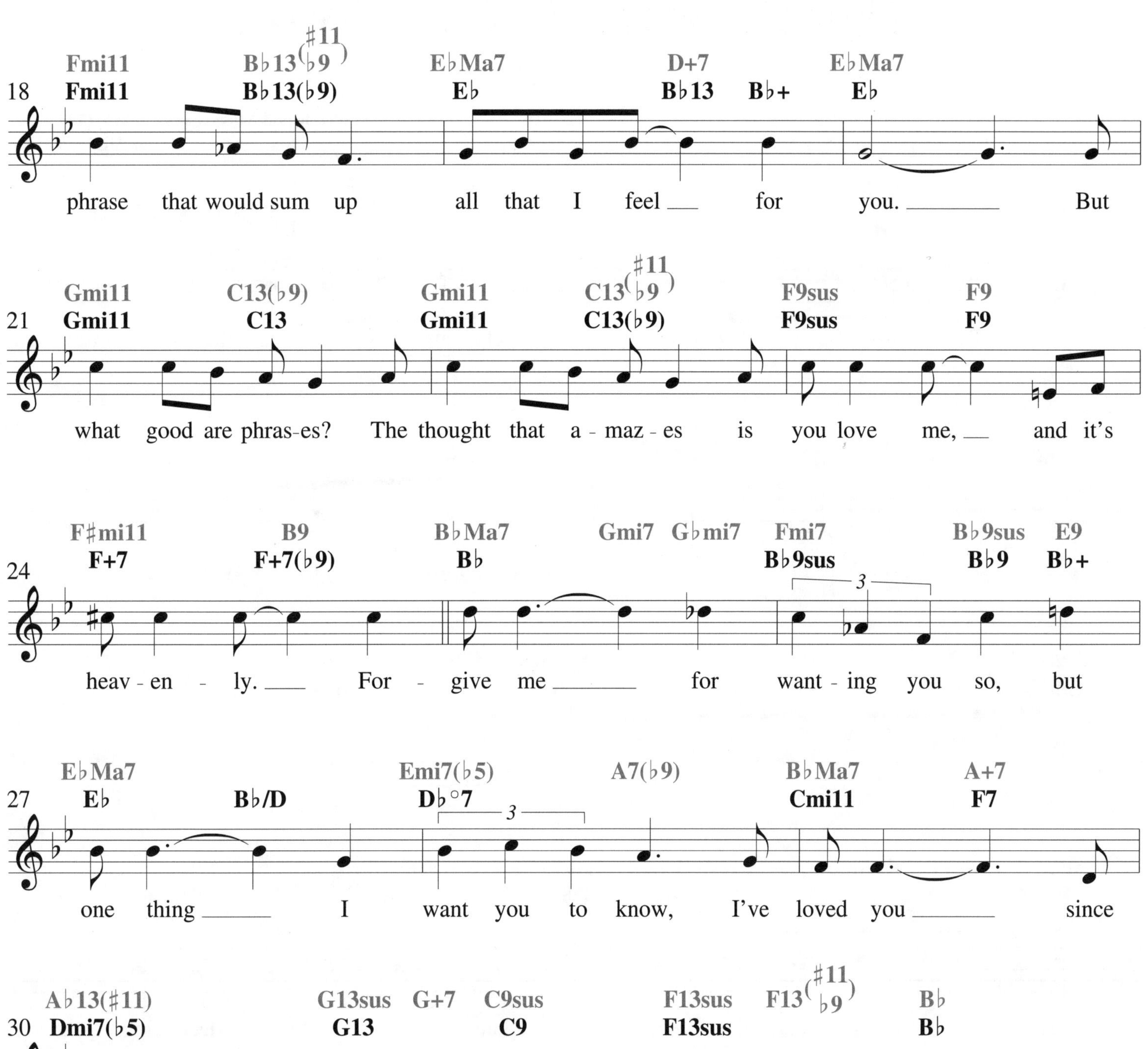
Fmi11 B♭13(♯11 ♭9) E♭Ma7 D+7 E♭Ma7
18 Fmi11 B♭13(♭9) E♭ B♭13 B♭+ E♭
phrase that would sum up all that I feel for you. But
Gmi11 C13(♭9) Gmi11 C13(♯11 ♭9) F9sus F9
21 Gmi11 C13 Gmi11 C13(♭9) F9sus F9
what good are phras-es? The thought that a-maz-es is you love me, and it's
F♯mi11 B9 B♭Ma7 Gmi7 G♭mi7 Fmi7 B♭9sus E9
24 F+7 F+7(♭9) B♭ B♭9sus B♭9 B♭+
3
heav-en-ly. For-give me for want-ing you so, but
E♭Ma7 Emi7(♭5) A7(♭9) B♭Ma7 A+7
27 E♭ B♭/D D♭°7 Cmi11 F7
3
one thing I want you to know, I've loved you since
A♭13(♯11) G13sus G+7 C9sus F13sus F13(♯11 ♭9) B♭
30 Dmi7(♭5) G13 C9 F13sus B♭
heav-en knows when, There! I've said it a-gain.

THERE MUST BE A WAY

Words and Music by SAMMY GALLOP
and DAVID SAXON

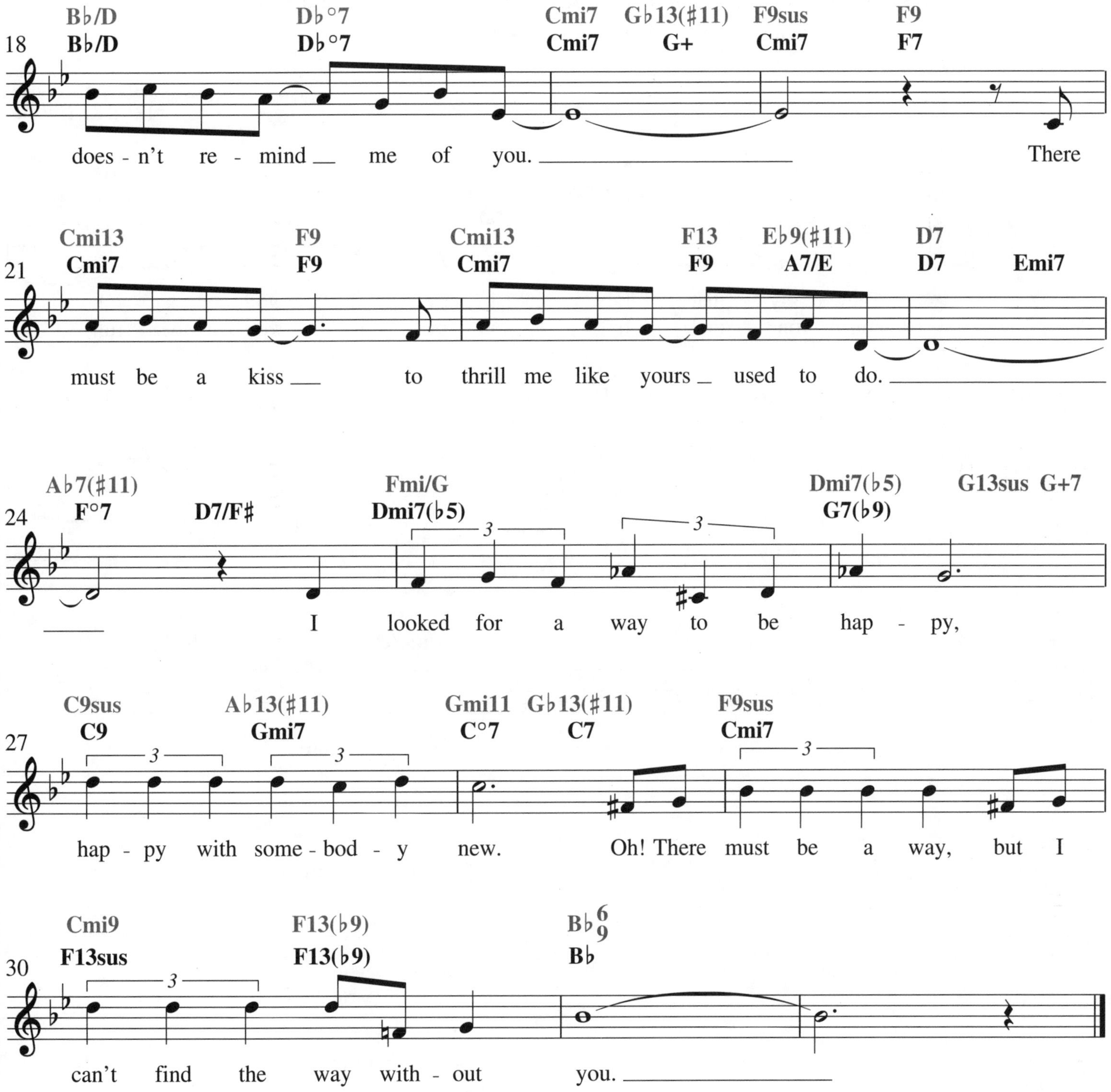

18
B♭/D Db°7 Cmi7 G♭13(♯11) F9sus F9
B♭/D D♭°7 Cmi7 G+ Cmi7 F7
does - n't re - mind __ me of you. ___ There

21
Cmi13 F9 Cmi13 F13 E♭9(♯11) D7
Cmi7 F9 Cmi7 F9 A7/E D7 Emi7
must be a kiss __ to thrill me like yours _ used to do. ___

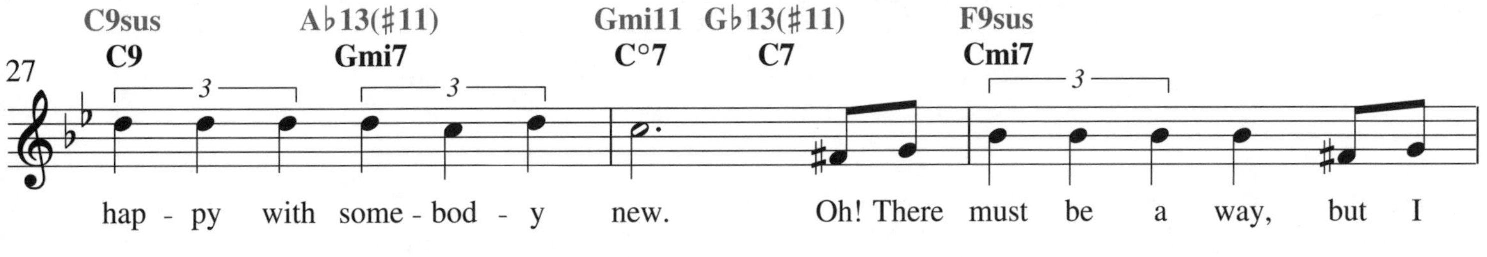

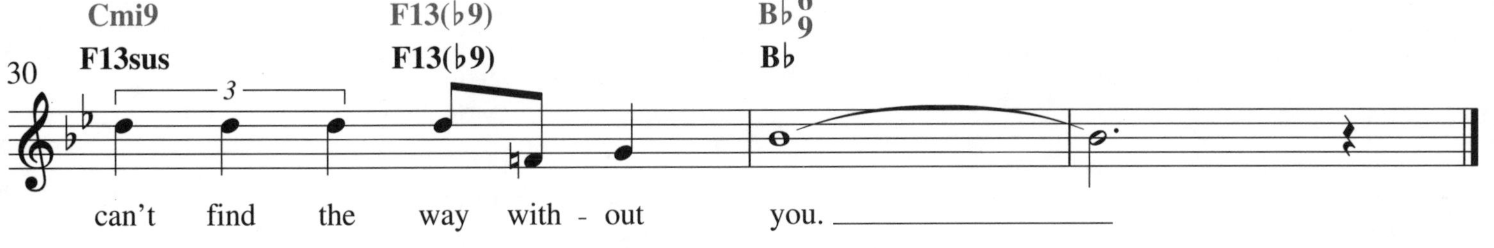

30
Cmi9 F13(♭9) B♭$^{6}_{9}$
F13sus F13(♭9) B♭
3
can't find the way with - out you. ___

THEY SAY IT'S WONDERFUL

from the Stage Production ANNIE GET YOUR GUN

Words and Music by
IRVING BERLIN

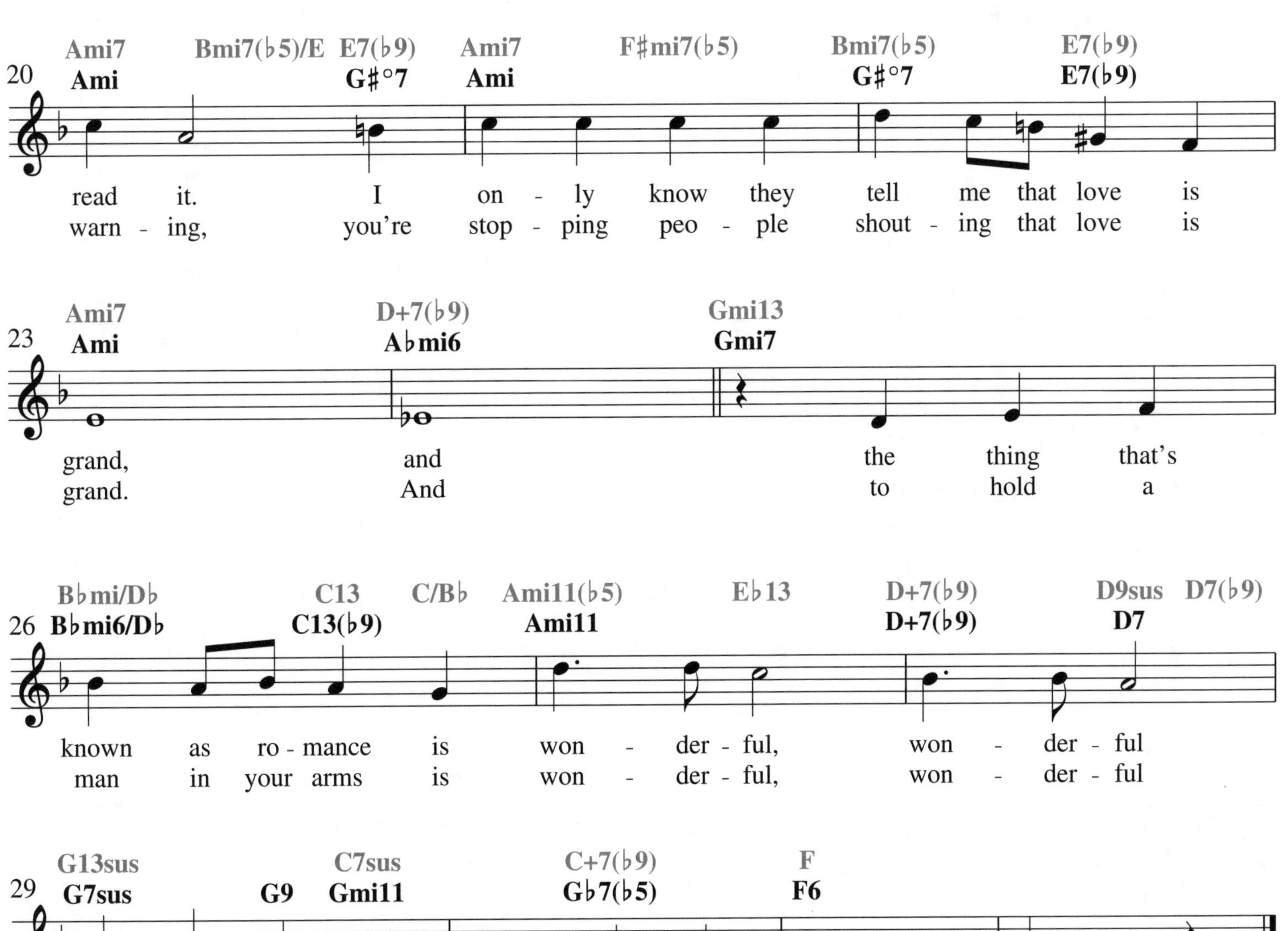
20
Ami7 Bmi7(♭5)/E E7(♭9) Ami7 F♯mi7(♭5) Bmi7(♭5) E7(♭9)
Ami G♯°7 Ami G♯°7 E7(♭9)
read it. I on - ly know they tell me that love is
warn - ing, you're stop - ping peo - ple shout - ing that love is
23
Ami7 D+7(♭9) Gmi13
Ami A♭mi6 Gmi7
grand, and the thing that's
grand. And to hold a
26
B♭mi/D♭ C13 C/B♭ Ami11(♭5) E♭13 D+7(♭9) D9sus D7(♭9)
B♭mi6/D♭ C13(♭9) Ami11 D+7(♭9) D7
known as ro - mance is won - der - ful, won - der - ful
man in your arms is won - der - ful, won - der - ful
29
G13sus C7sus C+7(♭9) F
G7sus G9 Gmi11 G♭7(♭5) F6
in ev - 'ry way, so they say.
in ev - 'ry way, so you say.

THREE COINS IN THE FOUNTAIN

from THREE COINS IN THE FOUNTAIN

Words by SAMMY CAHN
Music by JULE STYNE

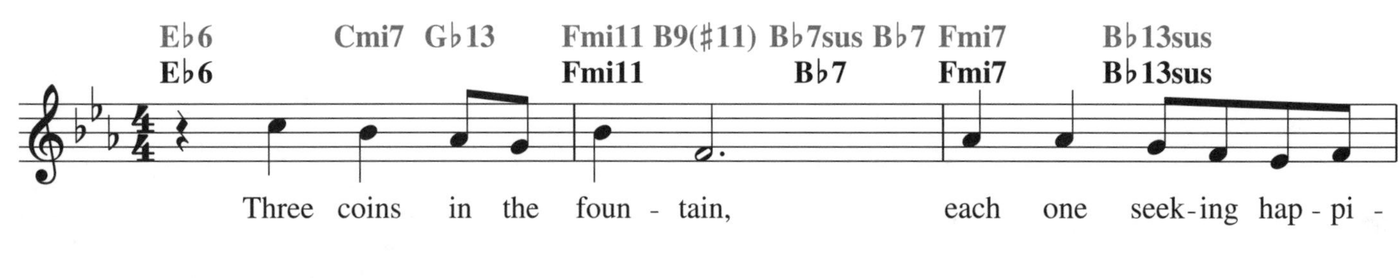

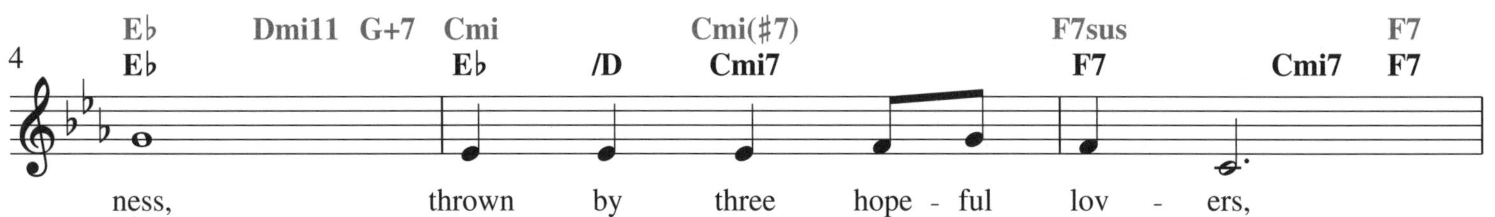

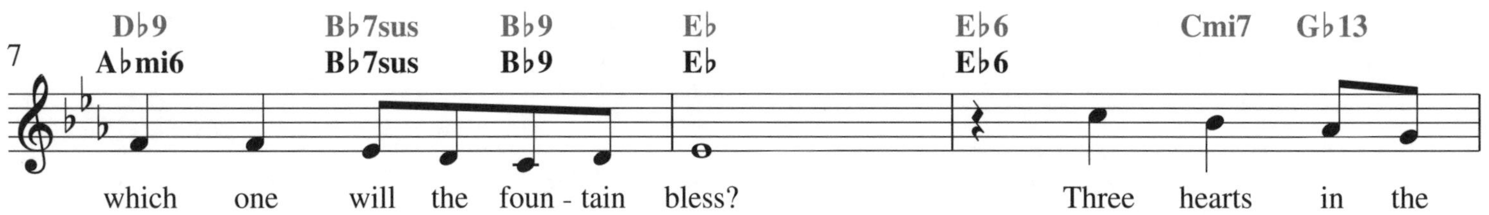

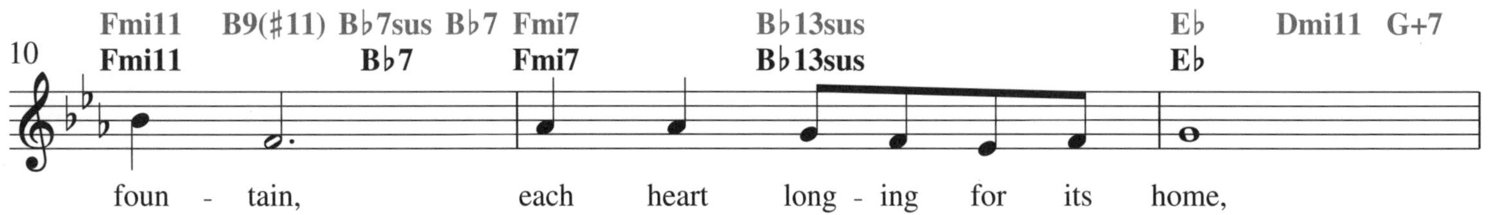

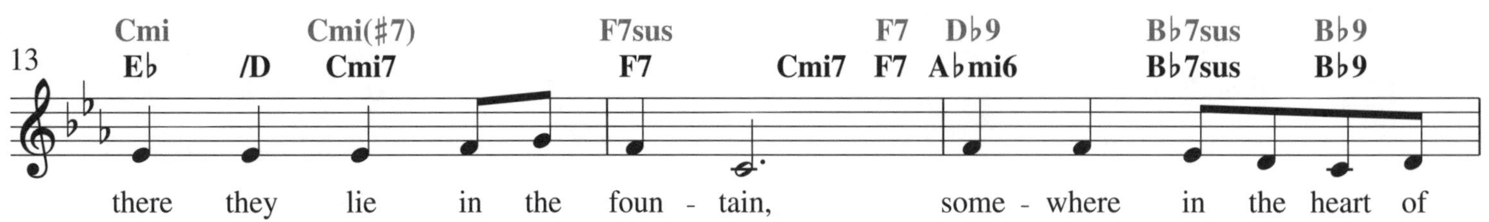

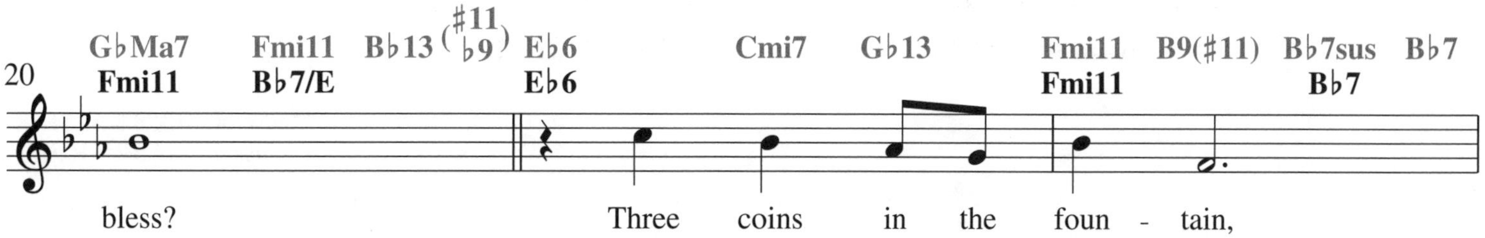

G♭Ma7 Fmi11 B♭13(♯11 ♭9) E♭6 Cmi7 G♭13 Fmi11 B9(♯11) B♭7sus B♭7
20
Fmi11 B♭7/E E♭6 Fmi11 B♭7
bless? Three coins in the foun - tain,

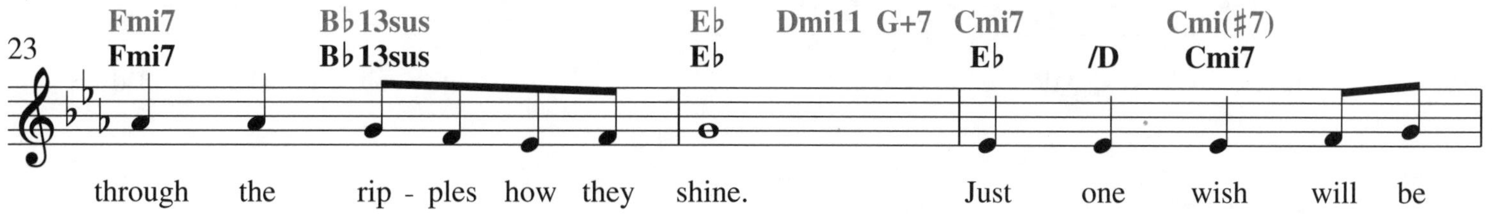

Fmi7 B♭13sus E♭ Dmi11 G+7 Cmi7 Cmi(♯7)
23
Fmi7 B♭13sus E♭ E♭ /D Cmi7
through the rip - ples how they shine. Just one wish will be

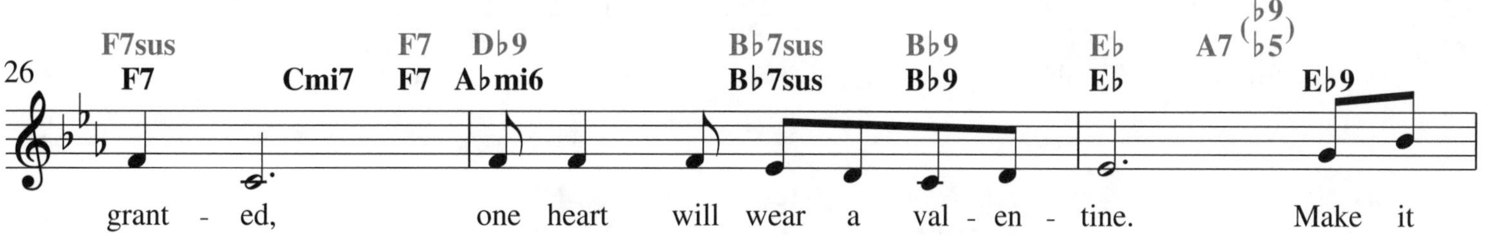

F7sus F7 D♭9 B♭7sus B♭9 E♭ A7(♭9 ♭5)
26
F7 Cmi7 F7 A♭mi6 B♭7sus B♭9 E♭ E♭9
grant - ed, one heart will wear a val - en - tine. Make it

A♭Ma9 /G Fmi7 B♭9sus E♭
29
A♭ Fmi7 B♭9sus E♭
mine! Make it mine! Make it mine!

THREE LITTLE WORDS

from the Motion Picture CHECK AND DOUBLE CHECK

Lyric by BERT KALMAR
Music by HARRY RUBY

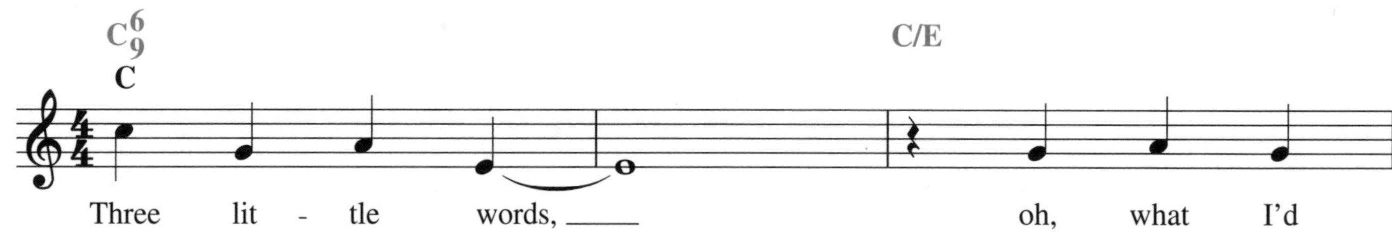

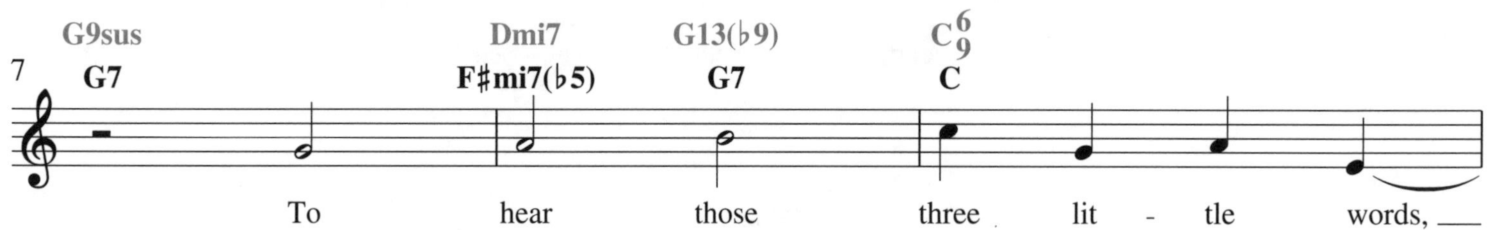

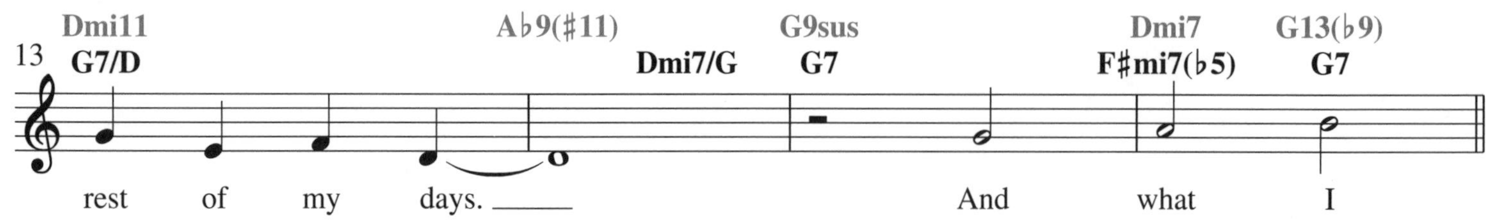

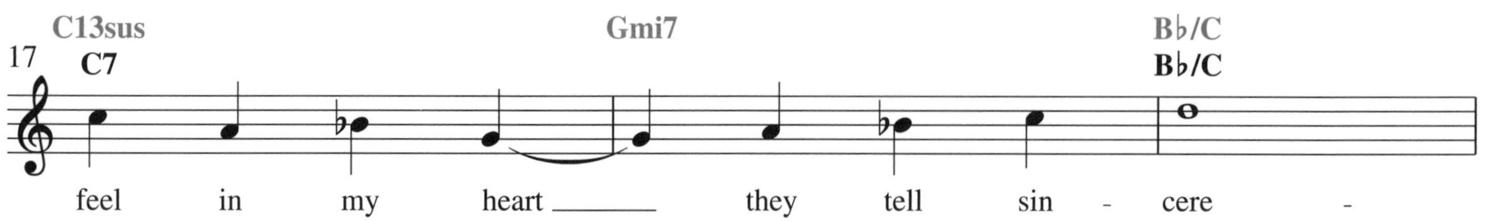

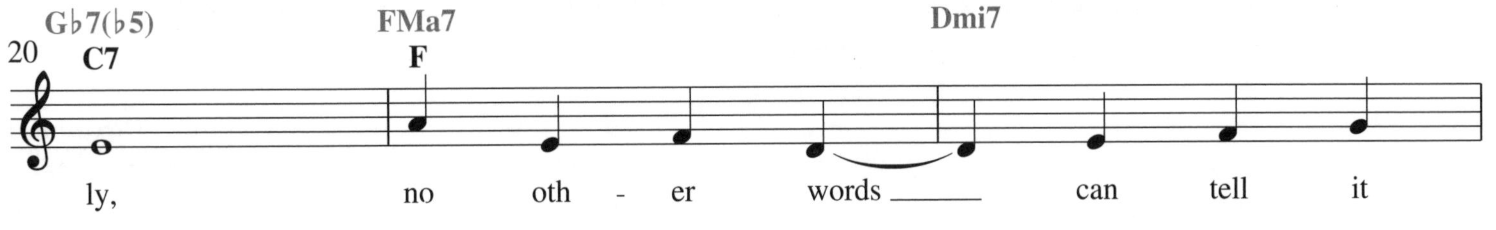
G♭7(♭5)
FMa7
Dmi7
20
C7
F
ly, no oth - er words can tell it

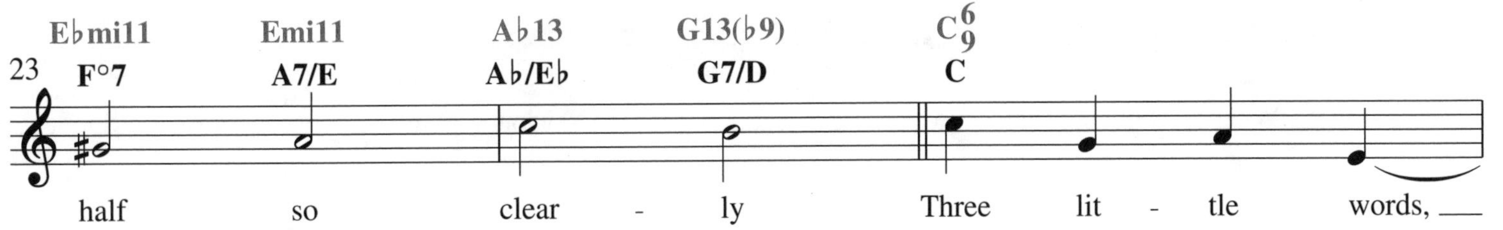
E♭mi11
Emi11
A♭13
G13(♭9)
C6/9
23
F°7
A7/E
A♭/E♭
G7/D
C
half so clear - ly Three lit - tle words,

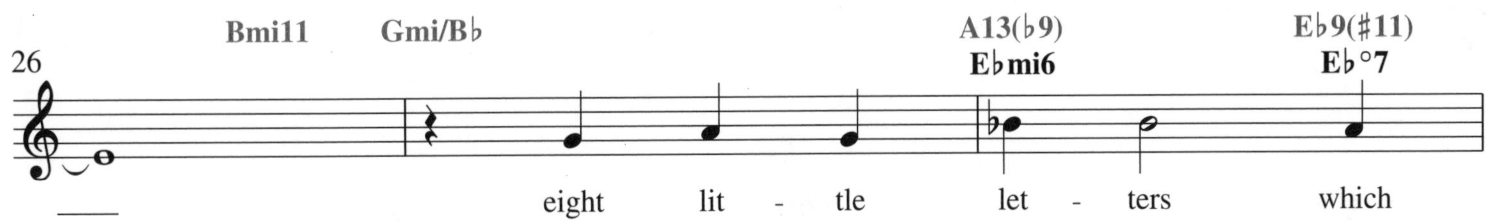
Bmi11
Gmi/B♭
A13(♭9)
E♭9(♯11)
26
E♭mi6
E♭°7
eight lit - tle let - ters which

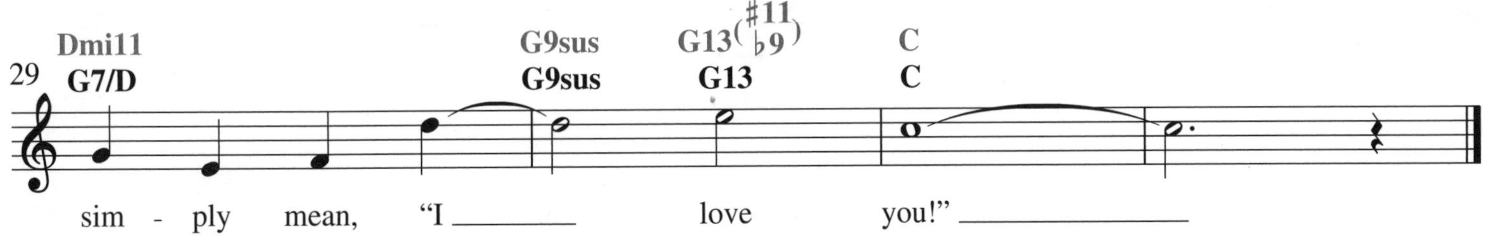
Dmi11
G9sus
G13(♯11 ♭9)
C
29
G7/D
G9sus
G13
C
sim - ply mean, "I love you!"

TOGETHER WHEREVER WE GO

from GYPSY

Words by STEPHEN SONDHEIM
Music by JULE STYNE

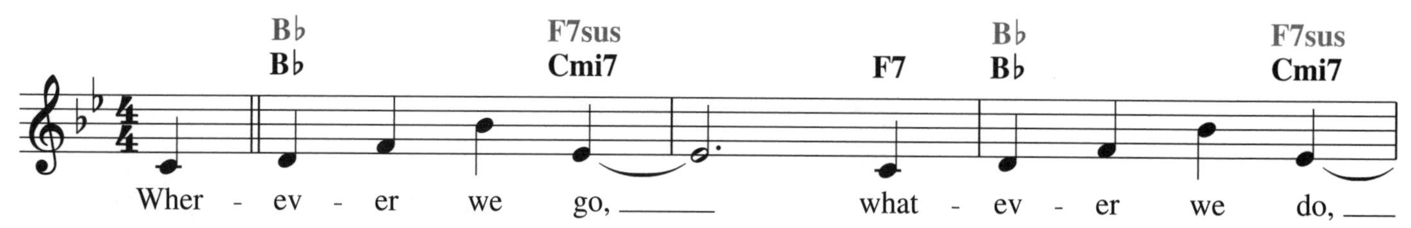

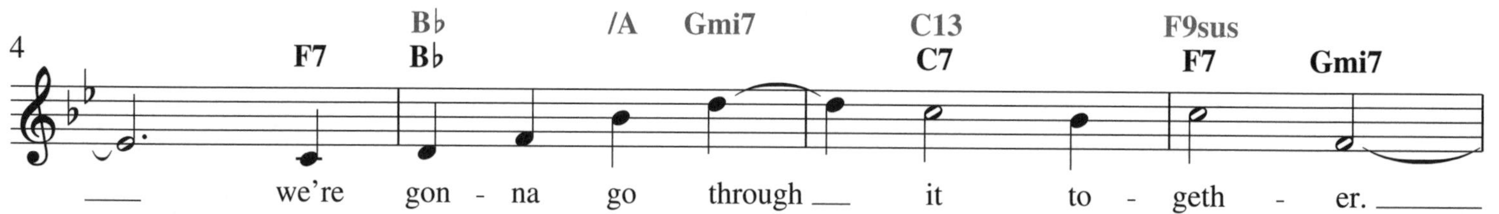

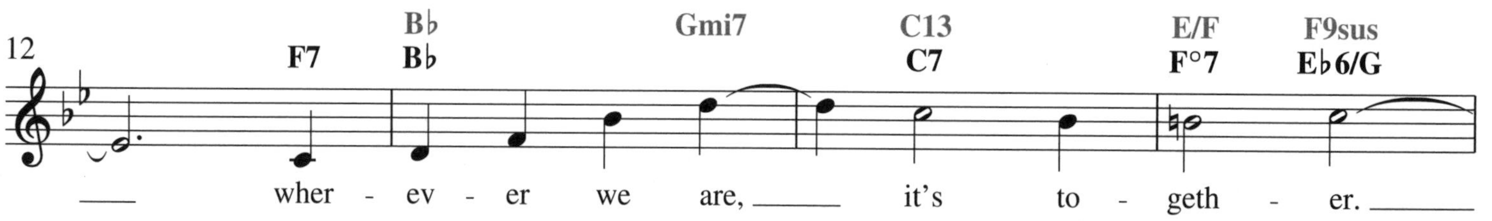

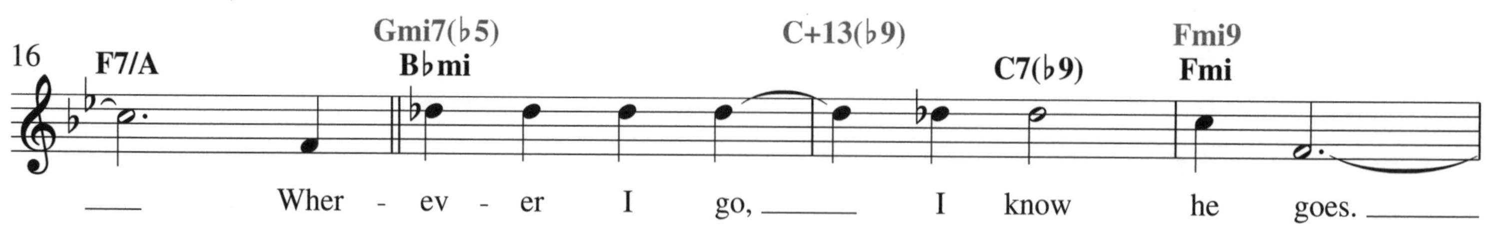

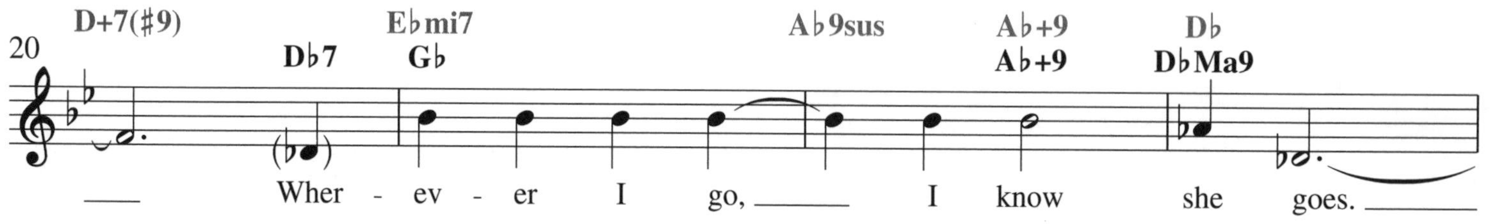

G♭Ma9
Cmi7(♭5)
C♭
F+7(♭9)
B♭mi9
B♭mi6
No fits no fights, no feuds and no e - goes
Gmi7(♭5)
C13sus
C7
C+7
F13sus
F13
Cmi9
a - mi - goes, to - geth - er!
Cmi11
F7
F7
B♭
B♭
F7sus
Cmi7
F7
Through thick and through thin, all
B♭
B♭
F7sus
Cmi7
F7
B♭
B♭
/A
Gmi7
Gmi11
C13
/B♭
out or all in, and wheth - er it's win, place, or
Ami7(♭5)
Ami7(♭5)
D7(♭9 ♭5)
D7(♭9)
Gmi
Gmi
show, with you for me and
Gmi(♯7)
Gmi(♯7)
C9sus
Gmi7
C13
C13
me for you, we'll mud - dle through what - ev - er we do to -
B♭/F
B♭/F
F13
Cmi9
F9
F9
B♭
B♭
geth - er, wher - ev - er we go!

UNCHAINED MELODY

from the Motion Picture UNCHAINED

Lyric by HY ZARET
Music by ALEX NORTH

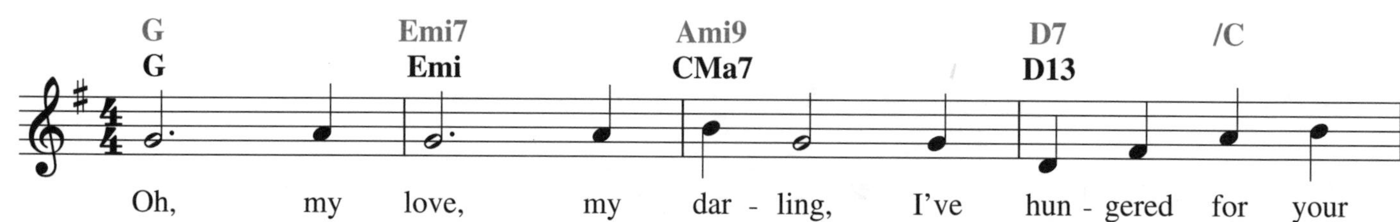
G Emi7 Ami9 D7 /C
G Emi CMa7 D13
Oh, my love, my dar - ling, I've hun - gered for your

G/B Emi7 Ami11 D7sus D7
5
G Emi D D7
touch a long, lone - ly time.

G Emi7 Ami9 D7 /C
9
G Emi CMa7 D13
Time goes by so slow - ly and time can do so

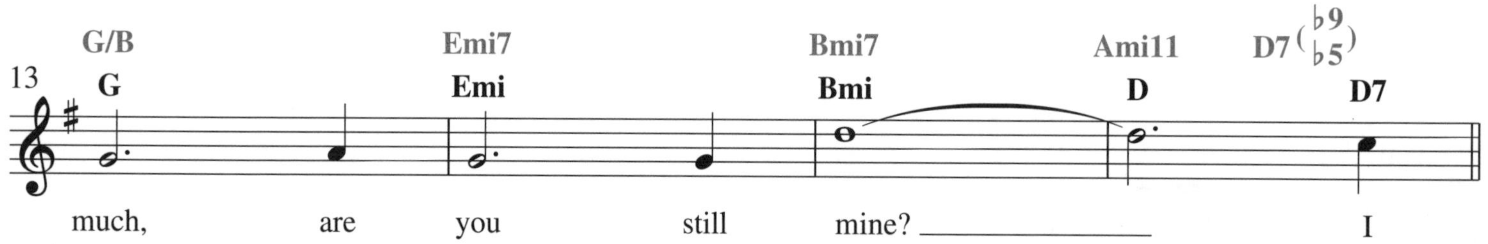
G/B Emi7 Bmi7 Ami11 D7(♭9 ♭5)
13
G Emi Bmi D D7
much, are you still mine? I

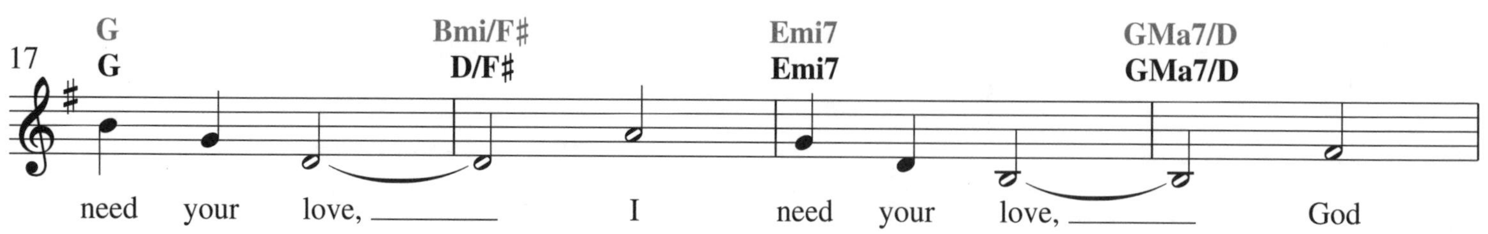
G Bmi/F♯ Emi7 GMa7/D
17
G D/F♯ Emi7 GMa7/D
need your love, I need your love, God

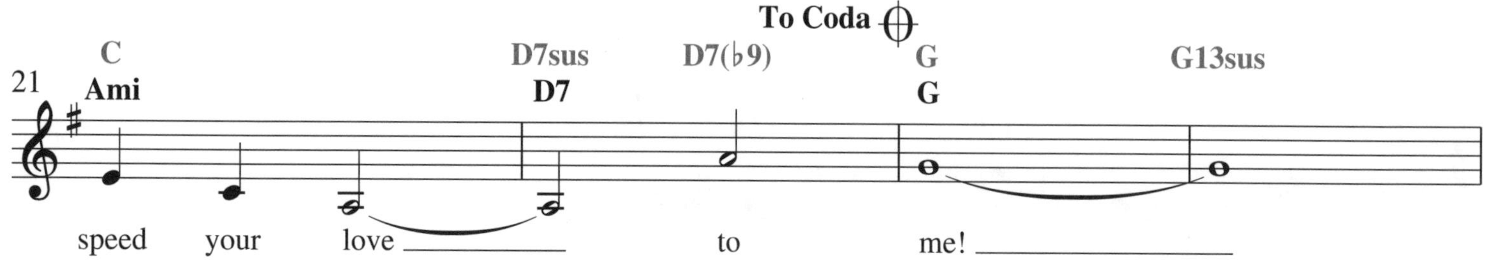
To Coda
C D7sus D7(♭9) G G13sus
21
Ami D7 G
speed your love to me!

25
C C D/C D C C B♭/C B♭
Lone - ly riv - ers flow to the sea, to the sea,
Lone - ly moun - tains gaze at the stars, at the stars,
29
C C D9sus D GMa9 G G9sus
to the o - pen arms of the sea.
wait - ing for the dawn of the day.
33
C C D/C D C C B♭/C B♭
Lone - ly riv - ers sigh, "Wait for me, wait for me!"
All a - lone, I gaze at the stars, at the stars,
37
C C D9sus D
1 G G
I'll be com - ing home, wait for me!
dream - ing of my love far a -
41
2 G G
D.C. al Coda
way.
CODA
G G
me!

UP, UP AND AWAY

Words and Music by
JIMMY WEBB

AMa9 G13sus G13(#11 b9) CMa9 Emi7 Ami11
A G6 FMa7 C Emi7
Sus - pend - ed un - der a twi - light
Dmi11 G13sus G+7 CMa9 Emi7 Ami11
Dmi11 G7 G/F C/E C
can - o - py we'll search the clouds for a star to
Dmi11 Ab13(#11) G9sus G/F EbMa9 Gmi7 Cmi11
Dmi11 G7 G/F Eb Gmi7
guide us. If by some chance you find your-self
Fmi11 B9(#11) Bb9sus GbMa9 Db/F Ebmi7 Ab13sus
Fmi11 Bb7 Gb Ab
lov - ing me we'll find a cloud to hide us,
D.C. al Coda
G G/F Eb13(#11) D13(#11 b9)
G F (Eb)
keep the moon be - side us.
CODA
Repeat and Fade
AMa9 G6 FMa7
A G6 FMa7
(fly)

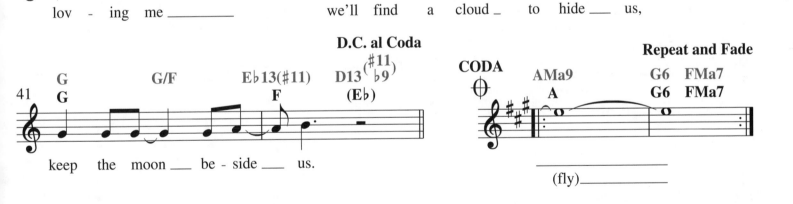

WAKE THE TOWN AND TELL THE PEOPLE

Words by SAMMY GALLOP
Music by JERRY LIVINGSTON

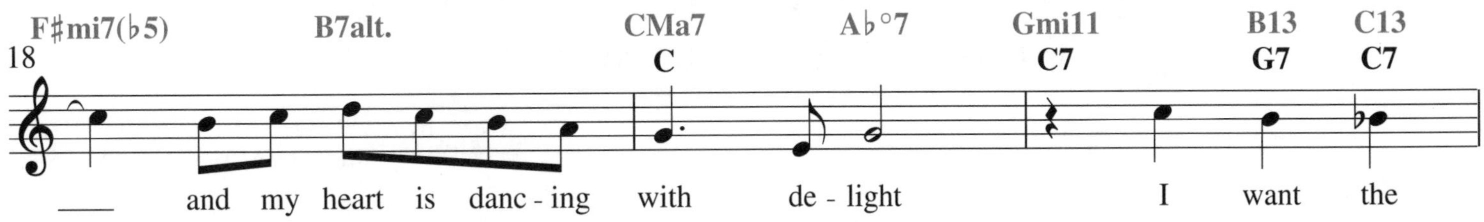
F♯mi7(♭5) B7alt. CMa7 A♭°7 Gmi11 B13 C13
18
C C7 G7 C7
and my heart is danc - ing with de - light I want the

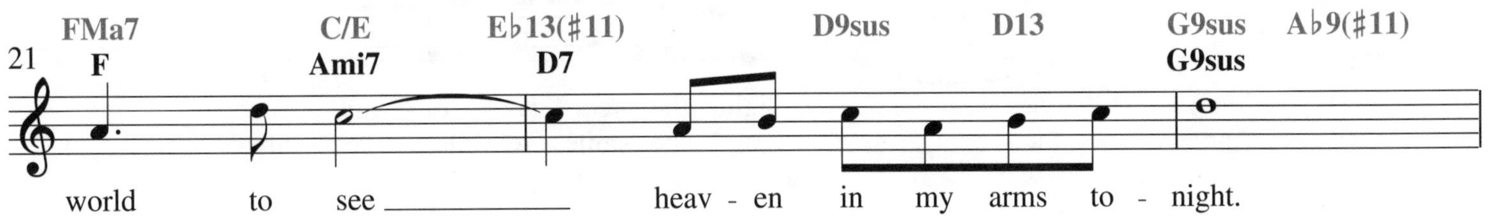
FMa7 C/E E♭13(♯11) D9sus D13 G9sus A♭9(♯11)
21
F Ami7 D7 G9sus
world to see heav - en in my arms to - night.

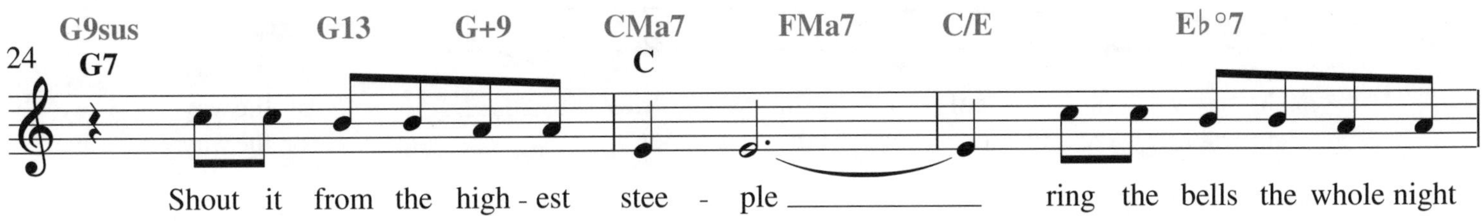
G9sus G13 G+9 CMa7 FMa7 C/E E♭°7
24
G7 C
Shout it from the high - est stee - ple ring the bells the whole night

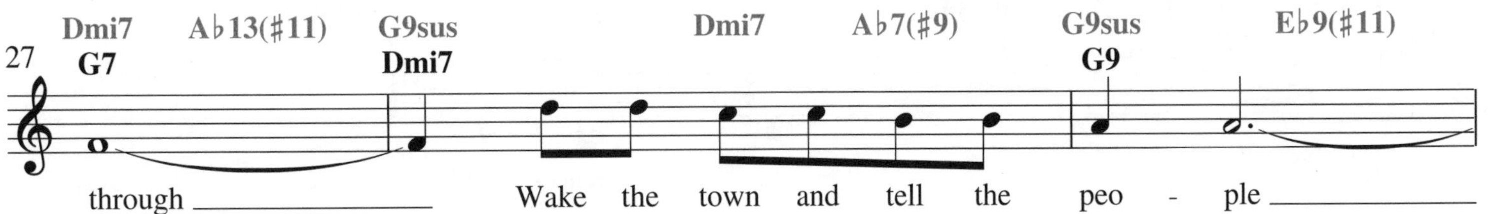
Dmi7 A♭13(♯11) G9sus Dmi7 A♭7(♯9) G9sus E♭9(♯11)
27
G7 Dmi7 G9
through Wake the town and tell the peo - ple

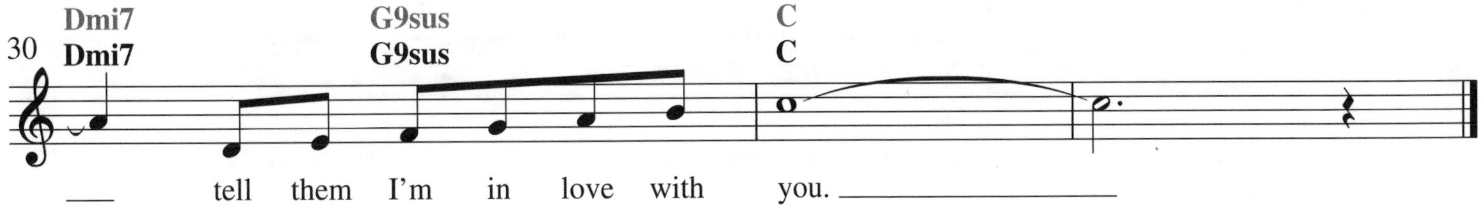
Dmi7 G9sus C
30
Dmi7 G9sus C
tell them I'm in love with you.

THE WAY WE WERE

from the Motion Picture THE WAY WE WERE

Words by ALAN and MARILYN BERGMAN
Music by MARVIN HAMLISCH

A 6/9 A(add2)/C♯ DMa9 F♯mi9 /E
19
A6 C♯mi DMa9 F♯mi9 /E
Mem - 'ries ___ may be beau - ti - ful, and yet,

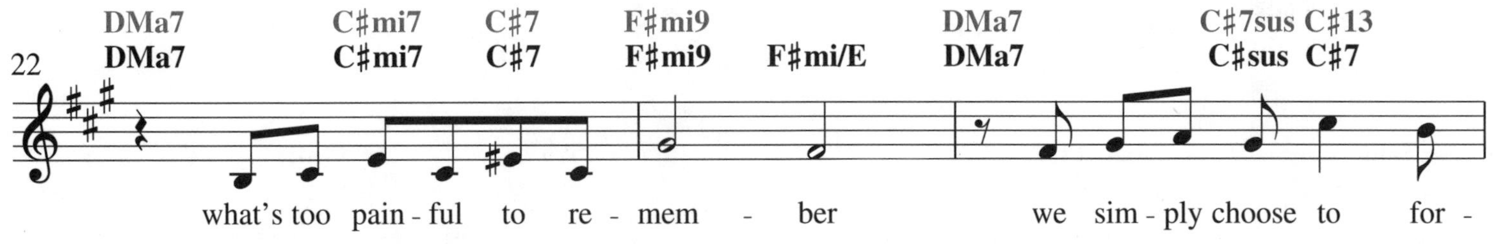
DMa7 C♯mi7 C♯7 F♯mi9 DMa7 C♯7sus C♯13
22
DMa7 C♯mi7 C♯7 F♯mi9 F♯mi/E DMa7 C♯sus C♯7
what's too pain - ful to re - mem - ber we sim - ply choose to for -

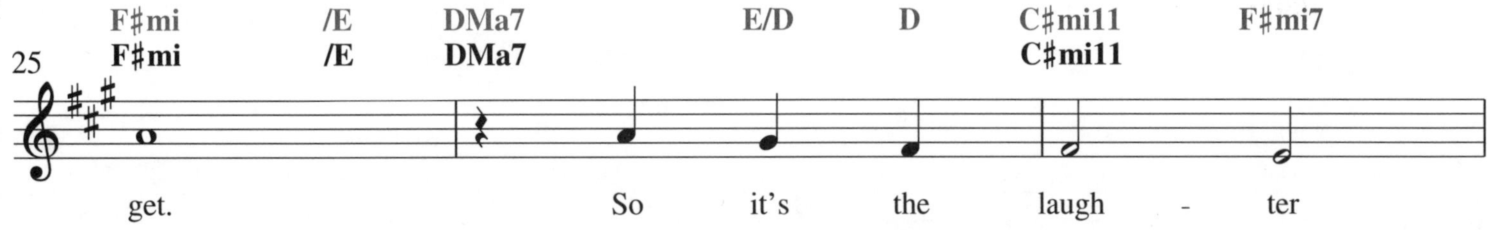
F♯mi /E DMa7 E/D D C♯mi11 F♯mi7
25
F♯mi /E DMa7 C♯mi11
get. So it's the laugh - ter

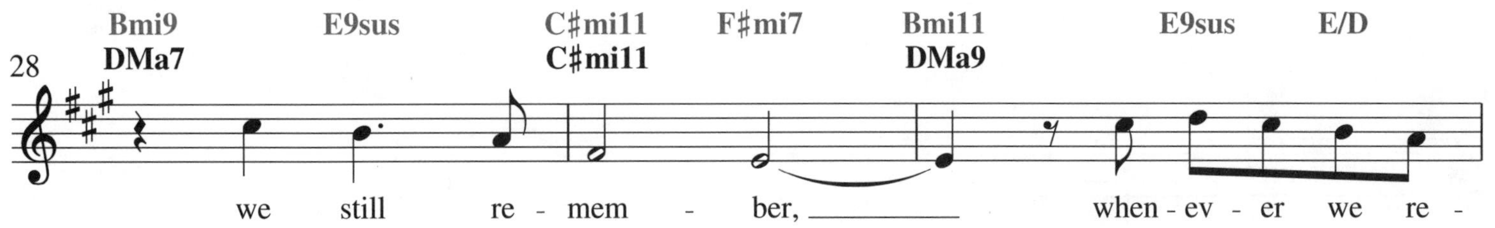
Bmi9 E9sus C♯mi11 F♯mi7 Bmi11 E9sus E/D
28
DMa7 C♯mi11 DMa9
we still re - mem - ber, ___ when - ev - er we re -

C♯mi11 F♯mi7 Bmi11 E7sus AMa7
31
C♯mi11 F♯mi7 Bmi11 E7sus AMa7 DMa7
mem - ber ___ the way we were;

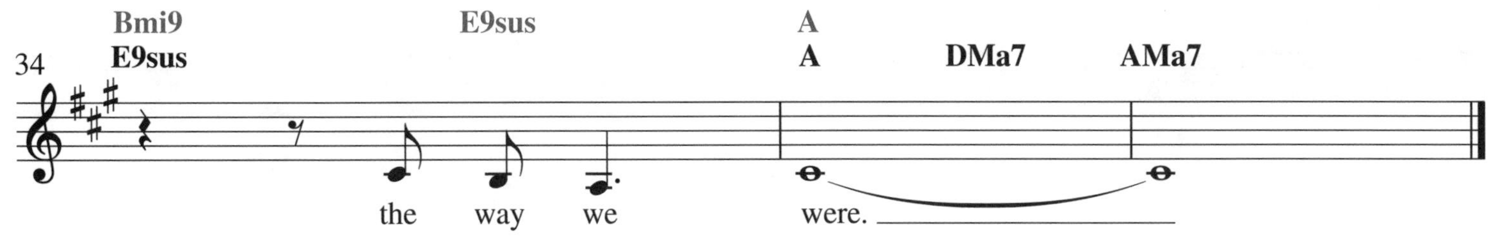
Bmi9 E9sus A
34
E9sus A DMa7 AMa7
the way we were. ___

WE KISS IN A SHADOW

from THE KING AND I

Lyrics by OSCAR HAMMERSTEIN II
Music by RICHARD RODGERS

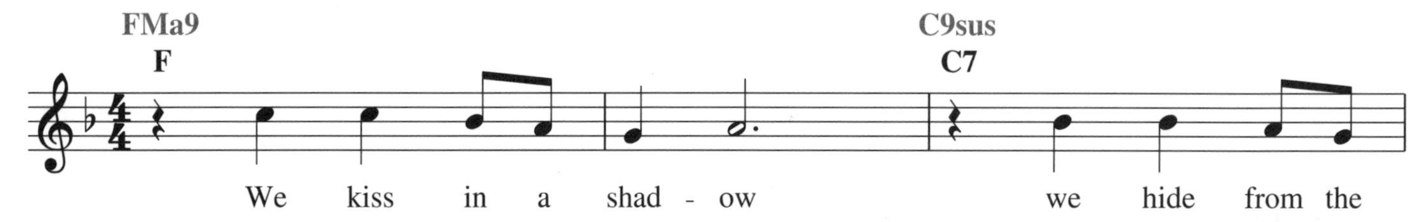

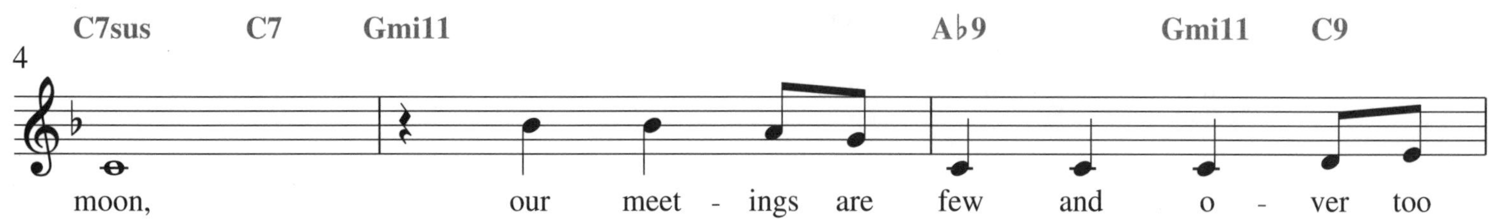

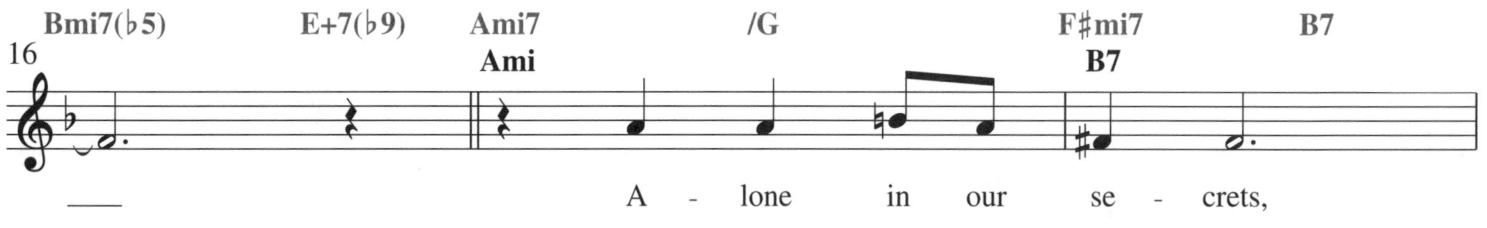

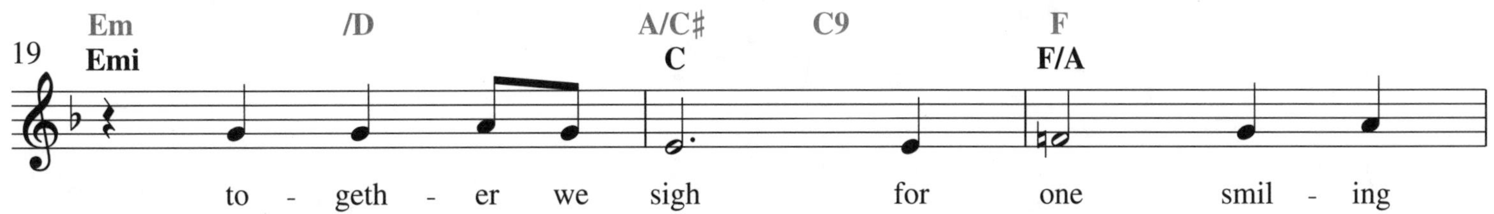
Em /D A/C♯ C9 F
19 Emi C F/A
to - geth - er we sigh for one smil - ing

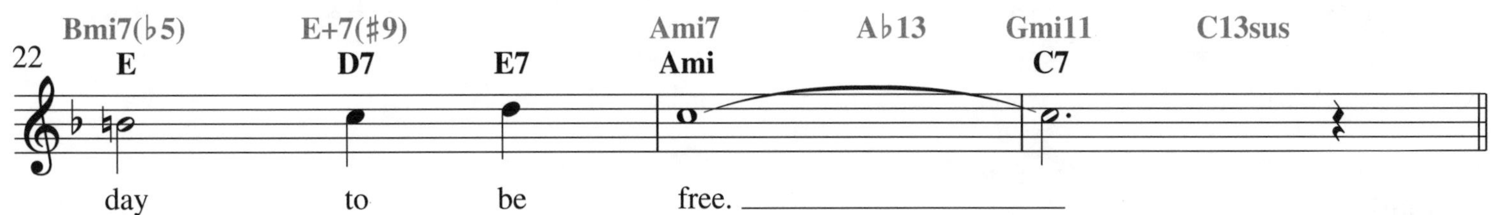
Bmi7(♭5) E+7(♯9) Ami7 A♭13 Gmi11 C13sus
22 E D7 E7 Ami C7
day to be free.

FMa9 C9sus
25 F C7
To kiss in the sun - light and say to the

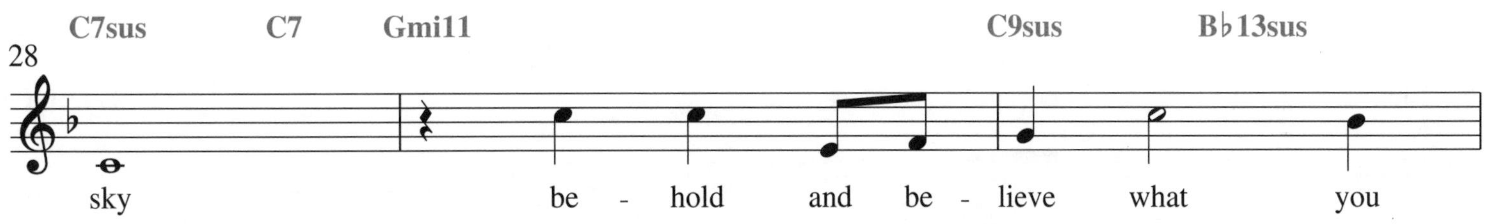
C7sus C7 Gmi11 C9sus B♭13sus
28
sky be - hold and be - lieve what you

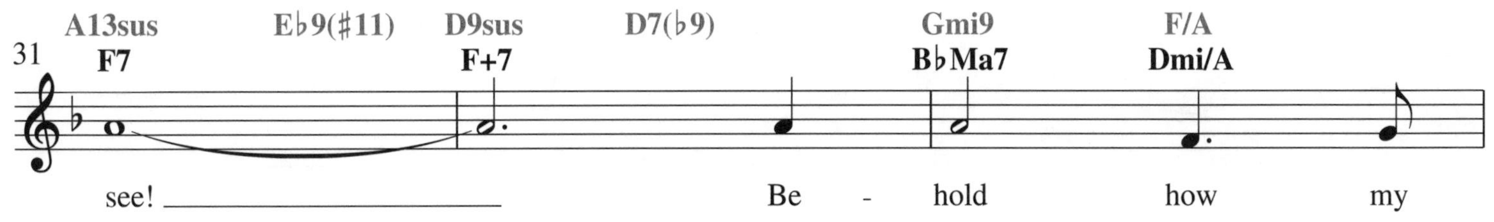
A13sus E♭9(♯11) D9sus D7(♭9) Gmi9 F/A
31 F7 F+7 B♭Ma7 Dmi/A
see! Be - hold how my

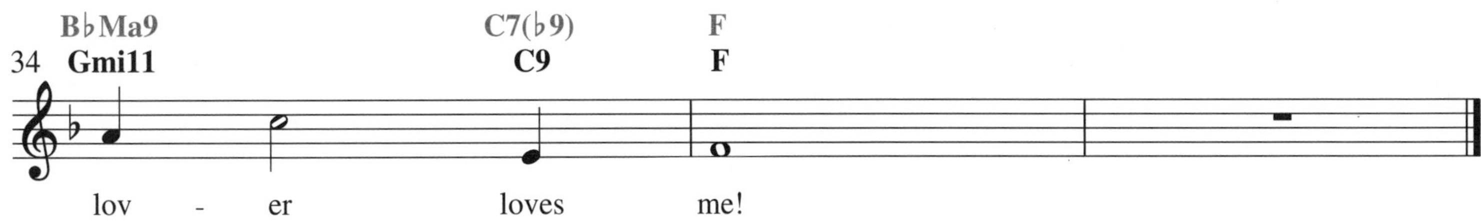
B♭Ma9 C7(♭9) F
34 Gmi11 C9 F
lov - er loves me!

WHAT THE WORLD NEEDS NOW IS LOVE

Lyric by HAL DAVID
Music by BURT BACHARACH
Bmi7 Emi7 Bmi7
What the world needs now is love, sweet
Emi7 CMa9 C6 C D13sus Bmi/D
love. It's the on - ly thing that there's just too
D13 C(add2) Bmi7 Emi7 Bmi7
lit - tle of. What the world needs now is love, sweet
Emi7 CMa9 C6 C
To Coda
love. No, not just for some, but for
F♯mi11 B F9(♯11) B7 Emi9 A13
ev - 'ry - one. Lord, we don't need an - oth - er
Emi9 A13 Dmi11 G9sus G9
moun - tain. There are moun - tains and hill - sides e -

23
CMa7
CMa7
Ami7
C6
Dmi11
Dmi11
nough to climb. There are o - ceans and

26
G9sus
G9
CMa7
CMa7
Emi7
Emi7
riv - ers e - nough to cross, e - nough to last,

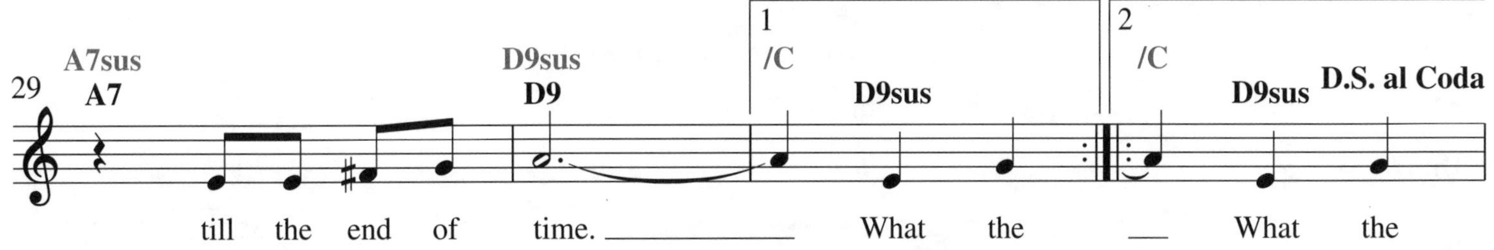
29
A7sus
A7
D9sus
D9
1
/C
D9sus
2
/C
D9sus
D.S. al Coda
till the end of time. What the What the

CODA
33
F♯mi11
B
B7
G/B7
E7
F/B7
CMa9
C6
ev - 'ry - one. No, not just for some,

36
C
Bmi7
Bmi7
Emi7
CMa7
oh, but just for ev -

39
D9sus
D9
G6
G
'ry - one.

WHAT'S NEW?

Words by JOHNNY BURKE
Music by BOB HAGGART

E♭mi9 A♭13(♭9) D♭Ma9 Gmi7(♭5) C7(♯11 ♭9)
19 A♭13 D♭Ma9 C+7(♭9) C7(♯11 ♭9)
Prob - a - bly I'm ___ bor - ing you, but see - ing you ___ is
Fmi9 D7(♭5) D♭13 C+7(♭9) Fmi9
22 Fmi9 C7(♯9) C+7(♭9) Fmi13
grand, and ___ you were sweet to of - fer your hand;
D7(♯11 ♯9) G13sus G13(♭9) C6/9 B13(♭9) B♭mi9 E♭13(♭9)
25 G7(♭9) G7(♭9 ♭5) C6 E♭13
I ___ un - der - stand. A - dieu! Par - don my ask - ing what's
A♭Ma9 Dmi(♭5) G+7(♭9) Cmi9 A7(♭5)
28 A♭Ma7 G7(♯9) G7(♭9) Cmi9(♯7) Ami7(♭5)
new. Of course, you ___ could - n't know;
A♭13 G+7(♭9) CMa9
31 Dmi7(♭5) G+7(♭9) Cmi9(♯7) C6 (Dmi7 G7)
I ___ have - n't changed, I still love you so. ___

WHEN SUNNY GETS BLUE

Lyric by JACK SEGAL
Music by MARVIN FISHER

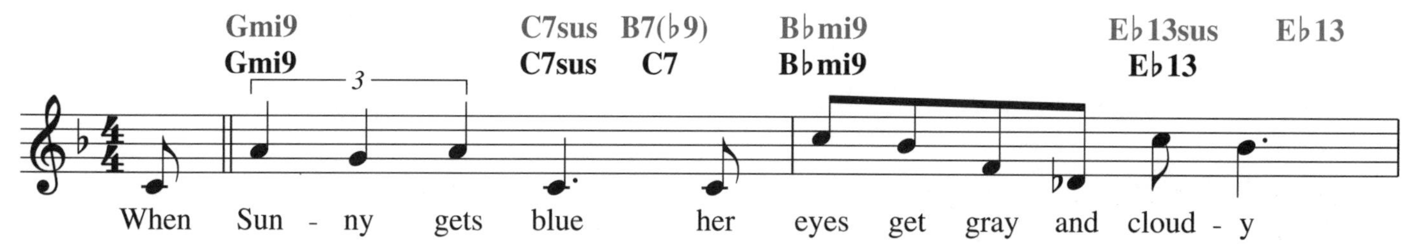

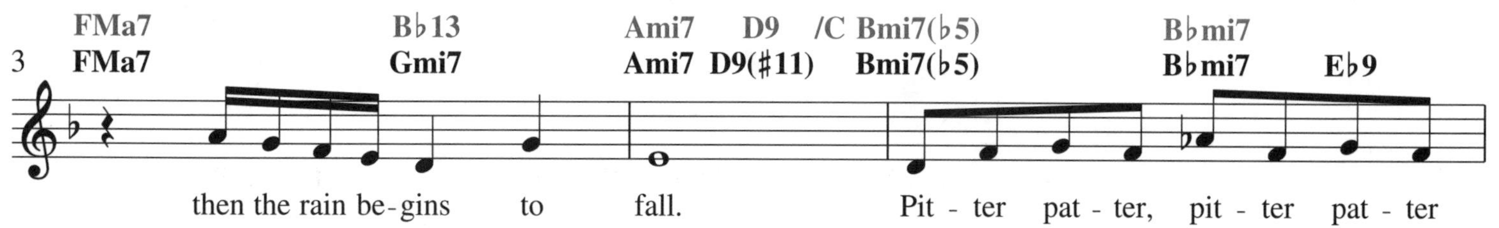

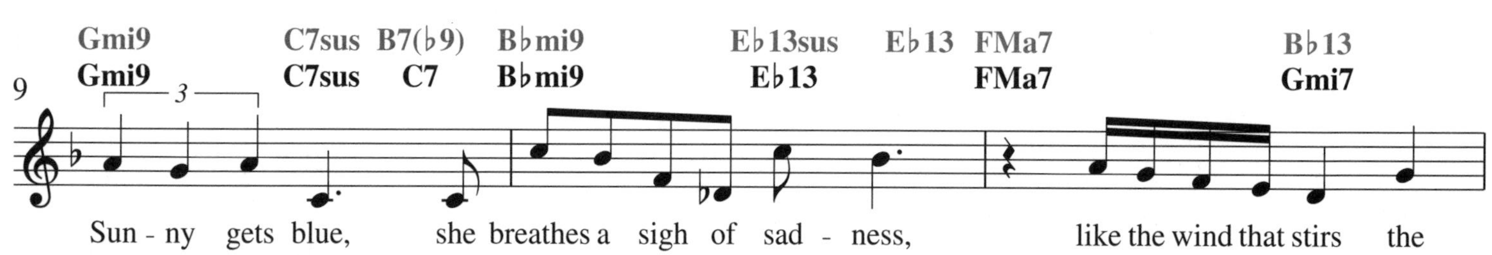

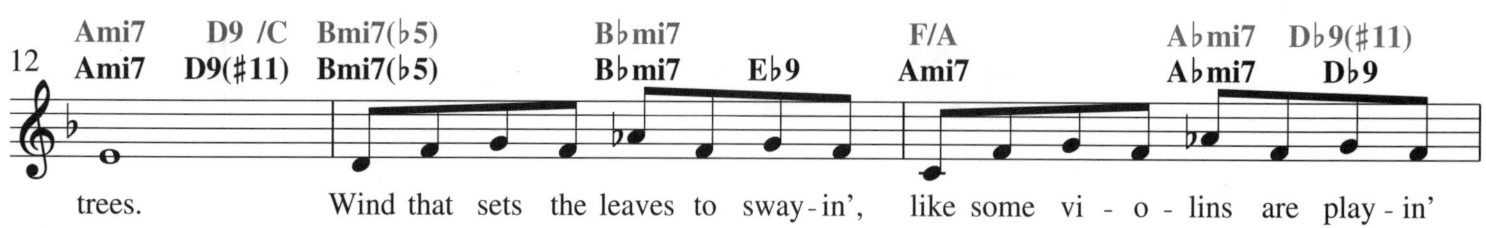

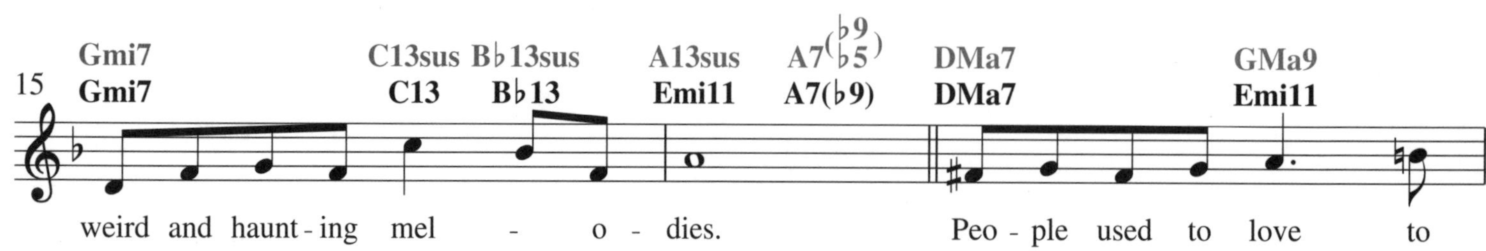

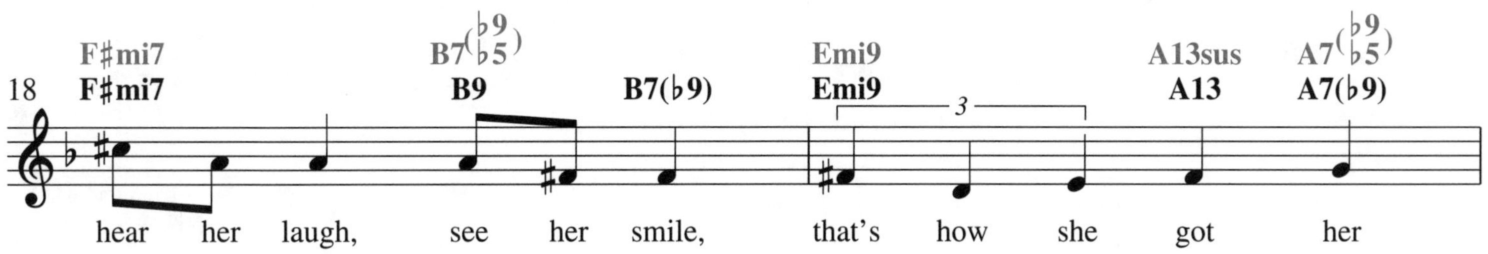
F♯mi7 B7(♭9 ♭5) Emi9 A13sus A7(♭9 ♭5)
18 F♯mi7 B9 B7(♭9) Emi9 A13 A7(♭9)
3
hear her laugh, see her smile, that's how she got her

DMa7 (A♭13sus) G13sus CMa9/G
20 DMa7 Dmi7 G13 G+9 CMa7 Ami7
name. Since that sad af - fair, she's lost her smile, changed her style,

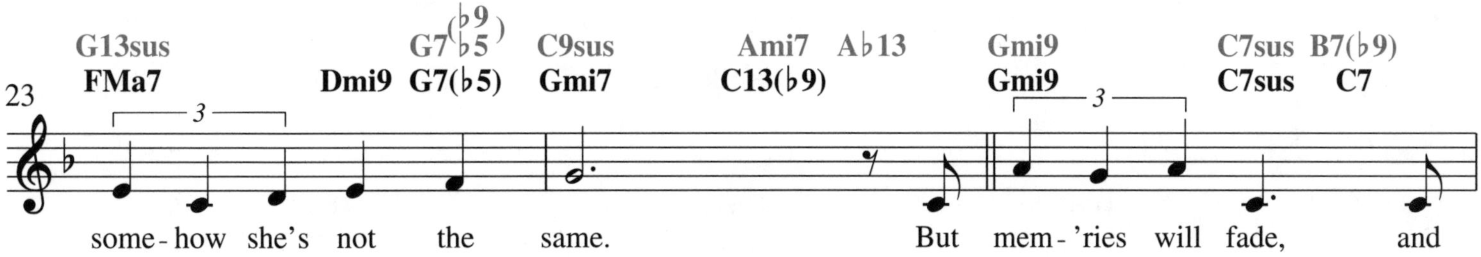
G13sus G7(♭9 ♭5) C9sus Ami7 A♭13 Gmi9 C7sus B7(♭9)
23 FMa7 Dmi9 G7(♭5) Gmi7 C13(♭9) Gmi9 C7sus C7
3 3
some - how she's not the same. But mem - 'ries will fade, and

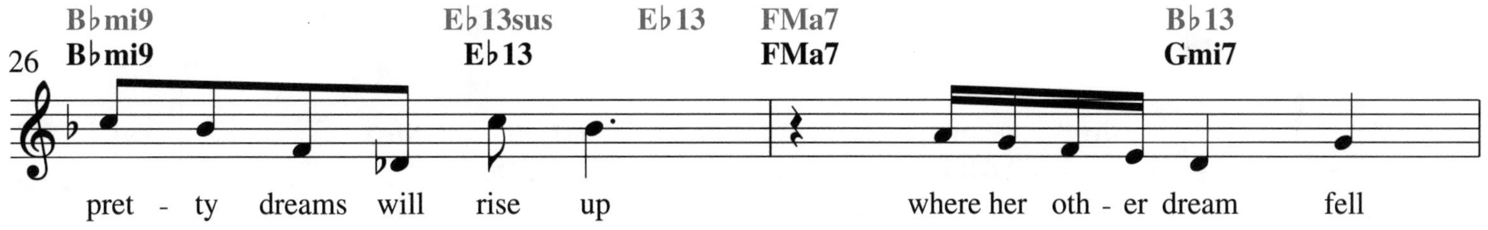
B♭mi9 E♭13sus E♭13 FMa7 B♭13
26 B♭mi9 E♭13 FMa7 Gmi7
pret - ty dreams will rise up where her oth - er dream fell

Ami7 D9 /C Bmi7(♭5) B♭mi7 F/A A♭mi7 D♭9(♯11)
28 Ami7 D9(♯11) Bmi7(♭5) B♭mi7 Ami7 A♭mi7 D♭9
3 3
through. Hur - ry new love, hur - ry here _ to kiss a - way each lone - ly tear, _ and

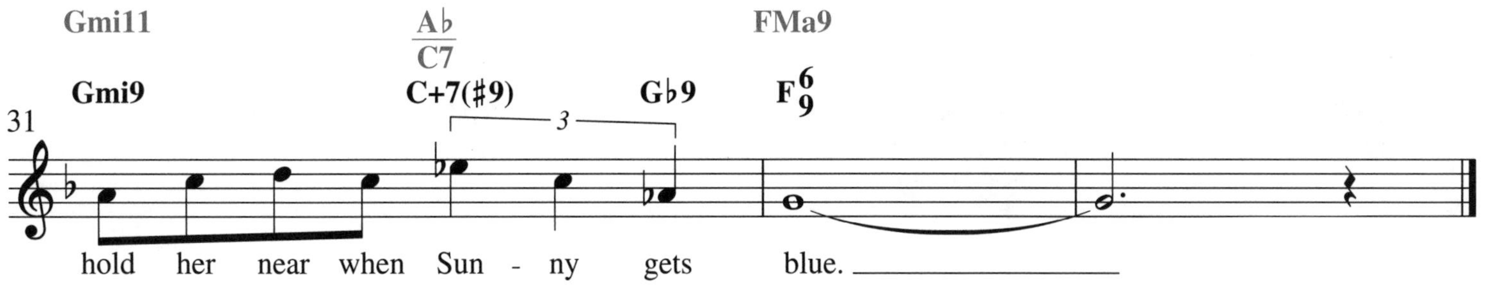
Gmi11 A♭/C7 FMa9
31 Gmi9 C+7(♯9) G♭9 F6/9
3
hold her near when Sun - ny gets blue.

WHEN THE RED, RED ROBIN COMES BOB, BOB BOBBIN' ALONG

from I'LL CRY TOMORROW

Words and Music by
HARRY WOODS

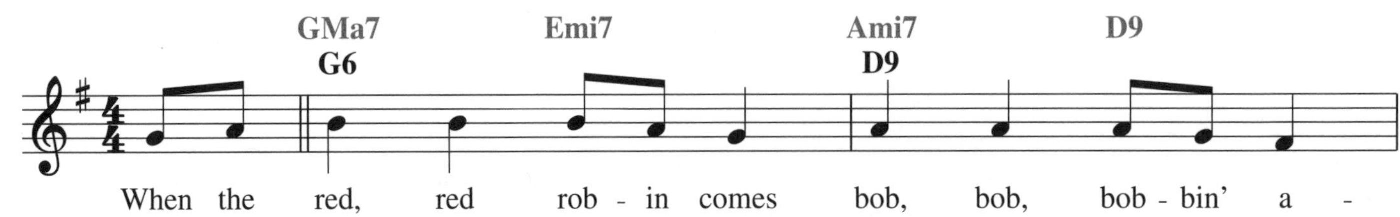
GMa7 Emi7 Ami7 D9
G6 D9
When the red, red rob - in comes bob, bob, bob - bin' a -

G6 Emi7 Ami9 D7sus GMa7 Emi7
3
G6
long, a - long, there'll be no more sob - bin' when

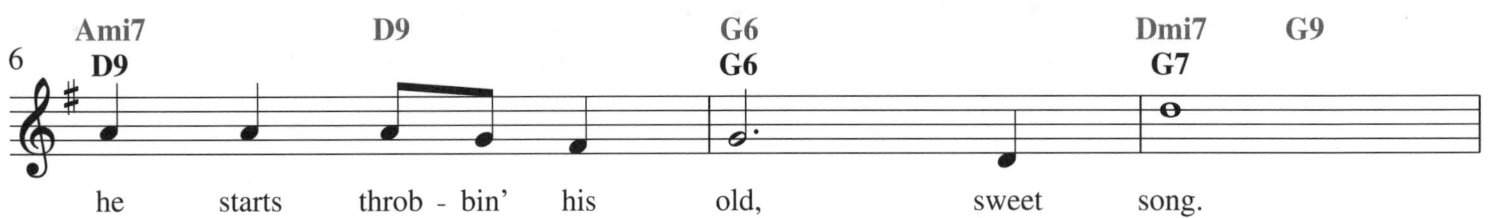
Ami7 D9 G6 Dmi7 G9
6
D9 G6 G7
he starts throb - bin' his old, sweet song.

C /B Ami7 D9sus D7(♭9) GMa7 D/F♯
9
C Ami7 Ami7(♭5) G
Wake up, wake up, you sleep - y head. Get up, get

Emi7 A9sus A9
12
Emi7 A9
up, get out ___ of bed. Cheer up, cheer up, the sun ___ is red.

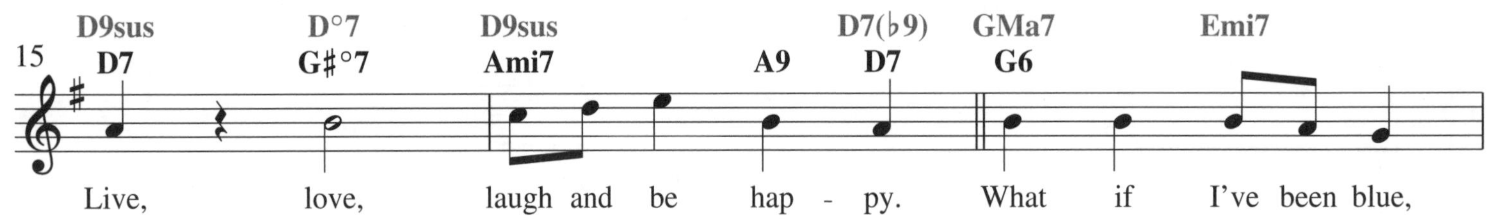
D9sus D°7 D9sus D7(♭9) GMa7 Emi7
15
D7 G♯°7 Ami7 A9 D7 G6
Live, love, laugh and be hap - py. What if I've been blue,

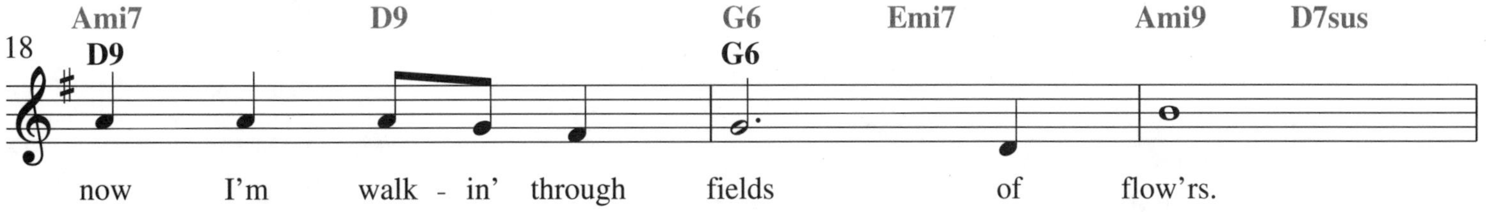
Ami7 D9 G6 Emi7 Ami9 D7sus
18
D9 G6
now I'm walk - in' through fields of flow'rs.

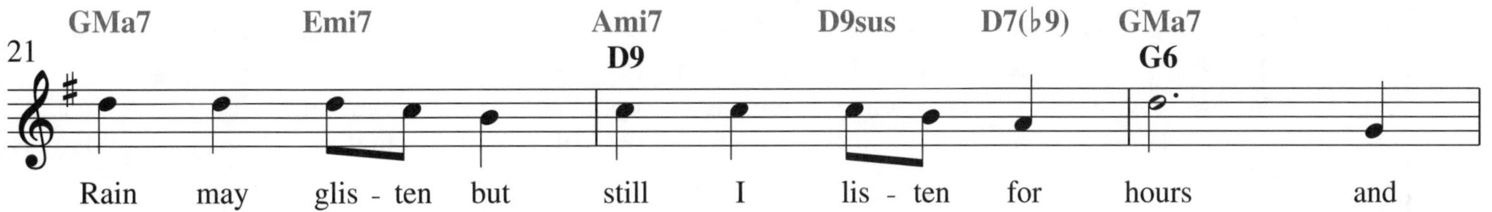
GMa7 Emi7 Ami7 D9sus D7(♭9) GMa7
21
D9 G6
Rain may glis - ten but still I lis - ten for hours and

B7 CMa7 F9sus F13
24
G+7 C Cmi
hours. I'm just a kid a - gain, do - in' what I did a - gain.

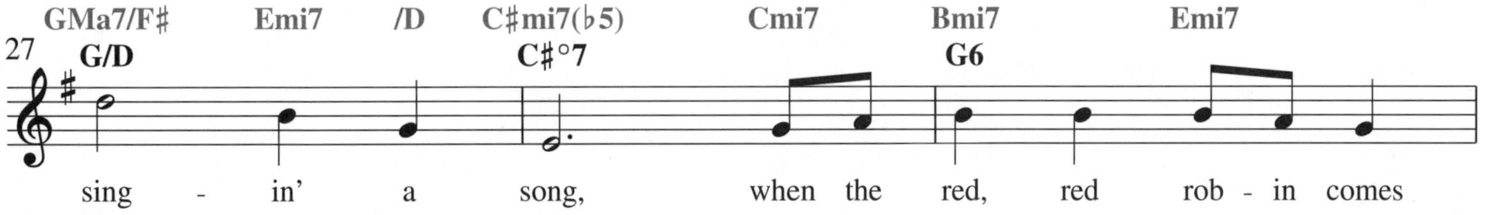
GMa7/F♯ Emi7 /D C♯mi7(♭5) Cmi7 Bmi7 Emi7
27
G/D C♯°7 G6
sing - in' a song, when the red, red rob - in comes

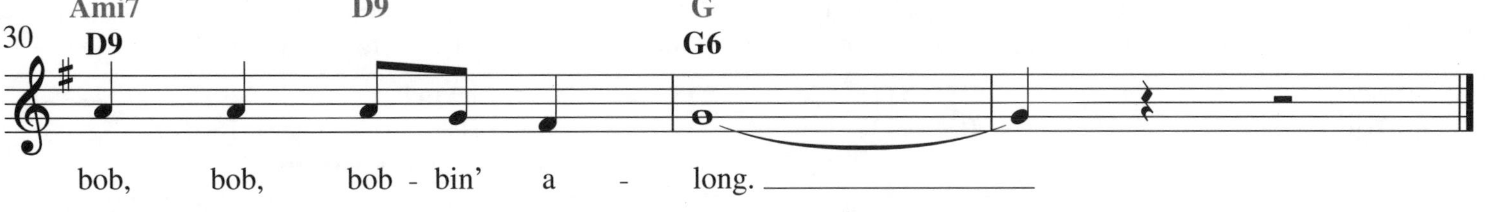
Ami7 D9 G
30
D9 G6
bob, bob, bob - bin' a - long.

WHEN THE WORLD WAS YOUNG

English Lyric by J. MERCER
French Lyric by A. VANNIER
Music by M. PHILIPPE-GERARD

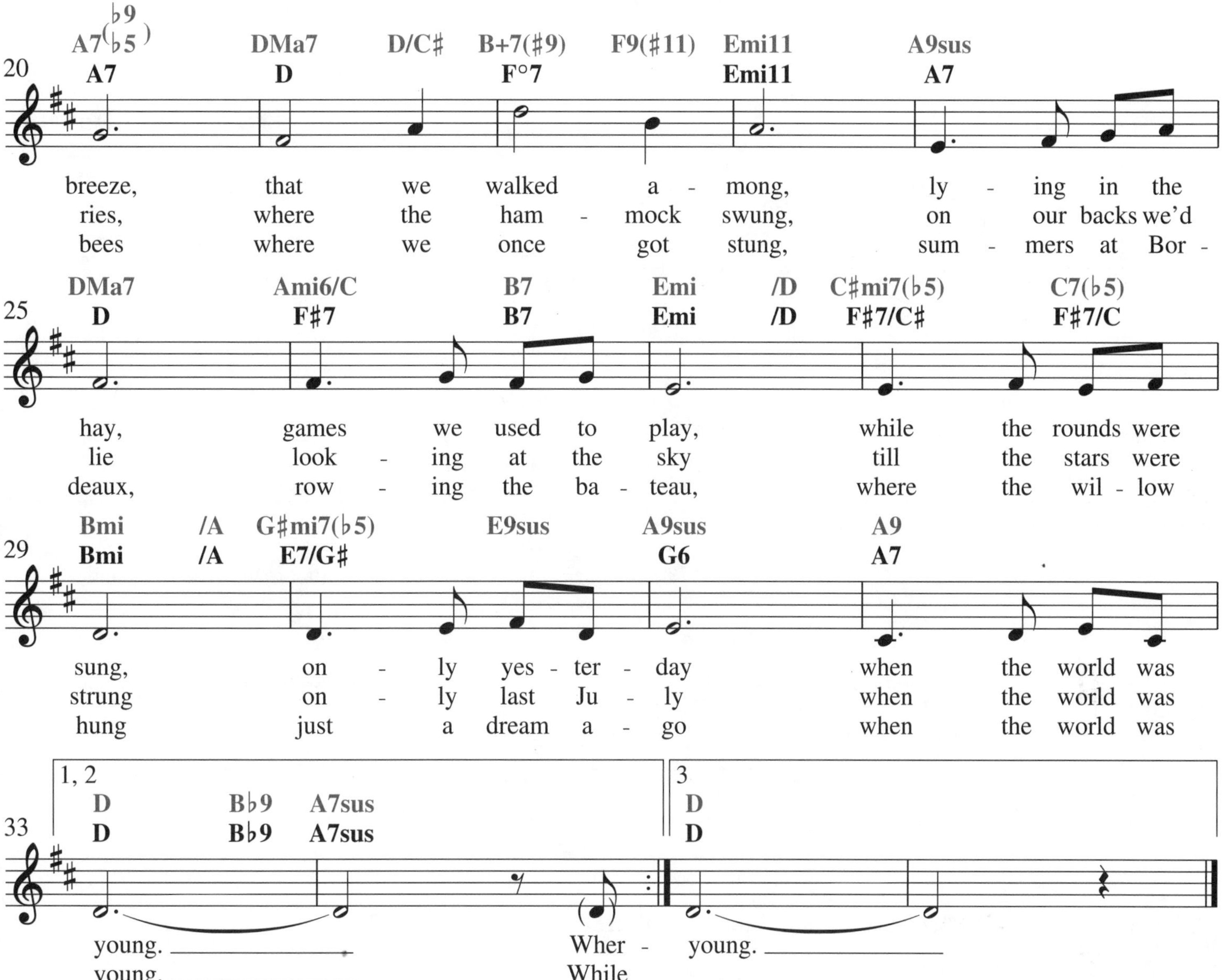
20
A7(♭9 ♭5) DMa7 D/C♯ B+7(♯9) F9(♯11) Emi11 A9sus
A7 D F°7 Emi11 A7
breeze, that we walked a - mong, ly - ing in the
ries, where the ham - mock swung, on our backs we'd
bees where we once got stung, sum - mers at Bor -
25
DMa7 Ami6/C B7 Emi /D C♯mi7(♭5) C7(♭5)
D F♯7 B7 Emi /D F♯7/C♯ F♯7/C
hay, games we used to play, while the rounds were
lie look - ing at the sky till the stars were
deaux, row - ing the ba - teau, where the wil - low
29
Bmi /A G♯mi7(♭5) E9sus A9sus A9
Bmi /A E7/G♯ G6 A7
sung, on - ly yes - ter - day when the world was
strung on - ly last Ju - ly when the world was
hung just a dream a - go when the world was
33
1, 2
D B♭9 A7sus
D B♭9 A7sus
young. Wher -
young. While
3
D
D
young.

WHISTLE WHILE YOU WORK

Words by LARRY MOREY
Music by FRANK CHURCH

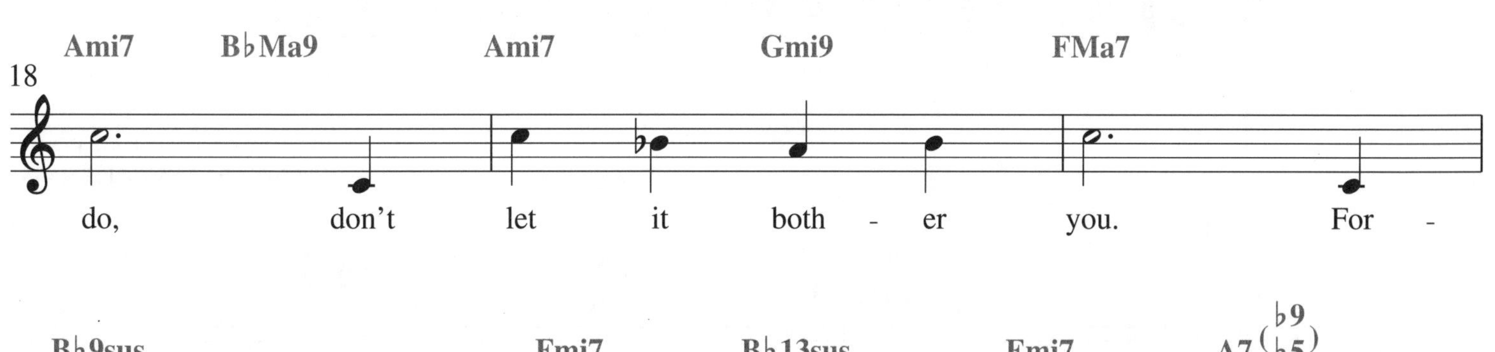
Ami7 B♭Ma9 Ami7 Gmi9 FMa7
18
do, don't let it both - er you. For -

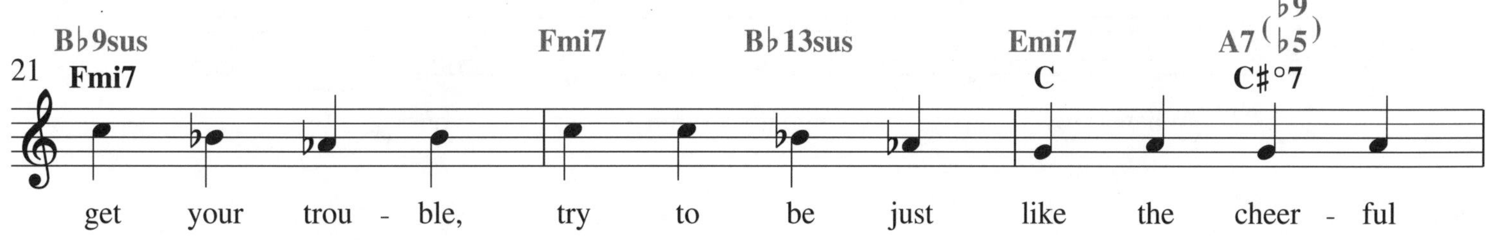
B♭9sus Fmi7 B♭13sus Emi7 A7(♭9 ♭5)
21 Fmi7 C C♯°7
get your trou - ble, try to be just like the cheer - ful

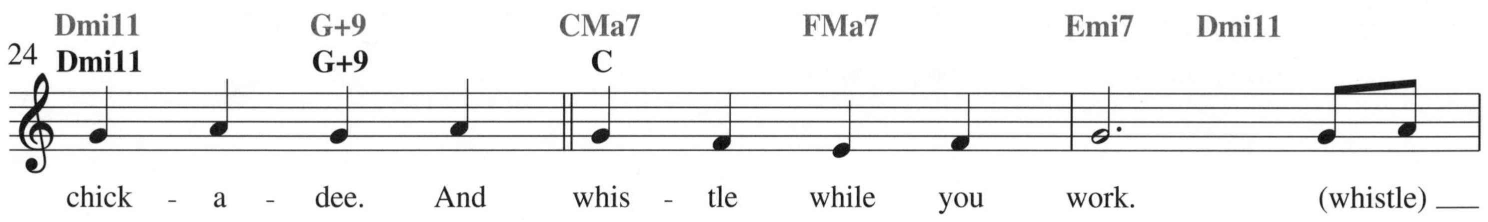
Dmi11 G+9 CMa7 FMa7 Emi7 Dmi11
24 Dmi11 G+9 C
chick - a - dee. And whis - tle while you work. (whistle)

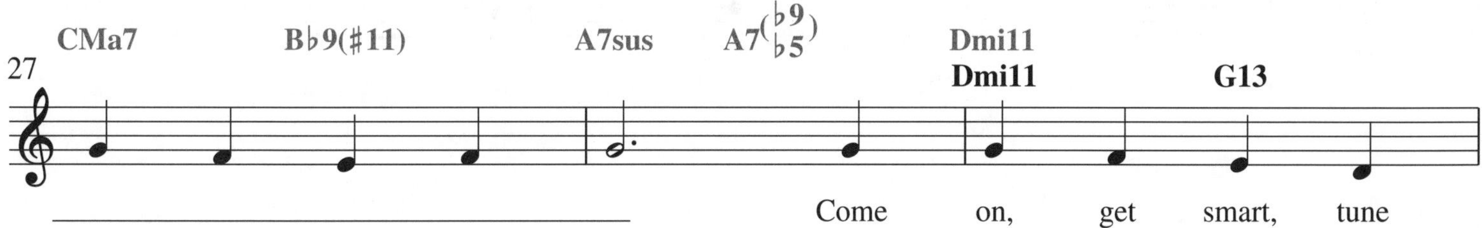
CMa7 B♭9(♯11) A7sus A7(♭9 ♭5) Dmi11
27 Dmi11 G13
Come on, get smart, tune

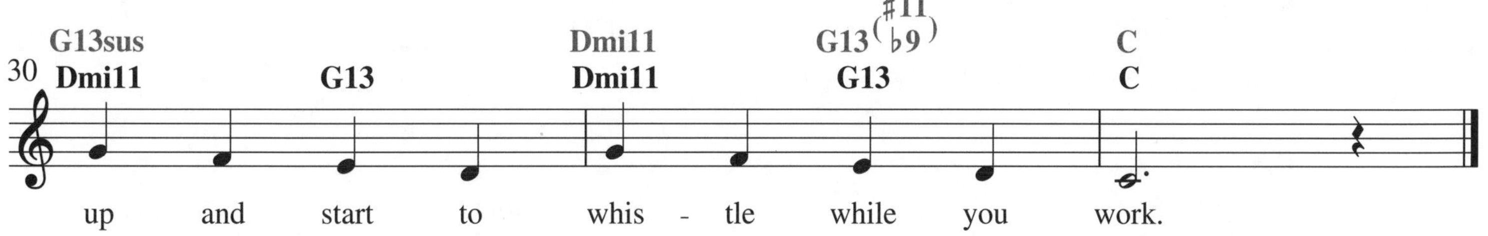
G13sus Dmi11 G13(♯11 ♭9) C
30 Dmi11 G13 Dmi11 G13 C
up and start to whis - tle while you work.

WILL YOU STILL BE MINE

Words by TOM ADAIR
Music by MATT DENNIS

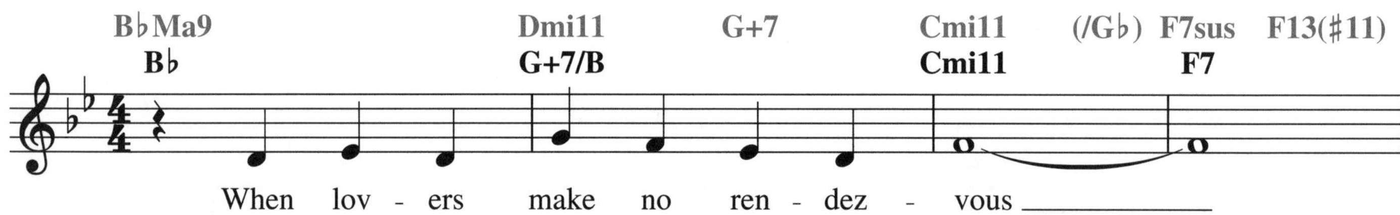
B♭Ma9 Dmi11 G+7 Cmi11 (/G♭) F7sus F13(♯11)
B♭ G+7/B Cmi11 F7
When lov - ers make no ren - dez - vous

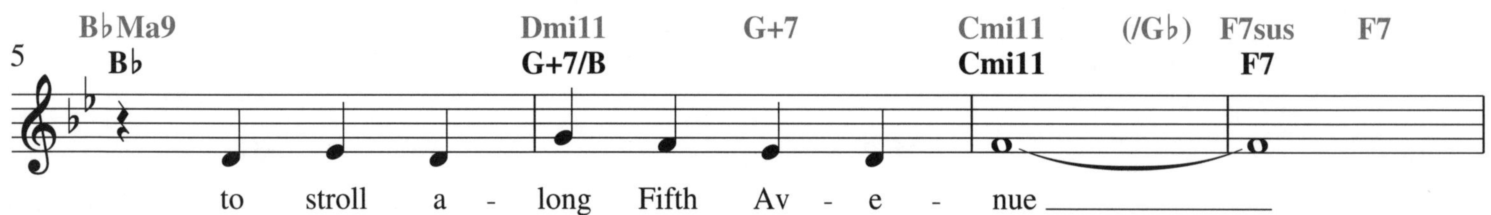
5
B♭Ma9 Dmi11 G+7 Cmi11 (/G♭) F7sus F7
B♭ G+7/B Cmi11 F7
to stroll a - long Fifth Av - e - nue

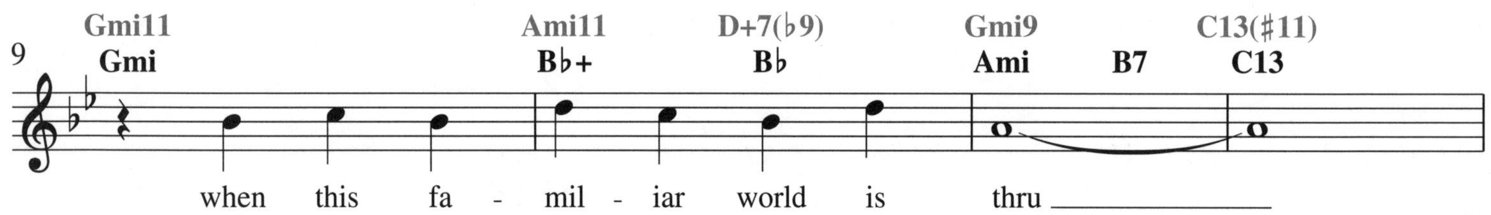
9
Gmi11 Ami11 D+7(♭9) Gmi9 C13(♯11)
Gmi B♭+ B♭ Ami B7 C13
when this fa - mil - iar world is thru

13
G♭9sus G♭9 F13sus F13(♯11)
G♭9 B♭6 B♭mi7 Cmi11 F7
will you still be mine?

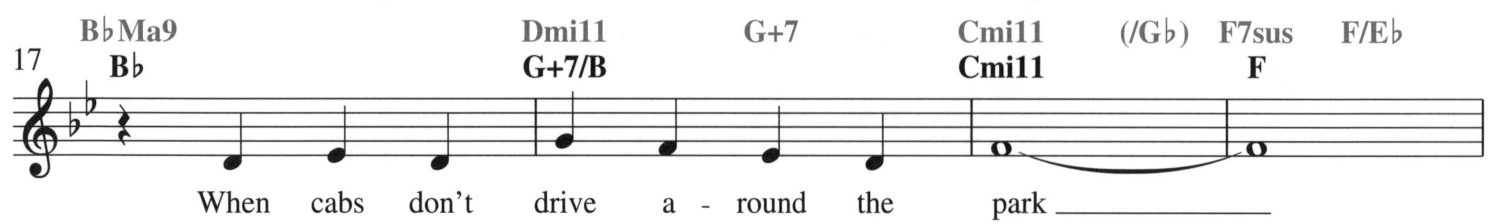
17
B♭Ma9 Dmi11 G+7 Cmi11 (/G♭) F7sus F/E♭
B♭ G+7/B Cmi11 F
When cabs don't drive a - round the park

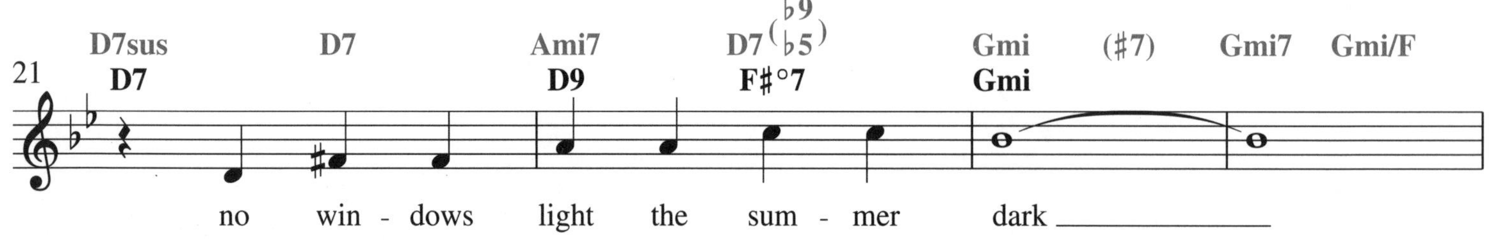
21
D7sus D7 Ami7 D7(♭9 ♭5) Gmi (♯7) Gmi7 Gmi/F
D7 D9 F♯°7 Gmi
no win - dows light the sum - mer dark

25
Emi7(♭5) Ami11 D+7(♭9) G13 G+9 C13sus C13(♭9)
Gmi B♭+ B♭ Ami B7 C13
when love has lost its se - cret spark
29
G♭9sus G♭9 F13sus F13 B♭9sus B♭+9
G♭9 Fmi7 B♭7 B♭+9
will you still be mine? When moon - light
33
E♭Ma9 G♭/A♭ A♭9(♯11) Gmi7
E♭Ma7 E♭ A♭9 (♯11) B♭6
on the Hud - son's not ro - man - cy and spring no
38
C9sus C13 D♭mi11 G♭9 F9sus F7(♭9) B♭Ma9
Gmi7 G♭7 Cmi7 F7 B♭
long - er turns a young man's fan - cy. When glam - our
42
Dmi11 G+7 Cmi11 (/G♭) F7sus F13(♯11) B♭Ma9 Dmi11 G+7
G+7/B Cmi11 F7 B♭ G+7/B
girls have lost their charms when si - rens just mean false a -
47
Cmi11 (/G♭) F7sus Gmi11 Ami11 D+7(♭9) Gmi9
Cmi11 F7 Gmi B♭+ B♭ Ami B7
larms when lov - ers heed no call to arms
52
C13(♯11) C9 F13sus F13(♯11 ♭9) B♭6
C13 Cmi9 B7(♯9) B♭6
will you still be mine?

WITHOUT A SONG

Words by WILLIAM ROSE and EDWARD ELISCU
Music by VINCENT YOUMANS

FMa7
B♭Ma9/F
FMa7
B♭Ma9/F
With - out a song the day would nev - er end; with - out a

FMa7
B♭/F
FMa7
Dmi7
3
FMa7
B♭
F/C
song the road would nev - er bend; when things go wrong a man ain't

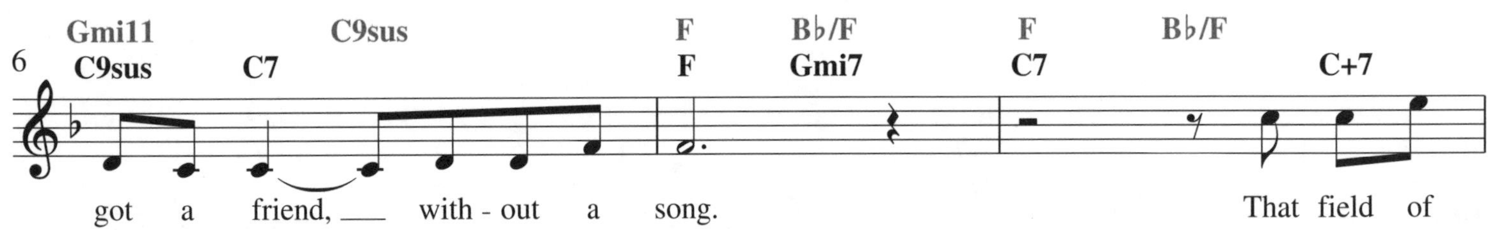
Gmi11
C9sus
F
B♭/F
F
B♭/F
6
C9sus
C7
F
Gmi7
C7
C+7
got a friend, with - out a song. That field of

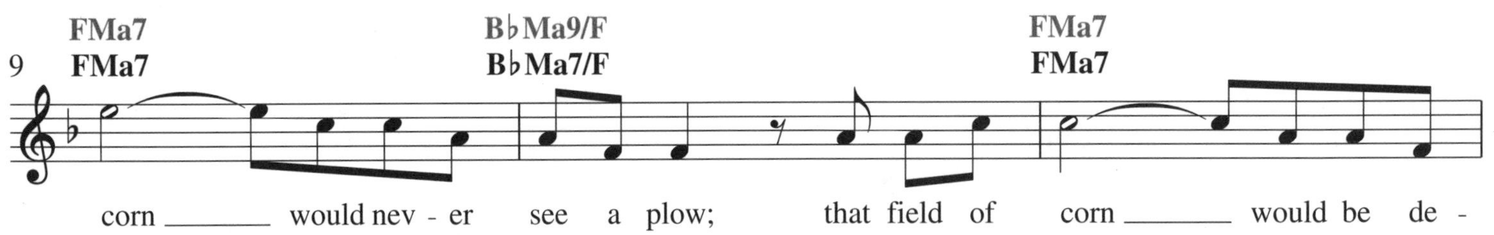
FMa7
B♭Ma9/F
FMa7
9
FMa7
B♭Ma7/F
FMa7
corn would nev - er see a plow; that field of corn would be de -

B♭/F
FMa7
Dmi7
Gmi11
C9sus
12
B♭
F/C
C9sus
C7
sert - ed now; a man is born, but he's no good no - how, with-out a

F
B♭/F
F
F9sus
F7
B♭
15
F
F9
B♭
F7
B♭
song. I got my trou - ble and woe, but

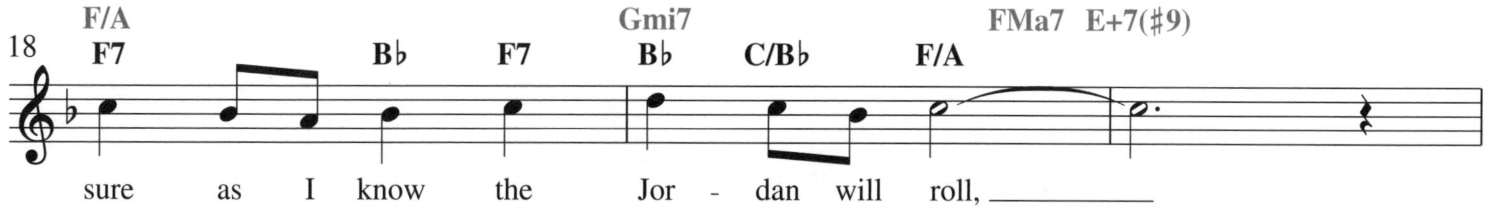
F/A Gmi7 FMa7 E+7(♯9)
18
F7 B♭ F7 B♭ C/B♭ F/A
sure as I know the Jor - dan will roll,

Ami7 /G F13 E+7(♯9) Ami7 A♭13 Gmi7
21
Ami E7/G♯ Ami7 D7 C/G G7 C F/C C9
I'll get a - long as long as a song is strong in my soul.

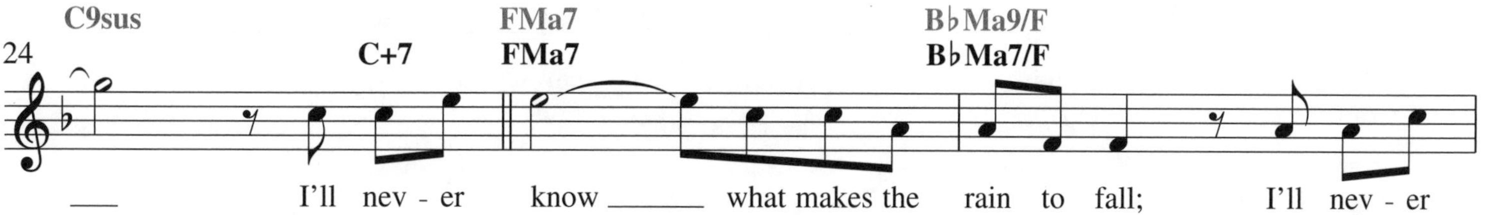
C9sus FMa7 B♭Ma9/F
24
C+7 FMa7 B♭Ma7/F
I'll nev - er know what makes the rain to fall; I'll nev - er

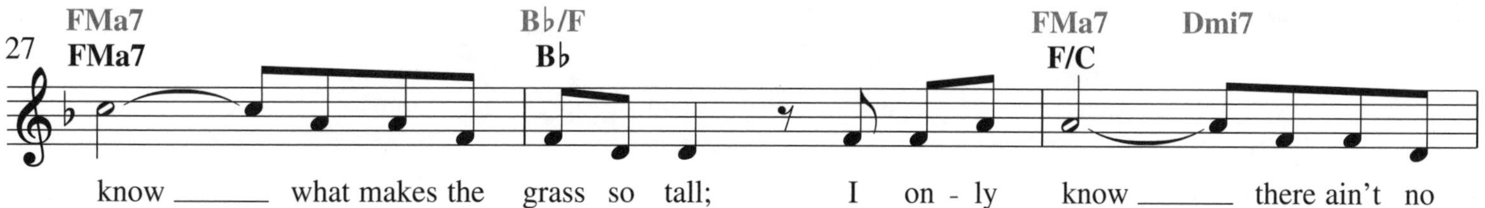
FMa7 B♭/F FMa7 Dmi7
27
FMa7 B♭ F/C
know what makes the grass so tall; I on - ly know there ain't no

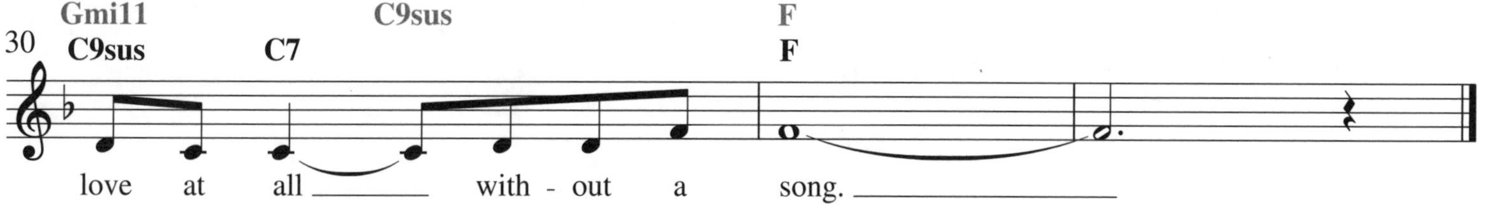
Gmi11 C9sus F
30
C9sus C7 F
love at all with - out a song.

A WONDERFUL DAY LIKE TODAY

from THE ROAR OF THE GREASEPAINT - THE SMELL OF THE CROWD

Words and Music by LESLIE BRICUSSE
and ANTHONY NEWLEY

26
E♭Ma7 A7(♭5) A♭ A♭+
E♭Ma7 A♭ A♭+
will. ___ Let me say fur - ther - more ___ I'd a -

30
A♭6 A♭13(♯11) Gmi7 C9sus
A♭6 B♭9 Gmi7 G♭+
dore ev - 'ry - bod - y to come and dine, the pleas - ure's mine, and

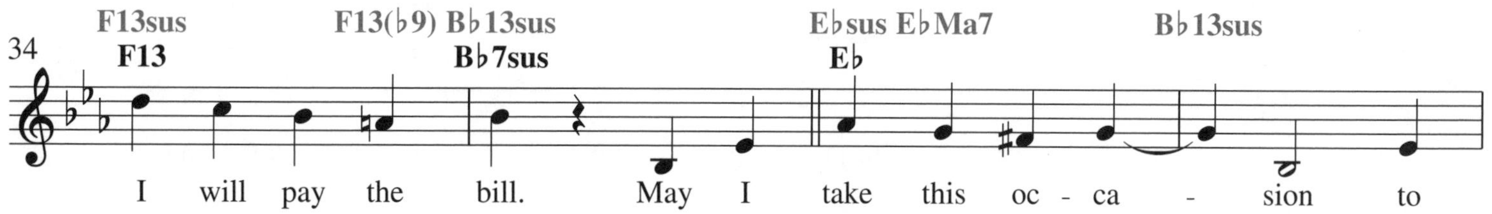
34
F13sus F13(♭9) B♭13sus E♭sus E♭Ma7 B♭13sus
F13 B♭7sus E♭
I will pay the bill. May I take this oc - ca - sion to

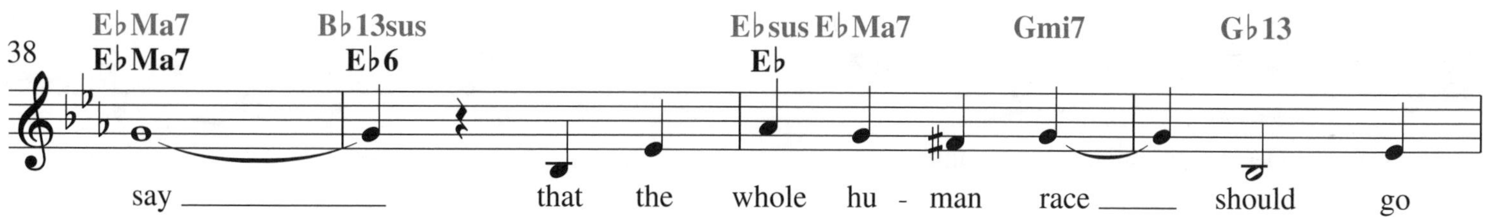
38
E♭Ma7 B♭13sus E♭sus E♭Ma7 Gmi7 G♭13
E♭Ma7 E♭6 E♭
say ___ that the whole hu - man race ___ should go

42
Fmi9 B♭7sus Fmi9 B♭7sus B♭13/A♭
Fmi9 B♭7 F9 B♭13
down on its knees, ___ show that we're grate - ful for

46
Gmi11 C7(♭9 ♭5) C+7 Fmi7 G9sus G7(♭9) Cmi7 G♭13
Gmi11 C7 C+7 A♭6 G7 Cmi7
morn - ings like these, ___ for the world's in a won - der - ful way, ___

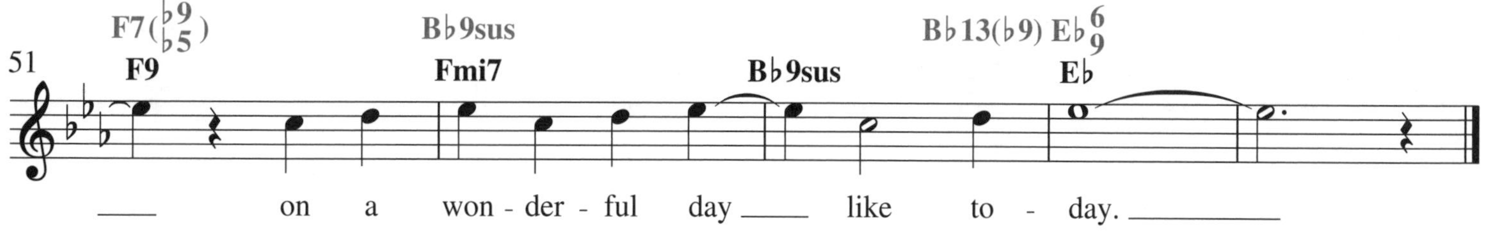
51
F7(♭9 ♭5) B♭9sus B♭13(♭9) E♭6/9
F9 Fmi7 B♭9sus E♭
___ on a won - der - ful day ___ like to - day. ___

THE WORLD IS WAITING FOR THE SUNRISE

Words by EUGENE LOCKHART
Music by ERNEST SEITZ

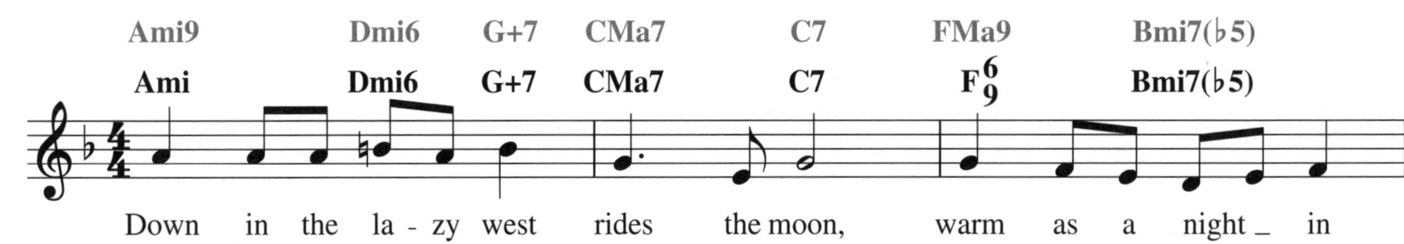
Ami9 Dmi6 G+7 CMa7 C7 FMa9 Bmi7(♭5)
Ami Dmi6 G+7 CMa7 C7 F6/9 Bmi7(♭5)
Down in the la - zy west rides the moon, warm as a night _ in

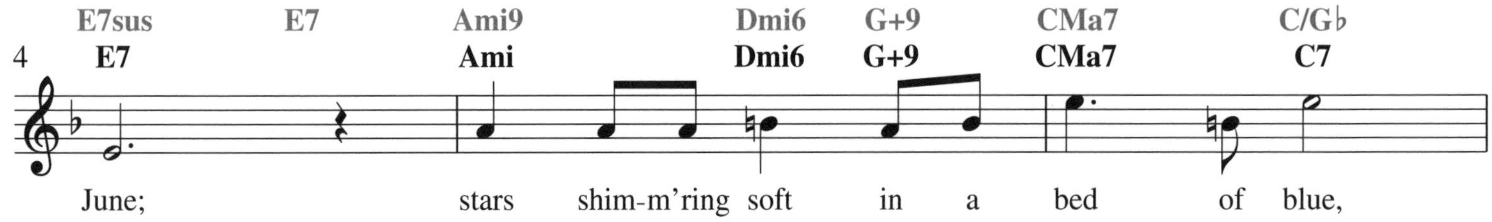
4
E7sus E7 Ami9 Dmi6 G+9 CMa7 C/G♭
E7 Ami Dmi6 G+9 CMa7 C7
June; stars shim-m'ring soft in a bed of blue,

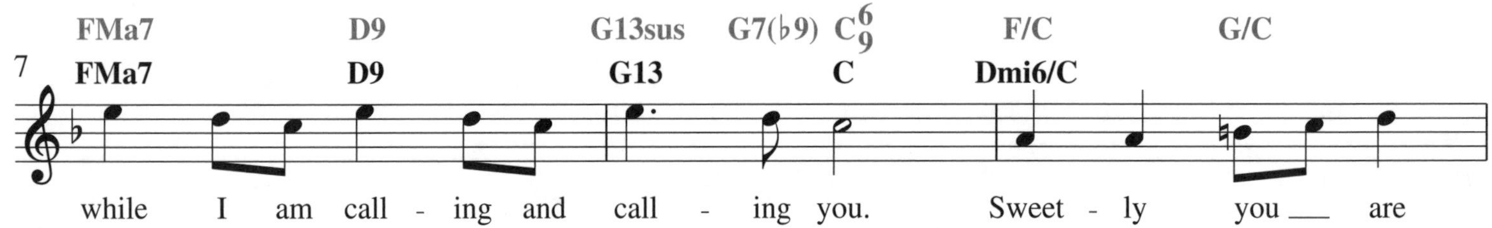
7
FMa7 D9 G13sus G7(♭9) C6/9 F/C G/C
FMa7 D9 G13 C Dmi6/C
while I am call - ing and call - ing you. Sweet - ly you ___ are

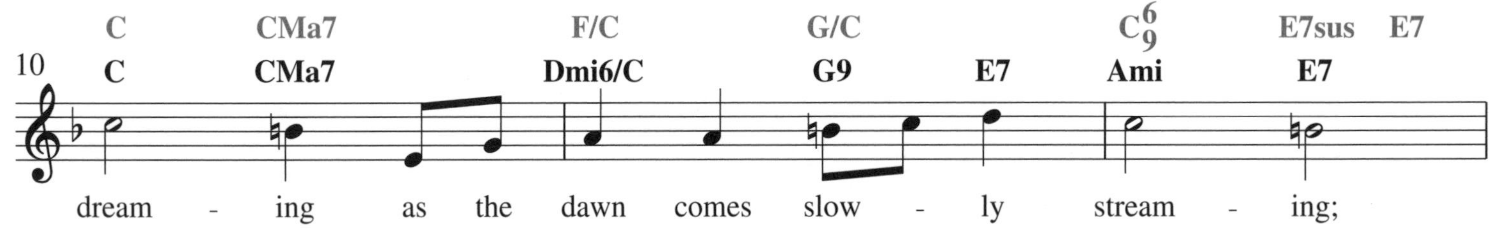
10
C CMa7 F/C G/C C6/9 E7sus E7
C CMa7 Dmi6/C G9 E7 Ami E7
dream - ing as the dawn comes slow - ly stream - ing;

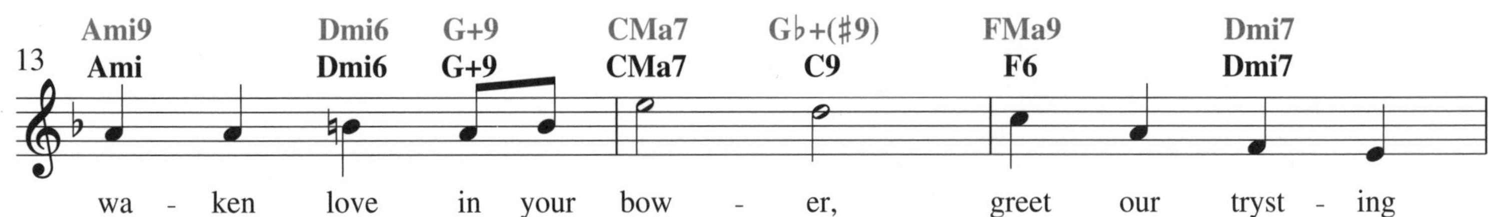
13
Ami9 Dmi6 G+9 CMa7 G♭+(♯9) FMa9 Dmi7
Ami Dmi6 G+9 CMa7 C9 F6 Dmi7
wa - ken love in your bow - er, greet our tryst - ing

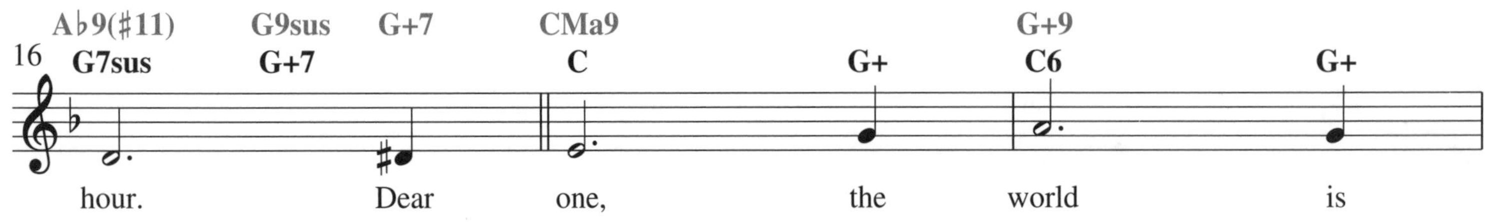
16
A♭9(♯11) G9sus G+7 CMa9 G+9
G7sus G+7 C G+ C6 G+
hour. Dear one, the world is

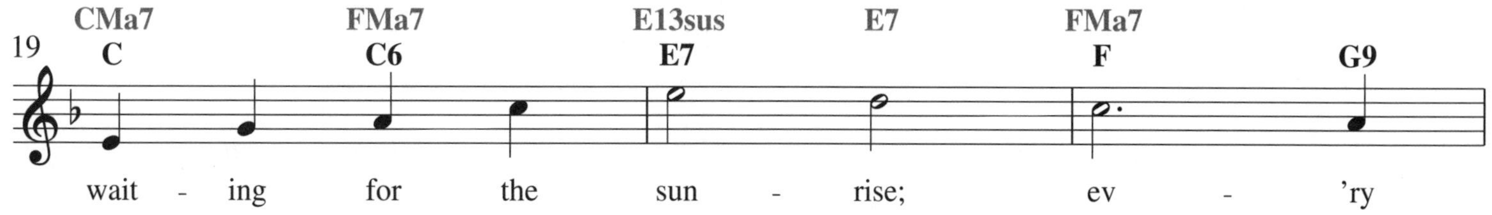
CMa7
FMa7
E13sus
E7
FMa7
19
C
C6
E7
F
G9
wait - ing for the sun - rise; ev - 'ry

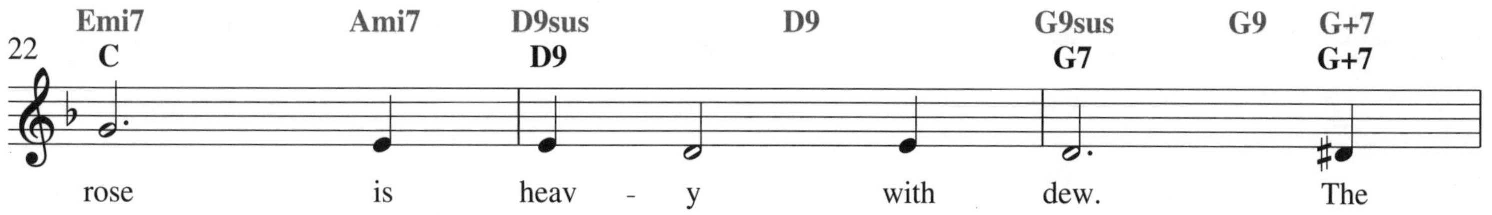
Emi7
Ami7
D9sus
D9
G9sus
G9
G+7
22
C
D9
G7
G+7
rose is heav - y with dew. The

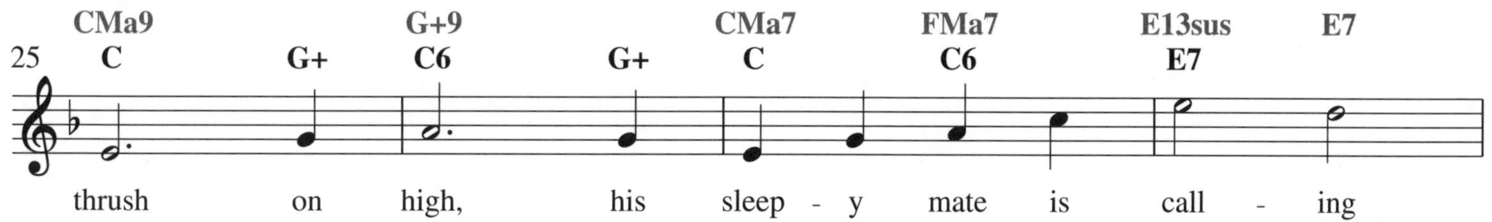
CMa9
G+9
CMa7
FMa7
E13sus
E7
25
C
G+
C6
G+
C
C6
E7
thrush on high, his sleep - y mate is call - ing

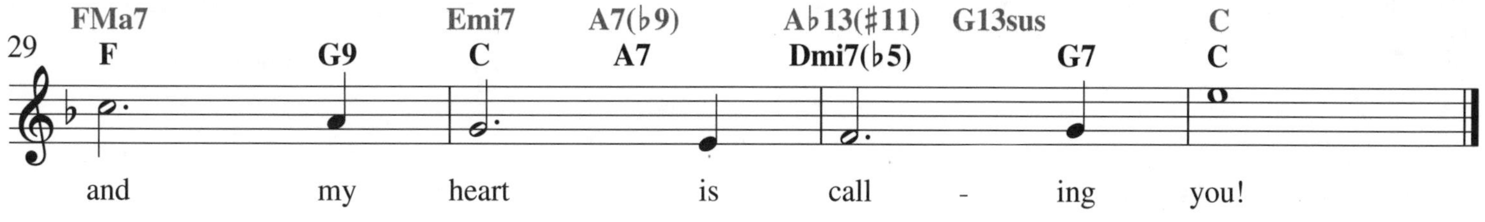
FMa7
Emi7
A7(♭9)
A♭13(♯11)
G13sus
C
29
F
G9
C
A7
Dmi7(♭5)
G7
C
and my heart is call - ing you!

WOULDN'T IT BE LOVERLY

from MY FAIR LADY

Words by ALAN JAY LERNER
Music by FREDERICK LOEWE

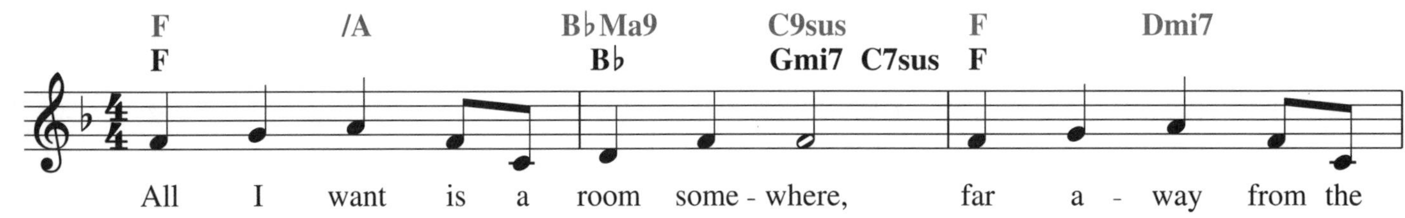
F F /A B♭Ma9 B♭ C9sus Gmi7 C7sus F F Dmi7
All I want is a room some - where, far a - way from the

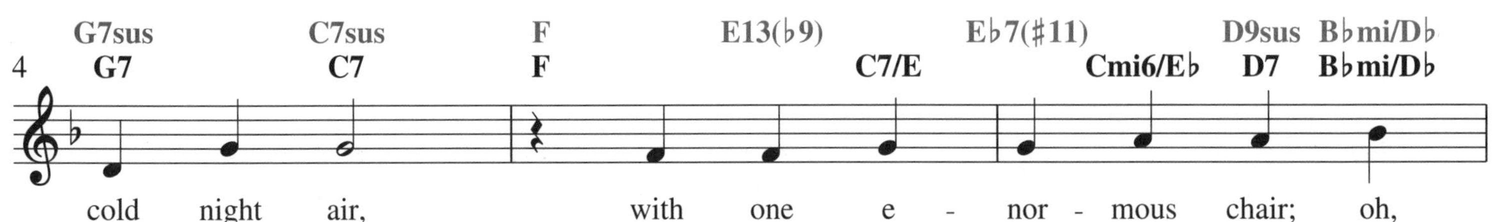
4
G7sus G7 C7sus C7 F F E13(♭9) C7/E E♭7(♯11) Cmi6/E♭ D9sus D7 B♭mi/D♭ B♭mi/D♭
cold night air, with one e - nor - mous chair; oh,

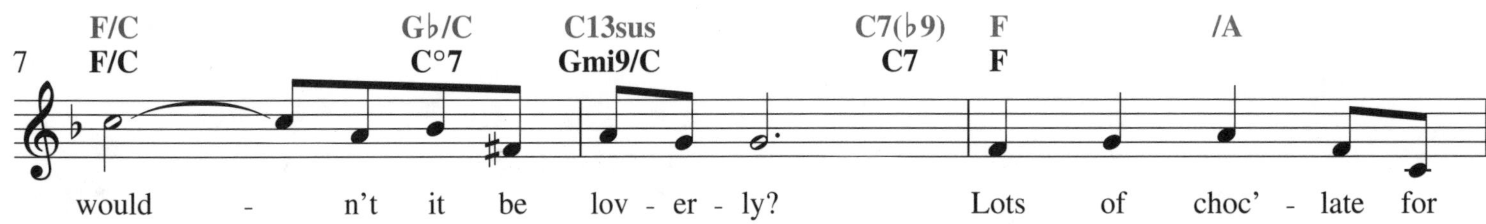
7
F/C F/C G♭/C C°7 C13sus Gmi9/C C7(♭9) C7 F F /A
would - n't it be lov - er - ly? Lots of choc' - late for

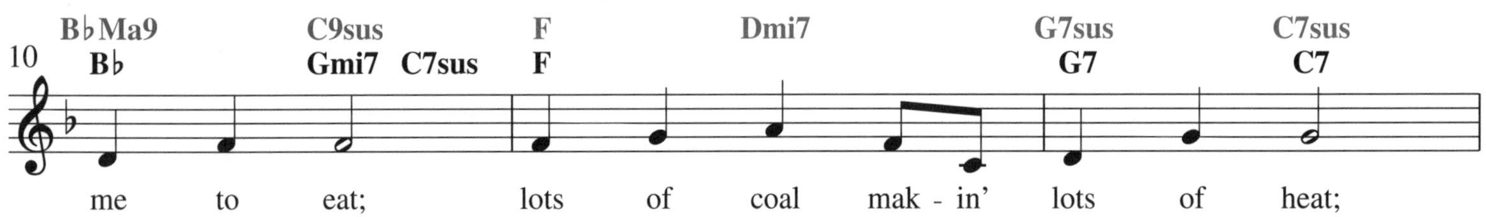
10
B♭Ma9 B♭ C9sus Gmi7 C7sus F F Dmi7 G7sus G7 C7sus C7
me to eat; lots of coal mak - in' lots of heat;

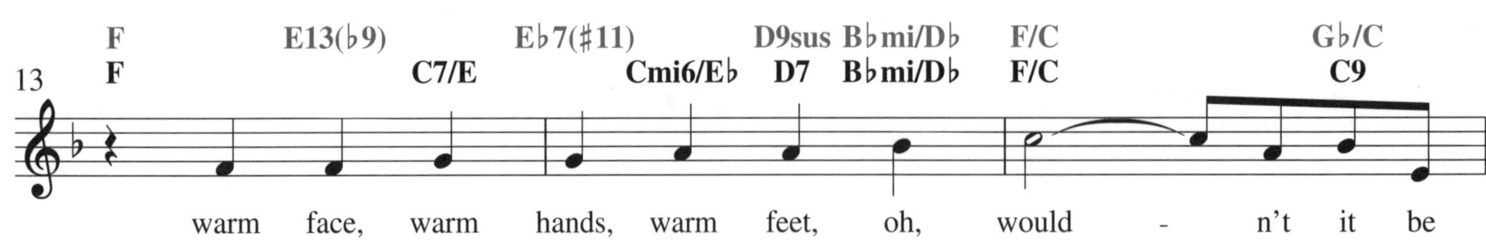
13
F F E13(♭9) C7/E E♭7(♯11) Cmi6/E♭ D9sus D7 B♭mi/D♭ B♭mi/D♭ F/C F/C G♭/C C9
warm face, warm hands, warm feet, oh, would - n't it be

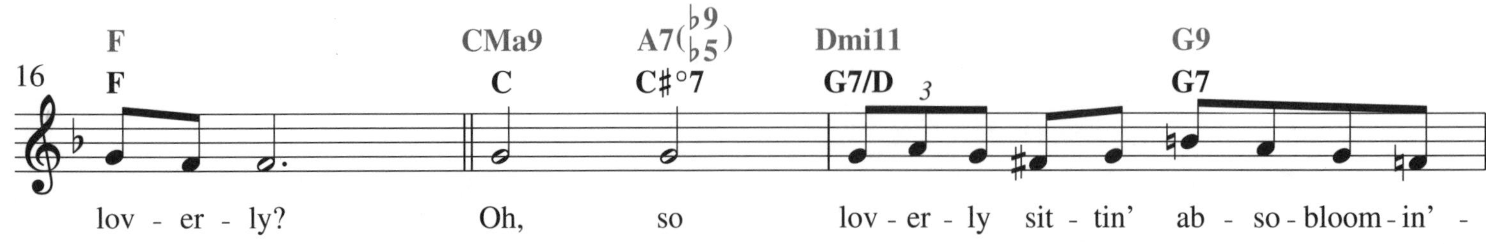
16
F F CMa9 C A7(♭9 ♭5) C♯°7 Dmi11 G7/D 3 G9 G7
lov - er - ly? Oh, so lov - er - ly sit - tin' ab - so - bloom - in' -

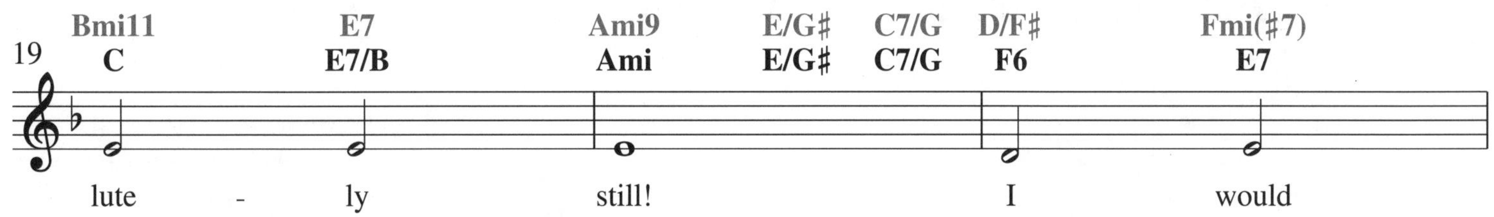
Bmi11 E7 Ami9 E/G♯ C7/G D/F♯ Fmi(♯7)
19
C E7/B Ami E/G♯ C7/G F6 E7
lute - ly still! I would

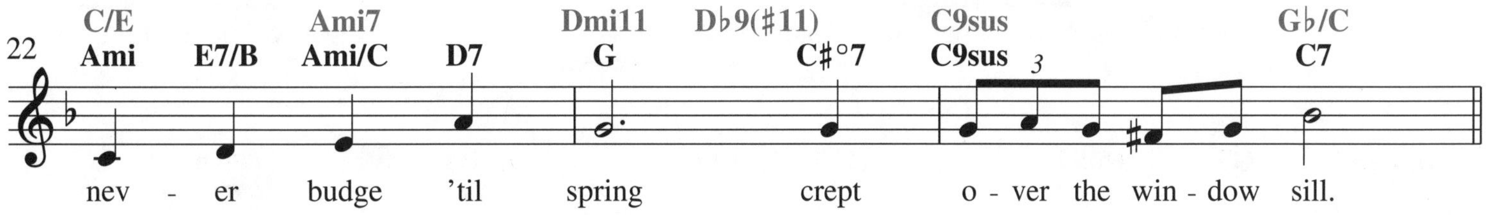
C/E Ami7 Dmi11 D♭9(♯11) C9sus G♭/C
22
Ami E7/B Ami/C D7 G C♯°7 C9sus C7
3
nev - er budge 'til spring crept o - ver the win - dow sill.

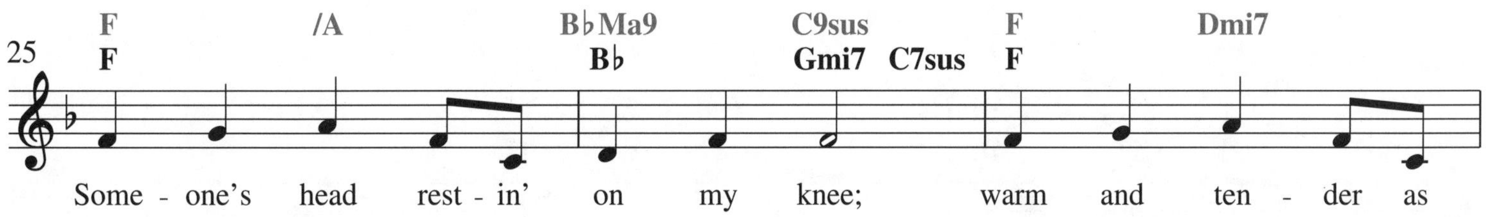
F /A B♭Ma9 C9sus F Dmi7
25
F B♭ Gmi7 C7sus F
Some - one's head rest - in' on my knee; warm and ten - der as

G7sus C7sus F E13(♭9) E♭7(♯11) D9sus B♭mi/D♭
28
G7 C7 F C7/E Cmi6/E♭ D7 B♭mi/D♭
he can be; who takes good care of me, oh,

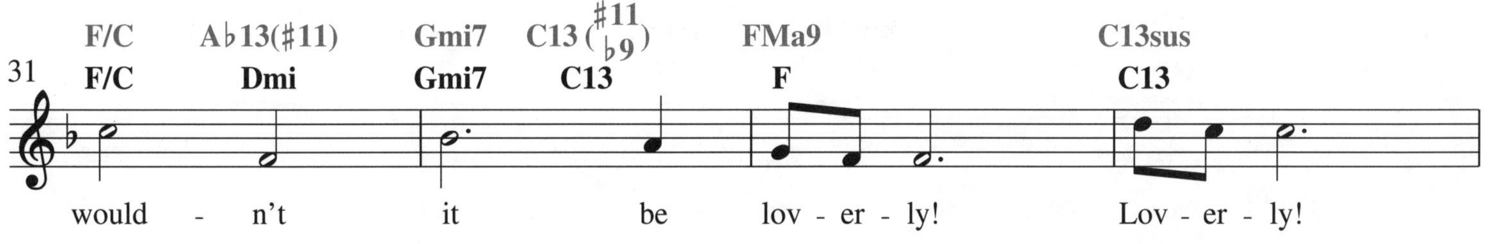
F/C A♭13(♯11) Gmi7 C13(♯11 ♭9) FMa9 C13sus
31
F/C Dmi Gmi7 C13 F C13
would - n't it be lov - er - ly! Lov - er - ly!

FMa9 E♭13sus E♭13 F
35
F B♭Ma9 F
Lov - er - ly! Lov - er - ly! Lov - er - ly!

YOU OUGHTA BE IN PICTURES

Words and Music by DANA SUESSE
and EDWARD HEYMAN

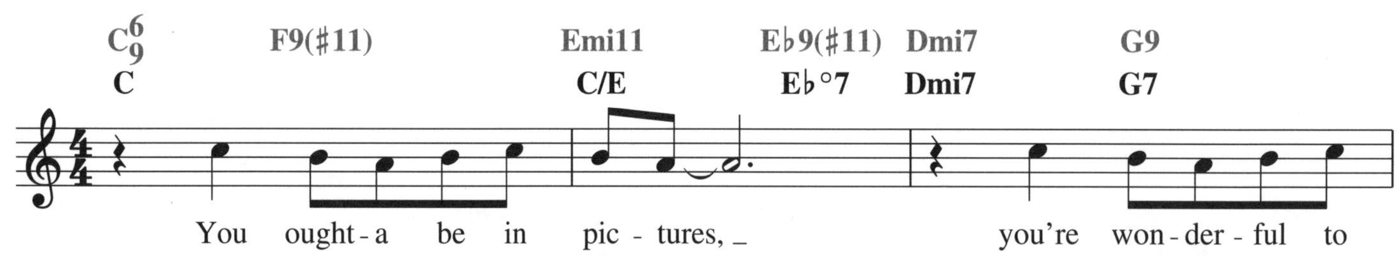

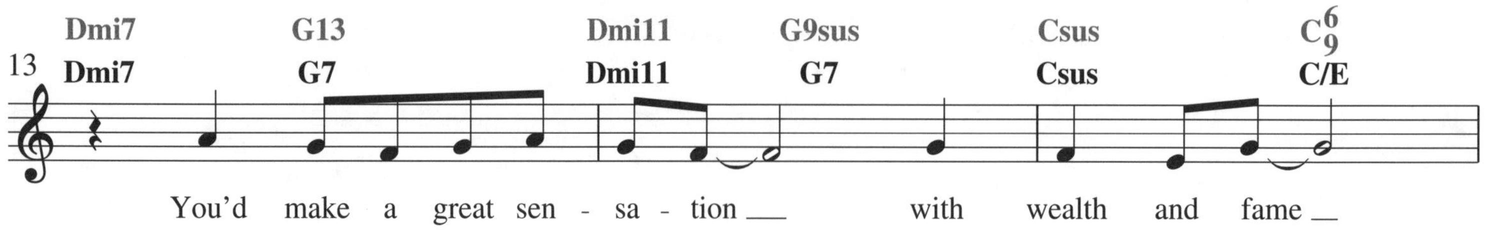

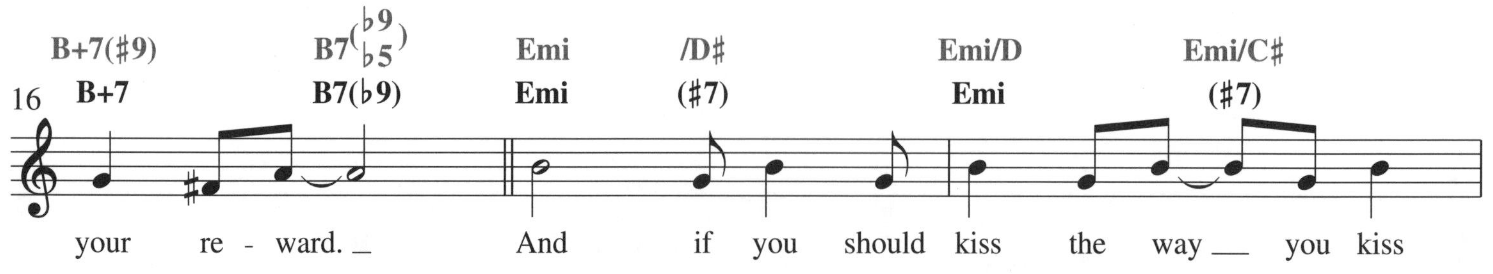

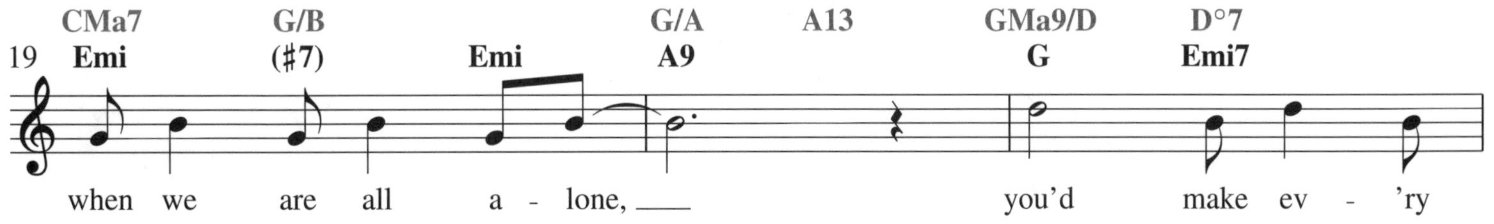
CMa7 G/B G/A A13 GMa9/D D°7
19 Emi (♯7) Emi A9 G Emi7
when we are all a - lone, you'd make ev - 'ry

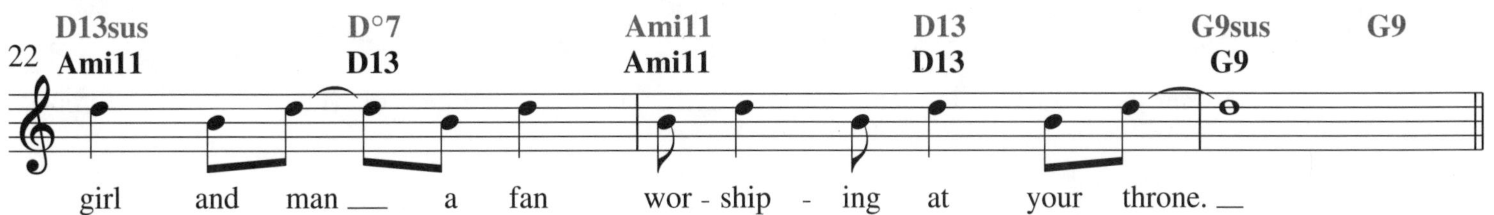
D13sus D°7 Ami11 D13 G9sus G9
22 Ami11 D13 Ami11 D13 G9
girl and man a fan wor - ship - ing at your throne.

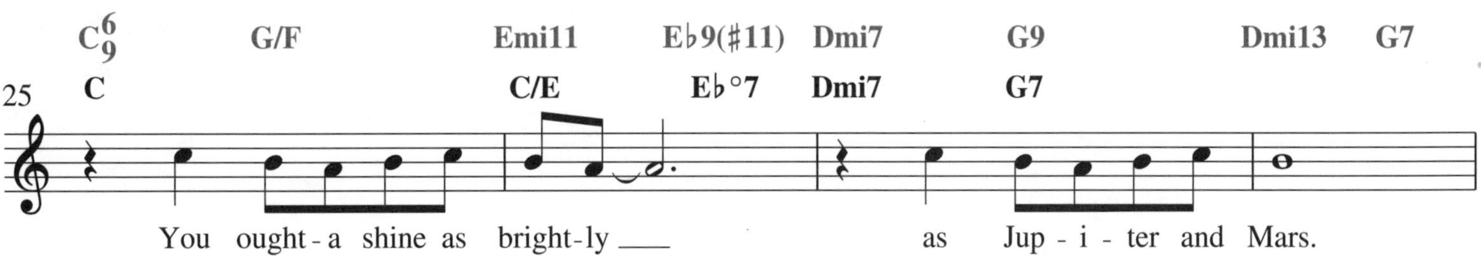
C6/9 G/F Emi11 E♭9(♯11) Dmi7 G9 Dmi13 G7
25 C C/E E♭°7 Dmi7 G7
You ought - a shine as bright - ly as Jup - i - ter and Mars.

Dmi7 G13 Dmi11 G9sus A♭13(♯11) G13(♯11 ♭9) C6/9
29 Dmi7 G7 Dmi11 G9sus G9sus G13 C
You ought - a be in pic - tures, my star of stars!

YOUNG AT HEART

from YOUNG AT HEART

Words by CAROLYN LEIGH
Music by JOHNNY RICHARDS

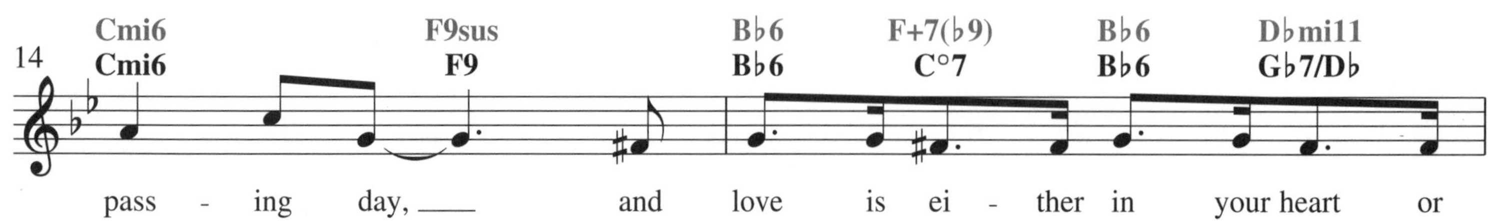

16
Cmi7 F7sus Bb BbMa9
Cmi7 F7 Bb
on the way. Don't you know that it's worth ev - 'ry
18
Bb Dmi7 G+ Cmi7 Cmi (#7) F9sus F9
BbMa7 Db°7 Cmi7
treas-ure on earth to be young at heart. For as
21
Cmi7 Cmi7 F7 F9sus F+9
F7 Cmi7 F7 F9 F+9
rich as you are it's much bet - ter by far to be
23
BbMa7 BbMa7 Eb13 Dmi7(b5) G13
BbMa7 Dmi7(b5) G7
young at heart. And if you should sur - vive to a
26
Dmi7(b5) G13sus G+ C9sus C13
Dmi7(b5) G7 G+ C9
hun - dred and five look at all you'll de - rive out of
28
C13 Ab9sus Bb/F Gmi7 Cmi7 F7
EbMa7 Ebmi Bb/F F7 Cmi7 F7
be - ing a - live. And here is the best part, you have a head start
31
Bb /D EbMa7 E°7 F9sus Bb
Bb /D Eb6 E°7 F11 F9 Bb
if you are a - mong the ver - y young at heart.

YOU'RE NOBODY 'TIL SOMEBODY LOVES YOU

Words and Music by RUSS MORGAN,
LARRY STOCK and JAMES CAVANAUGH

F♯mi7 B7 E7 Bmi7(♭5) B♭13(♯11)
18 B7 E7(♭9) E7 Bmi7 E7 B7 E7
same, you'll nev - er change it as
Ami7 Bmi7(♭5) E7 Ami7 E7/B
21 Ami7 E7 Ami7 E7/B
sure as the stars shine a - bove.
Ami/C C♯°7 D/C
24 Ami/C C C♯°7
You're no - bod - y 'til some - bod - y loves
Bmi7 G/F Bmi7(♭5)/E B♭7(♯11) Ami7 G/B Ami/C
27 G E7 Ami7 E7 Ami
you, so find your - self some -
C♯°7 D7 D13(♯11 ♯9) G 6 9
30 A13 D13 G
bod - y to love.

THE BEST CHORD CHANGES

Every song is based on a basic chord structure upon which the melody relies for overall feeling and sound. Altered chords (variations of the original chords) make a song sound even more rich and professionally arranged. Frank Mantooth has written this series of books to give pianists the very best chord changes for some of the most beautiful songs ever written. Each book includes 100 songs with the melody line, chord symbols, lyrics, and a second line of altered chords printed in red above the original chords.

THE BEST CHORD CHANGES FOR THE BEST KNOWN SONGS

arr. by Frank Mantooth

100 songs musicians need to know, including: Alfie • April in Paris • Be Careful, It's My Heart • Blue Skies • The Girl from Ipanema • I Remember You • Let's Fall in Love • Mood Indigo • Satin Doll • Song for My Father • Unforgettable • The Very Thought of You • Willow Weep for Me • You Took Advantage of Me • and more.

00240028 .... $22.95

THE BEST CHORD CHANGES FOR THE BEST STANDARDS EVER

arr. by Frank Mantooth

100 classics, including: Alice In Wonderland • All of You • Body and Soul • Cheek to Cheek • Harlem Nocturne • If I Loved You • In a Sentimental Mood • It's Impossible • Look for the Silver Lining • Mona Lisa • Moon River • My Blue Heaven • So in Love • Tangerine • Waltz for Debby • We Kiss in a Shadow • You're My Everything • and more.

00240029 .... $22.95

BEST CHORD CHANGES FOR THE MOST POPULAR SONGS

arr. by Frank Mantooth

100 standards, including: Ain't She Sweet • The Birth of the Blues • By the Time I Get to Phoenix • The Christmas Song (Chestnuts Roasting on an Open Fire) • Dream a Little Dream of Me • Get Me to the Church on Time • Getting to Know You • I Love Paris • In the Mood • Oklahoma • The Rainbow Connection • Star Dust • Sunrise Serenade • Take the "A" Train • Unchained Melody • Up, Up and Away • The Way We Were • Whistle While You Work • You Oughta Be in Pictures • and more.

00240101 .... $22.95

THE BEST CHORD CHANGES FOR THE WORLD'S GREATEST STANDARDS

arr. by Frank Mantooth

100 songs, including: Ain't Misbehavin' • Easy Street • Gone with the Wind • Here's That Rainy Day • I Left My Heart in San Francisco • The Lady Is a Tramp • My Favorite Things • My Funny Valentine • Opus One • People • Skylark • Somewhere out There • Stompin' at the Savoy • Summertime • and many more. Historic annotations by Dr. David N. Baker are also featured.

00359124 .... $22.95

BEST CHORD CHANGES FOR THE MOST REQUESTED STANDARDS

arr. by Frank Mantooth

This features 100 more favorite standards, including: All the Things You Are • Button Up Your Overcoat • Chances Are • Hello, Young Lovers • It's Only a Paper Moon • Just the Way You Are • Misty • On a Clear Day (You Can See Forever) • Quiet Nights of Quiet Stars • Smoke Gets in Your Eyes • Tuxedo Junction • What a Diff'rence a Day Made • and many more.

00359125 .... $22.95

For More Information, See Your Local Music Dealer, Or Write To:

7777 W. Bluemound Rd. P.O. Box 13819 Milwaukee, WI 53213

Prices, contents, and availability subject to change without notice.
Some products may not be available outside the U.S.A.

1197